CONTENTS

ACKNOWLEDGEMENTS

The editor and publishers wish to thank the following, who have kindly given permission for the use of copyright material:

A. Alvarez, extract from *The School of Donne* by permission of Curtis Brown Ltd on behalf of the author; Sir Edmund Chambers, extract from review of the Muses' Library edition of *Marvell's Poems* (1892) by permission of Oxford University Press; Rosalie L. Colie, extracts from 'Pictorial Traditions' from '*My Echoing Song*', *Andrew Marvell's Poetry of Criticism* © 1970 by permission of Princeton University Press; J. V. Cunningham, 'Logic and Lyric' from *Collected Essays of J. V. Cunningham* © 1976, by permission of The Swallow Press and the author; T. S. Eliot, extract from 'Andrew Marvell' in *Selected Essays* (1932) by permission of Faber & Faber Ltd; D. M. Friedman, extracts from 'Upon Appleton House' in *Marvell's Pastoral Art* (1970) by permission of Routledge & Kegan Paul Ltd; F. Kermode, 'The Argument of Marvell's Garden' from *Essays in Criticism* (1952) by permission of the author and editors; J. B. Leishman, 'Some Themes and Variations in the Poetry of Andrew Marvell' from *Proceedings of the British Academy*, XLVII (1961), by permission of the British Academy; Maren-Sofie Røstvig, extract from 'Marvell and the Caroline Poets' in *English Poetry and Prose, 1540–1674* vol. 2 of *Sphere History of English Literature*, by permission of the author; J. H. Summers, extract from 'Marvell's Nature' from *English Literacy History*, xx, no. 2 (1953) by permission of The Johns Hopkins University Press; E. W. Tayler, 'Marvell's Garden of the Mind' from *Nature and Art in Renaissance Literature* (1964), by permission of Columbia University Press; A. J. N. Wilson, ' "An Horation Ode Upon Cromwell's Return from Ireland" The Thread of the Poem and Its Use of Classical Allusions' in *Critical Quarterly*, 11, no. 4 (winter 1969), by permission of the author.

GENERAL EDITOR'S PREFACE

The Casebook series, launched in 1968, has become a well-regarded library of critical studies. The central concern of the series remains the 'single-author' volume, but suggestions from the academic community have led to an extension of the original plan, to include occasional volumes on such general themes as literary 'schools' and genres.

Each volume in the central category deals either with one well-known and influential work by an individual author, or with closely related works by one writer. The main section consists of critical readings, mostly modern, collected from books and journals. A selection of reviews and comments by the author's contemporaries is also included, and sometimes comment from the author himself. The Editor's introduction charts the reputation of the work or works from the first appearance to the present time.

Volumes in the 'general themes' category are variable in structure but follow the basic purpose of the series in presenting an integrated selection of readings, with an Introduction which explores the theme and discusses the literary and critical issues involved.

A single volume can represent no more than a small selection of critical opinions. Some critics are excluded for reasons of space, and it is hoped that readers will pursue the suggestions for further reading in the Select Bibliography. Other contributions are severed from their original context, to which some readers may wish to turn. Indeed, if they take a hint from the critics represented here, they certainly will.

A. E. DYSON

Note on Texts

The text used by the writers in Part Three is that of H. M. Margoliouth, *The Poems and Letters of Andrew Marvell* (Clarendon Press, 1927). In the earlier sections, though typography and, in some places, spelling may differ, the text has been harmonised with this edition and any differences noted.

For
Jan

INTRODUCTION

Marvell has a unique history of poetic reputation—first, neglected for so long, and then to soar to such eminence on the basis of so small an output. Though he wrote prolifically in the area of political controversy as Member of Parliament for Hull (biographical details will be found in the article by Maren-Sofie Røstvig in Part Three, below), he did not even bother to publish his poems. They had to wait for their appearance until his housekeeper, Mary Palmer, claiming doubtfully to be his widow, published them in 1681, over two years after his death. Marvell was republished only twice in the eighteenth century in Cooke's edition of 1726 and Thompson's in 1776. He was valued more for his politics than his poetry.

The poems are to be found in the third volume of Thompson's edition and include some that were not, in fact, Marvell's, but the work of Addison and Watts among others. To be the victim of incorrect attribution was one indignity: to be quoted in anthologies so narrowly from so small a corpus was another. To compound the insult Cooke and Thompson themselves adopted capricious alterations from the anthologists. The poems did not matter so much; for them Marvell was pre-eminently the British Aristides, the spokesman for political liberty. It is not therefore surprising that he became the choice of another Hull poet, William Mason, as hero for his 'Ode to Independence'.

Marvell's progress to recognition was for long a matter of halting steps and slow. The second-rate Romantic poets (Campbell and Bowles) and some of the essayists (Lamb, Hazlitt and Leigh Hunt) liked him or at least what they knew of him. The essayists together cover only nine of the poems, and Hazlitt was content to praise 'An Horatian Ode' by its repute rather than by his acquaintance with it. None of them appreciated the Metaphysical quality in Marvell; Lamb's well-known reference to 'witty delicacy' came nearest. This should not surprise us; for the Romantic temperament, what was most appreciated were such qualities as tenderness, pathos and response to nature. The poet's increasing fame was marked by the mingled biographical-critical article in *The Retrospective Review*, 1824–25[*] and the two lives—by John Dove and Hartley Coleridge[*]—some seven years later. Across the Atlantic Marvell was recognised by such writers as Poe[*], Emerson and Whittier.

The anthologising continued, and most important in this regard was the place which Palgrave assigned to 'An Horatian Ode', 'The Garden' and 'Bermudas' in his influential *Golden Treasury* (1861). In doing this he responded to the bidding of Tennyson, who also thought highly of 'To his Coy Mistress'[*]: a poem no doubt inadmissible by virtue of Victorian suscepti-bilities. This 'less known' poem was, however, quoted by John Ormsby in his important *Cornhill* article of 1869[*], the first study really to take much account of Marvell's poems as well as his life.

The way was open for new editions. Grosart's, 'prepared', says John Carey, 'with his usual grandiose incompetence',[1] appeared in 1872, followed by that of Aitken (Muses' Library) in 1892. Edmund Gosse, amid much that was wrong-headed, recognised Marvell as the last of 'the school of Donne'[*], while Gerard Manley Hopkins with his customary sensitivity considered him 'a most rich and nervous poet' (letter to R. W. Dixon, 27 February 1879). The rich profusion of conceit which earlier critics had noticed and felt uncomfortable about was now on its way to recognition. Grosart, for all his editorial faults, justifies a critical quotation:

And yet beneath the conceit, when you come to look lovingly and lingeringly, you find that it is sprung out of a vital thought or emotion or fancy.

Two articles on Marvell in 1892 show the look backward and the view ahead. A. C. Benson[*] is still not fully at ease, though recognising the poet's originality, whereas E. K. Chambers[*] really leads us forward. Besides identifying what he calls 'the music of Puritanism' and appreciating Marvell's poetry of nature, not least in the lesser-known poems, Chambers speaks out

---

* Here and elsewhere in the Introduction, an asterisk within square brackets refers to material excerpted in the relevant Part of this Casebook.

boldly against 'the indiscriminate condemnation of conceits in poetry'. In tone and manner recalling Wordsworth's dismissal in the Preface to *Lyrical Ballads* of Samuel Johnson's ill choice of doggerel lines for condemnation as verse in simple language, Chambers writes:

A conceit is only an analogy, a comparison, a revealing of likeness in things dissimilar, and therefore of the very essence of poetic imagination. Often it illumines, and where it fails, it is not because it is a conceit, but because it is a bad conceit.

This sentence indeed would suffice to refute Johnson's notorious denunciation of the Metaphysical mode in the *Life* of Cowley.

Writing at the beginning of the present century H. C. Beeching provides a systematic survey of what had by them become the prevailing critical view of Marvell.[*] The revival of the Metaphysicals generally had progressed through the middle and later nineteenth century. In 1912 came Sir Herbert Grierson's monumental edition of Donne, followed in 1921 by his influential anthology, *Metaphysical Poetry: Donne to Butler*, which not only placed Marvell squarely alongside the other Metaphysical poets, but even went so far as declaring

> The grave's a fine and private place,
> But none, I think, do there embrace

to be 'the very roof and crown of the Metaphysical love-lyric, at once fantastic and passionate'.

We are ready for T. S. Eliot. Marvell's modern fame rests on a three-fold foundation—textually, Margoliouth's edition of the *Poems and Letters* (1927); biographically, Legouis's comprehensive *André Marvell: poète, puritain, patriote* (1928); and critically, Eliot's *Times Literary Supplement* article[*] celebrating the tercentenary of the poet's birth (31 March 1921). As John Carey has reminded us, Eliot, as with Milton, spoke twice on Marvell, the second time (and the likeness to the view he took of Milton will be obvious) declaring him not 'a safe model to study' and even adding that he was inferior to Bishop King; but, in Carey's

words: 'The [late] review was not reprinted. Eliot's "Andrew
Marvell" remained as the permanent influence.'[2] It remained so,
above all, for such key-phrases as 'the alliance of levity and
seriousness' and the 'tough reasonableness beneath the slight
lyric grace'. J. E. Duncan in *The Revival of Metaphysical Poetry*
(1959) has suggested that earlier critics, Benson among them,
had prefigured Eliot's pronouncement. What matters, however,
is that Eliot said what he did when he did and said it more
distinctly than it had been said before.

Of what has followed it would be easy to paraphrase Churchill
and say that never has so much been written by so many about so
little. If there is therefore a justification for a book of this kind, it
must be in its selection of the useful from the mass. Those who
have commented on this mass have usually found their task
unedifying. Legouis in a conservative approach in 1957[3] identified the source of all the trouble in Empson's *Seven Types of
Ambiguity* (1930) and pursued it through American 'New Critics'
like Cleanth Brooks and Milton Klonsky, even going so far as to
include in his censure Frank Kermode's essay of 1952 on 'The
Garden'.[*] Kermode himself has also commented (in 1966) on
over-ingenious Marvell criticism;[4] and so too, more recently, has
another Marvell scholar, Miss Muriel Bradbrook.[5]

Much the most detailed and outspoken treatment, however, is
that of John Carey, who concludes, in *Andrew Marvell: A Critical
Anthology* (1969):

Obscurity and misplaced erudition are pervasive faults in modern
Marvell criticism. Some critics are misled by a desire to appear
scholarly. Others by a suspicion that their subject does not seem difficult
enough. Some write obscurely because they have not fully thought out
what they wish to say, and hope that the reader will discover profundity
where there is only muddle. Crudity is another fault. Criticism is taken
to consist in showing that a poem 'really means' something entirely
different from what had been assumed. Often it is apparent that the
critic is criticising a prose paraphrase of the poem.

Eliot's essay did two things above all else: it placed Marvell
historically within the context of European culture and the
poetry of his own century in England; and it grappled with and
defined wit in such a way that the discomfort of previous

generations with the metaphysical conceit was dispersed. In his chapter on 'The Line of Wit' (*Revaluation*, 1936) Leavis acknowledged that 'the work has been done, the re-orientation effected', not least by 'Mr Eliot's extraordinarily pregnant and decisive essay on Marvell'. Leavis also, however, directed attention to the fact that Marvell was not just the last in the acknowledged school of Donne, but that there was another line of seventeenth-century poetry 'from Ben Jonson (and Donne) through Carew and Marvell to Pope'.[6] He was as much concerned to suggest a new line to Pope (to stand beside that of Waller—Denham—Dryden—Pope) as to trace one up to Marvell. The terminus in Pope has been criticised (e.g., by F. W. Bateson), but the presence of Carew before and Pope after does emphasise that quality which is but rarely associated with the Metaphysicals and which is supremely one of Marvell's own, namely, his urbanity.

If Leavis represents one direction in 'practical criticism' from its origins in I. A. Richards, William Empson typifies another, that of lexicographical versatility. He devoted several pages of *Seven Types of Ambiguity* mainly to some of the minor poems, though the most memorable comment there is that on the lines from 'An Horatian Ode':

> But with his keener eye
> The Axes edge did try

about which Empson remarks: 'There is a sort of mental association which gains strength because it has been crystallised into a pun elsewhere; [Marvell] . . . seems to be remembering the Latin *acies*, "eyesight" and "sharp edge".'[7] It was, however, in the first volume of Leavis's periodical, *Scrutiny*, that Empson's own first comments on 'The Garden' appeared. They were to be followed by his essay on the poem in *Some Versions of Pastoral* (1936), where his pursuit of multiple meanings produced the since famous 'from the lessening of pleasure' and 'made less by pleasure' as alternative and joint meanings of 'From pleasure less' in the sixth stanza of the poem. Empson, however, omitted what Legouis has since claimed to be the 'real meaning'—'from a pleasure that is inferior'. (On these possibilities see Kermode's essay herein[*].) Empson's essay was valuable in its time for making us look at poetry, not just Marvell's, in a different way, but it labours under the weight of excessive ingenuity. I have always found it hard to believe that there could be really much relevant connection for literary purposes between

> Annihilating all that's made
> To a green thought in a green shade

and the seventh Buddhist state of enlightenment, little though I know of this latter.

Cleanth Brooks pursued a different line in ingenuity (in 1947), rejecting 'the obvious way to understand the [Horatian] "Ode" . . . to ascertain by historical evidence—by letters and documents of all kinds—what Marvell really thought of Cromwell . . . [as] a relatively coarse method which can hope to give no more than a rough approximation of the poem'. He will have nothing of 'what Marvell as poet consciously intended to say in his poem'. He asks us to trust the poem (or his interpretation of it) rather than the poet or the evidence of history—'A poem has a life of its own . . . it provides in itself the only criterion by which it can be judged.'[8] Brooks, however, does rely considerably on history. Douglas Bush, pointing this out, went on to state that Brooks, as a modern liberal, does not 'fully understand the providential conception of history which was traditional in Marvell's age . . . and which was indeed a necessary part of Christian belief and Marvell, however liberal and emancipated, from common prejudices, was a Christian'. Moreover, when he really cannot close his modern liberal eyes to what to him are uncomfortable views in Marvell, Brooks resorts, says Bush, to 'the desperate solution of finding the lines ironical'.[9]

If critics like Empson and Brooks represent the esoteric approach, there has been a parallel and prolific group of exoteric critics. In 1947 Rosemund Tuve wrote about *Elizabethan and Metaphysical Imagery*, placing great emphasis on rhetorical and logical influences on poetry. More notable, however, have been those who have searched for philosophical influences on Marvell. These have generally been identified with forms of Neo-Platonism, stretching from Plotinus himself (e.g. Klonsky, Lawrence Hyman and Patrick Hogan[10]), through such medieval Catholics as Hugo of St Victor and St Bonaventura (Ruth

Wallerstein[11]) and Hermes Trismegistus (M. S. Røstvig[12]),
down to Marvell's contemporaries, the Cambridge Platonists
(H. E. Toliver[13]). Of these commentators Miss Røstvig wisely
notes Hermes's 'syncretistic way of thinking about divine
revelation, according to which the same truths may be discovered everywhere—in Nature . . . , in pagan myth and philosophy when properly interpreted, and in the Bible'.

This is a phrase to remind us also that Marvell himself may
have been syncretistic. This search for philosophical (or perhaps,
more accurately, history-of-ideas) influences prompts two warn-
ings to the student: one, of being careful not to lose sight of the
poem in the critics' pursuit of the influence; the other, of
watching to see that poem and influence do not find themselves in
some kind of forced and unconvincing union. Frank Kermode
proposes a third: the possibility of the scholar's using the same
label to describe different phenomena.[*]

There is yet another set of influences to recognise and critics
who have used them. Margoliouth in the notes to his edition
points to some of Marvell's literary borrowings and similarities.
J. B. Leishman with his immense knowledge of seventeenth-
century poetry developed this approach both in his article of
1961[*] and his book, *The Art of Marvell's Poetry* (1966). Both
show Marvell's indebtedness to his immediate predecessors and
contemporaries and the ways in which both he and they worked
within the classical tradition. Kermode has a good phrase about
'An Horatian Ode', asking us to see it 'not only in historical
breadth—the precise moment, summer 1650—but also in historical depth, back to Lucan's Caesar and Horace's Octavius'.[14]
This is precisely what Miss Rosemary Syfret does in dwelling on
what was at once a classical and a contemporary source, May's
translation of Lucan.[15] With somewhat broader reference A. J.
N. Wilson[*] directs our notice to the rich textual saturation of
the Ode by classical allusions. Likewise, Miss Bradbrook and
Miss Lloyd Thomas drew attention in 1940 to the French *libertin*
poets in reading 'The Garden':[16], a suggestion given fuller
consideration by Frank Kermode in his interpretation of the
poem.[*]

There are yet other significant influences, of the emblems, for
instance, studied by Rosalie Colie[*] or the *hortus conclusus*, the
enclosed garden of happy solitude (cf. S. Stewart, *The Enclosed*

Garden, 1966). This latter traces an idea through from the Song of Songs to 'The Garden', and, in so doing, it is arguing for the interpretation of Marvell through genre. In a similar way D. M. Friedman concentrates on Marvell's pastoral art and explores 'Upon Appleton House'[*] within the tradition of the country-house poem. Likewise, E. W. Tayler[*] examines the poet's 'personal response to the paired terms of Nature and Art', which go together to compose pastoral. Both these critics seek to show how Marvell modified and extended the form in his own treatment of it.

Eliot's essay insisted that 'the business of criticism' lies in its need to isolate in literature 'a quality of a civilisation'. With this in mind Kermode in his *Encounter* article emphasised that scholarship for its part in this pursuit 'needs a sense of the civilised probabilities'.[17] In choosing the material for this collection I have sought a variety of approaches: some critical surveys, such as those of Røstvig and Alvarez; some studies of cultural and intellectual backgrounds, as those of Leishman, Colie and Wilson; some of generic interpretation, as Friedman and Tayler—but all, I hope, within the range of civilised probabilities.

Within these various approaches the several recurrent characteristics of Marvell's poetry are demonstrated—his wit and irony, his urbanity and detachment, his concern with nature and art, his love of landscape, his contrasts of retirement and action, of body and soul, to mention no more than these. But when all has been said, there will be much left unsaid. Legouis believed that in the end nothing will *explain* Marvell. The criticism falls short; the poetry remains always that distance ahead.

NOTES

1. John Carey, *Andrew Marvell: A Critical Anthology* (1969), p. 30.
2. Ibid, p. 33.
3. P. Legouis, 'Marvell and the New Critics', *Review of English Studies*, new series, 8 (1957), pp. 382–9.

4. Frank Kermode, 'Marvell Transprosed', *Encounter* (Nov. 1966), pp. 77–84.

5. Muriel Bradbrook, 'Marvell Our Contemporary', in R. L. Brett (ed.), *Andrew Marvell: Essays on the Tercentenary of His Death* (1979).

6. F. R. Leavis, *Revaluation* (1936), pp. 10, 24, 29.

7. W. Empson, *Seven Types of Ambiguity* (1930; rev. edn 1947), p. 166.

8. Cleanth Brooks, 'Criticism and Literary History: Marvell's "Horatian Ode"', *Sewanee Review*, 55 (1947), pp. 192–222.

9. Douglas Bush, 'Marvell's "Horatian Ode"', *Sewanee Review*, 60 (1952), pp. 363–76.

10. M. Klonsky, 'A Guide through the Garden', *Sewanee Review*, 58 (1950), pp. 16–35; Lawrence Hyman, in *English Literary History*, 25, pp. 15–22; Patrick Hogan, in *Studies in Philology*, 60, pp. 1–11.

11. Ruth Wallerstein, *Studies in Seventeenth-Century Poetic* (1950).

12. M.–S. Røstvig, *The Happy Man: Studies in the Metamorphosis of a Classical Ideal* 2 vols (1958), 1.

13. H. E. Toliver, *Marvell's Ironic Vision* (1965).

14. Kermode, 'Marvell Transprosed' p. 79.

15. Rosemary Syfret, Marvell's "Horatian Ode"', *Review of English Studies*, new series, 12 (1961), pp. 160–72.

16. M. C. Bradbrook and M. G. Lloyd Thomas, *Andrew Marvell* (1940).

17. Kermode, op. cit., p. 80.

PART ONE

Comments, 1776–1885

Edward Thompson (1776)

... The poem to his *Coy Mistress* is sweet, natural and easy, and bespeaks his heart to be high in love; and perhaps his not being married might arise from her coldness, and want of the compleat composition of love-enraptured and cœlestial mutuality; without which the partial passion on one side, produces every evil which attends on marriage. There is no sublime rapture without reciprocation; and when the flame is mutual and general, it is above all earthly blisses, and only inferior to heavenly. His little poem of the *Gallery* loosely and pleasantly depicts this beloved fair one, whom he follows through all his pastoral dialogues, and in a most pleasing and epigrammatical manner in that of *Thyrsis and Dorinda*. ...

SOURCE: extract from *The Works of Andrew Marvell* (1776).

William Hazlitt (1825)

... Marvell is a writer almost forgotten; but undeservedly so. His poetical reputation seems to have sunk with his political party. His satires were coarse, quaint and virulent; but his other productions are full of a lively, tender, and elegant fancy. His verses leave an echo on the ear, and find one in the heart. See

those entitled BERMUDAS, TO HIS COY MISTRESS, ON THE DEATH OF A
FAWN, &c. . . .

SOURCE: extract from *Select Poets of Great Britain* (1825).

Anonymous (1825)

. . . As a poet, Marvell was certainly unequal; and some of his
most beautiful passages are alloyed with vulgarism and commonplace similes. His poem of the Nymph lamenting the Death of
Her Fawn, is, perhaps, the most finished, and, on the whole, the
best of the collection. All the poems, however, contain more or
less of poetic beauty; some, great tenderness of feeling and
expression; and others, successful descriptions of nature and
pastoral scenes. [Quotes 'Upon Appleton House', 497–512, 561–
776—Ed.]

SOURCE: extract from article in *Retrospective Review*
(1825).

John Dove (1832)

. . . As a *Poet*, Marvell was certainly unequal, and some of his
most beautiful passages are alloyed with vulgarism and commonplace similes. His early poems express a fondness for the charms of
rural and pastoral scenes, with much delicacy of sentiment; and

are full of fancy, after the manner of Cowley and his contemporaries. Marvell's *wit* was debased, indeed, by the coarseness of the time, and his *imagination* by its conceits; but he had a
true vein of poetry. . . .

SOURCE: extract from *The Life of Andrew Marvell* (1832)

Hartley Coleridge (1832)

. . . The poems of Marvell are, for the most part, productions of
his early youth. They have much of that over-activity of fancy,
that remoteness of allusion, which distinguishes the school of
Cowley; but they have also a heartfelt tenderness, a childish
simplicity of feeling, among all their complication of thought,
which would atone for all their conceits, if conceits were indeed as
great an offence against poetic nature as Addison and other
critics of the French school pretend. But though there are cold
conceits, a conceit is not necessarily cold. The mind, in certain
states of passion, finds comfort in playing with occult or casual
resemblances, and dallies with the echo of a sound.

We confine our praise to the poems which he wrote for himself.
As for those he made to order, for Fairfax or Cromwell, they are
as dull as every true son of the muse would wish these things to
be. . . .

SOURCE: extract from *The Worthies of Yorkshire and
Lancashire* (1832).

S. C. Hall (1836)

. . . As a poet Andrew Marvell was true, and this is the grand point in poetry. He was not of the highest order, not perhaps in even a high order, but what he did was genuine. It is sweetness speaking out in sweetness. In the language there is nothing more exquisitely tender than the 'Nymph complaining for the loss of her Fawn'. Such poems as this and 'the Bermudas' may live, and deserve to live, as long as the longest and the mightiest. Of as real a quality are the majority of the poems of Marvell. In a playful and fantastic expression of tender and voluptuous beauty, they are well nigh unrivalled. His fancy indeed some times over-masters him, but it is always a sweet and pleasant mastery. His strong love of the actual at times bursts forth, but his poetry still survives it, and will not be fairly clogged and over-laden with the body corporate.

SOURCE: extract from *The Book of Gems* (1836).

Edgar Allan Poe (1836)

. . . We copy a portion of Marvell's 'Maiden lamenting for her Fawn'—which we prefer not only as a specimen of the elder poets, but in itself as a beautiful poem abounding in pathos, exquisitely delicate imagination and truthfulness, to anything of its species. [Quotes 63–92—Ed.]

How truthful an air of lamentation hangs here upon every syllable! It pervades all. It comes over the sweet melody of the words—over the gentleness and grace which we fancy in the little maiden herself—even over the half-playful, half-petulant air with which she lingers on the beauties and good qualities of her favorite—like the cool shadow of a summer cloud over a bed of lilies and violets, 'and all sweet flowers'. The whole is redolent with poetry of the very loftiest order. Every line is an idea— conveying either the beauty and playfulness of the fawn, or the artlessness of the maiden, or her love, or her admiration, or her grief, or the fragrance and warmth and *appropriateness* of the little nest-like bed of lilies and roses which the fawn devoured as it lay upon them, and could scarcely be distinguished from them by the once happy little damsel who went to seek her pet with an arch and rosy smile on her face. Consider the great variety of truthful and delicate thought in the few lines we have quoted—the *wonder* of the maiden at the fleetness of her favorite—the 'little silver feet'—the fawn challenging his mistress to a race with 'a pretty skipping grace', running on before, and then, with head turned back, awaiting her approach only to fly from it again—can we not distinctly perceive all these things? How exceedingly vigorous, too, is the line,

And trod as if [*sic*] on the four winds!—

a vigor fully apparent only when we keep in mind the artless character of the speaker and the four feet of the favorite—one for each wind. Then consider the garden of 'my own,' so over grown—entangled—with roses and lilies, as to be 'a little wilderness'—the fawn, loving to be there, and there 'only'—the maiden seeking it 'where it *should* lie'—and not being able to distinguish it from the flowers until 'itself would rise'— the lying among the lilies 'like a bank of lilies'—the loving to 'fill itself with roses',

And its pure virgin limbs to fold
In whitest sheets of lilies cold,

and these things being its 'chief' delights—and then the preeminent beauty and naturalness of the concluding lines—whose very hyperbole only renders them more true to nature when we consider the innocence, the artlessness, the enthusiasm, the passionate grief, and more passionate admiration of the bereaved child—

> Had it lived long, it would have been
> Lilies without—roses within.

SOURCE: extract from review of S. C. Hall's *Book of Gems*, in *Southern Literary Messenger* (August 1836).

Leigh Hunt (1837)

. . . He unites wit with earnestness and depth of sentiment, beyond any miscellaneous writer in the language. Glorious Andrew's partisanship did not hinder his being of the party of all mankind, and doing justice to what was good in the most opposite characters. In a panegyric on Cromwell he has taken high gentlemanly occasion to record the dignity of the end of Charles the First. [Quotes 9–16, 21–36–Ed.] The emphatic cadence of this couplet,

> —Bow'd his comely head
> *Down*, as upon a bed,

is in the best taste of his friend Milton, with greater simplicity than the latter usually evinced.

SOURCE: extract from article in *The Monthly Repository*, New Series, 1 (1837–8).

Mary Russell Mitford (1852)

. . . As a poet, he is little known, except to the professed and unwearied reader of old folios. And yet his poems possess many of the finest elements of popularity: a rich profusion of fancy which almost dazzles the mind as bright colours dazzle the eye; an earnestness and heartiness which do not always, do not often belong to these flowery fancies, but which when found in their company add to them inexpressible vitality and savour; and a frequent felicity of phrase, which when once read, fixes itself in the memory and *will* not be forgotten.

Mixed with these dazzling qualities is much carelessness and a prodigality of conceits which the stern Roundhead ought to have left with other frippery to his old enemies, the Cavaliers. But it was the vice of the age—all ages have their favourite literary sins—and we must not blame Marvell too severely for falling into an error to which the very exuberance of his nature rendered him peculiarly prone. His mind was a bright garden, such a garden as he has described so finely, and that a few gaudy weeds should mingle with the healthier plants does but serve to prove the fertility of the soil.

SOURCE: extract from *Recollections of a Literary Life* (1852)

Alfred Tennyson (c.1860)

I

. . . Tennyson once said to me [Fitzgerald], some thirty years ago, or more, in talking of Marvell's 'Coy Mistress', where it breaks in

> But at my back I always hear
> Time's winged chariot hurrying near

—'*That* strikes me as sublime, I can hardly tell why.' Of course, this partly depends on its place in the Poem.

SOURCE: extract from *Letters and Literary Remains of Edward Fitzgerald*, vol. I (1889).

II

. . . With most by far of the pieces submitted [to the *Golden Treasury of Songs and Lyrics*—Ed.] he was already acquainted; but I [Palgrave] seem to remember more or less special praise of Lodge's 'Rosaline', of 'My Love in her attire . . .' and the 'Emigrants' Song' by Marvell. For some poems by that writer, then with difficulty accessible, he had a special admiration: delighting to read, with a voice hardly yet to me silent, and dwelling more than once on the magnificent hyperbole, the powerful union of pathos and humour in the lines 'To his Coy Mistress' where Marvell says

> Had we but world enough, and time,
> This coyness, lady, were no crime
> . . .

[Quotes 7–10, 21–4.] Youth, therefore, Marvell proceeds, is the time for love:

> Let us roll all our strength, and all
> Our sweetness up into one ball,
> And tear our pleasures with rough strife
> Through the iron gates of life:

on this line remarking that he could fancy *grates* would have intensified Marvell's image.

SOURCE: extract from F. T. Palgrave, *Personal Recollections, 1849–92*; quoted in H. Tennyson, *Alfred, Lord Tennyson: A Memoir*, vol. II (1897).

John Ormsby (1869)

. . . As a poet he is generally classed among the poets of Charles the Second's reign; but in reality he belongs to an earlier age, and has nothing whatever in common with Waller, Sedley, Dorset or Rochester. He is, in fact, no more one of the Restoration poets than Milton. His true place is with the men of the preceding period—with Herrick, Habington, Suckling, Lovelace, and Wither, to each of whom occasional resemblances may be traced in his poetry. But the poet that influenced him most, probably, was Donne. When Marvell was a student at Cambridge the influence of Donne's poetry was at its height, and it acted in the same way as the influence of Spenser in the preceding generation, of Cowley some thirty years later, and of Byron and Tennyson in modern times. Donne was the accepted poet with the young men, the orchestra-leader from whom they took their time and tone, and whose style, consciously or unconsciously, they assimilated. Marvell's earliest poem is an illustration of this. His satire on

'Fleckno, an English Priest at Rome', might easily pass for one of Donne's, so thoroughly has he caught not only the manner and rugged vigorous versification of Donne's satires, but also his very turns of thought, and the passion for elaborate conceits, recondite analogies, and out-of-the-way similitudes with which his poetry is so strongly imbued.

Few of the poets of the time of Charles I, and the Commonwealth escaped the infection of this, the metaphysical school of poetry, as Dryden somewhat awkwardly called it, which Donne is generally accused of having founded. In truth, neither he in England, nor Marino in Italy, nor Gongora in Spain, can be properly said to have founded a school. They were simply the most prominent masters of a certain style or method of writing, which came into fashion from causes independent of the example or teaching of any man, and affected prose as well as poetry. Its essential characteristic may be described as wit run to seed, or rather, perhaps, an unnatural growth of wit produced by the very richness and high cultivation of the literature of the period; for in each case the phenomenon made its appearance in, or immediately after, a period eminently rich in literature, that of Shakspeare, of Tasso, or of Cervantes and Lope de Vega. Metaphysical poets, Marinisti, or Conceptistas, all wrote under the same inspiration—a desire of being distinguished for wit and fancy at a time when wit and fancy were especially held in honour; a nervous dread of being thought trite, unoriginal, and commonplace, if they should be found treading in the footsteps of others; and a sort of suspicion that the legitimate fields of imagination were already worked out, and that now nothing was left to the poet but to fall back upon ingenuity. Traces of the prevailing fashion are to be met with frequently in Marvell's poems; and that they are not more abundant is probably owing to the fact that he wrote simply to please himself, 'for his own hand', and not with any ambition of one day claiming a place among the poets. But in this respect there is a difference between his earlier and later verses. For instance, his 'Nymph complaining for the Death of her Fawn', written, it would seem, before the close of the civil war, graceful, simple, and tender as the lines are, is not free from those *tours de force* of fancy which disfigure so much of the poetry of that day. Even the lowest, the mere verbal form of this forced wit, breaks out, *e.g.*

But Sylvio soon had me beguiled.
This waxèd tame; while he grew wild,
And, quite regardless of my smart,
Left me his *fawn*, but took his *heart*.   [33–6]

On the other hand, the poem on the 'Bermudas' produced, we may fairly presume, several years later, when Marvell was in daily communication with John Oxenbridge,—one of those very exiles to the Bermudas whose feelings the poem is supposed to express,—is as direct, natural, and unaffected as a poem of Wordsworth's could be. Both of these pieces have been of late frequently printed in collections of old poetry and works on English literature, especially the last, which a critic whose taste and judgment no one will dispute, has called 'a gem of melody, picturesqueness, and sentiment, nearly without a flaw'. They are therefore probably, too familiar already to the majority of our readers to justify quotation here, however tempting they may be as specimens of Marvell at his best; and we shall take, instead, a few illustrations from less-known poems. In the verses addressed 'To his Coy Mistress', the extravagant fancy, that in the graver sort of poetry is a blemish, becomes an ornament, employed as it is to push a kind of *argumentum ad absurdum* to the farthest possible limits, and its effect is heightened by the exquisite assumption of gravity in the opening lines. [Quotes 1–24.] The conclusion, therefore, is to the same effect as Herrick's advice, 'Then be not coy, but use your time'. [Quotes 33–46.]

The little poem of which we have here quoted the greater part is characteristic of Marvell in many ways, but more especially of that peculiarity of his which has been before alluded to, his trick—if anything so obviously natural and spontaneous can be called a trick—of passing suddenly from a light, bantering, trivial tone, to one of deep feeling, and even as in the instance just quoted, of solemnity. Nothing in Suckling, or Carew, or any other of the poets to whom love-making in verse was a pastime, is more gay, folâtre, careless, and at the same time, profoundly obsequious, than the first part; but lightly and playfully as the subject is treated, it suggests thoughts that lead to a graver and more impassioned strain. A few pages further on we find a poem which is in truth only a conceit expanded into a poem, but which in its very flimsiness shows a rare lightness of hand, and neatness

of execution. It is a sort of miniature idyll cast in the amœbean
form, and entitled 'Ametas and Thestylis making Hay-
ropes'. . . .

Nothing could be more designedly trifling than this, and yet
what a finished elegance there is about it. It is not the highest art,
perhaps, but there is a certain antique grace in the workmanship
that reminds one, somehow, of a cameo or an old engraved gem.
Charles Lamb, with his own peculiar felicity of expression, has hit
off the precise phrase when he speaks of 'a witty delicacy,' as the
prevailing quality in Marvell's poetry. If he did sin, as it must be
confessed he did occasionally, in forcing wit beyond its legitimate
bounds, he made amends for the offence by the graceful turn he
gave to a conceit. To take an instance from the lines 'To a Fair
Singer': poets have again and again tasked their ingenuity to
compliment ladies who are fortunate enough to add skill in music
to their other charms, but we doubt if it has been ever done with
greater elegance than here. [Quotes 7–12.]

The taste for subtleties, ingenuities, and prettinesses, which
here and there breaks out in Marvell's verse, is, however, his only
artificiality. He had, what was very rare among his contemporaries, a genuine love and reverence for nature. Most of the
poets of his day seem to treat nature in a somewhat patronizing
spirit, as a good sort of institution, deserving of support, especially
from poets, as being useful for supplying illustrations, comparisons, and descriptions available for poetic purposes. They,
we suspect, regarded it very much as the cook does the shrubbery,
from which he gets the holly and laurel leaves to garnish his
dishes. Marvell is one of the few men of that time who appear to
have delighted in nature for its own sake, and not merely for its
capabilities in the way of furnishing ideas. He enjoyed it
thoroughly and thankfully, and in the poems written during his
residence with Lord Fairfax at Nun-Appleton, he shows a keen
sense of pleasure in natural beauty and scenery, and, what was
even rarer in those days, close observation and study of nature.
The longest, that upon Appleton House, for an adequate
specimen of which we have not sufficient space, is an ample proof
of this, and from beginning to end 'breathes'—to use a phrase of
Washington Irving's—'the very soul of a rural voluptuary'. One
of his most graceful little poems, evidently belonging to this
time, is a protest against the artificial gardening then coming into

fashion. . . . [Quotes 'The Mower Against Gardens', 31–40.] . . .

SOURCE: extract from article in *Cornhill Magazine*, XX (July 1869).

Edmund Gosse (1885)

. . . Marvell is the last of the school of Donne, and in several respects he comes nearer to the master than any of his precursors. . . . The note, however, is not so sharply struck in him as in Donne; there is more suavity and grace. The conceits are perhaps as wild. . . . His style, when he can put his conceits behind him, is extremely sharp and delicate, with a distinction of phrase that is quite unknown to most of his contemporaries. . . . He is the last of the English romantic poets for several generations, and no one of them all, early or late, has regarded nature with a quicker or more loving attention than he. He is an alien indeed among the men of periwigs and ruffles. . . .

SOURCE: extracts from *From Shakespeare to Pope* (1885).

PART TWO

Revival of Interest, 1892–1921

A. C. Benson (1892)

'A Young Man Trying His Wings'

. . . Whatever the faults of Marvell's poems may be, and they are patent to all, they have a strain of originality. He does not seem to imitate, he does not even follow the lines of other poets; never—except in a scattered instance or two, where there is a faint echo of Milton—does he recall or suggest that he has a master. At the same time the poems are so short and slight that any criticism upon them is apt to take the form of a wish that the same hand had written more, and grown old in his art. There is a monotony for instance about their subjects, like the song of a bird recurring again and again to the same phrase; there is an uncertainty, an incompleteness not so much of expression as of arrangement, a tendency to diverge and digress in an unconcerned and vagabond fashion. There are stanzas, even long passages, which a lover of proportion such as Gray (who excised one of the most beautiful stanzas of the Elegy because it made too long a parenthesis) would never have spared. It is the work of a young man trying his wings, and though perhaps not flying quite so directly and professionally to his end, revelling in the new-found powers with a delicious ecstasy which excuses what is vague and prolix; especially when over all is shed that subtle precious quality which makes a sketch from one hand so unutterably more interesting than a finished picture from another—which will arrest with a few commonplace phrases, lightly touched by certain players, the attention which has wandered throughout a whole sonata. The strength of his style lies in its unexpectedness. You are arrested by what has been well called a 'predestined' epithet, not a mere otiose addition, but a word which turns a noun into a picture; the 'hook-shouldered' hill 'to abrupter greatness thrust', the 'sugar's uncorrupting oil', 'the vigilant patrol of stars', 'the squatted thorns', 'the oranges like golden lamps in a green night', 'the garden's fragrant innocence'—these are but a few random instances of a tendency that meets you in every poem. Marvell had in fact the qualities of a consummate artist, and only needed to repress his luxuriance and to confine his expansiveness. . . .

SOURCE: extract from article in *Macmillan's Magazine*, LXV (January 1892).

E. K. Chambers (1892)

'Complete Absorption in Nature'

. . . Marvell hold a unique place in the seventeenth century. He stands at the parting of the ways, between the extravagancies of the lyrical Jacobeans on the one hand, and the new formalism initiated by Waller on the other. He is not unaffected by either influence. The modish handling of the decasyllable couplet is very marked here and there. You have it, for instance, in the poem on Blake:

> Bold Stayner leads; this fleet's designed by fate
> To give him laurel, as the last did plate.   [117–18]

And elsewhere, of course, he has conceits which cry aloud in their flagrancy. But his real affinities are with a greater than Waller or Suckling. Milton in those days 'was like a star, and dwelt apart'; but of all who 'called him friend', Marvell is the one who can claim the most of spiritual kinship. The very circumstances of their lives are curiously similar. Each left poetry for statecraft and polemic: for Milton the flowering time came late; for Marvell, never. And their poetic temper is one: it is the music of

Puritanism,—the Puritanism of Spenser and Sidney, not un-cultivated, not ungracious, not unsensuous even, but always with the same dominant note in it, of moral strength and moral purity. Marvell is a Puritan; but his spirit has not entered the prison-house, nor had the key turned on it there. He is a poet still, such as there have been few in any age. The lyric gift of Herrick he has not, nor Donne's incomparable subtlety and intensity of emotion; but for imaginative power, for decent melody, for that self-restraint of phrase which is the fair half of art, he must certainly hold high rank among his fellows. The *clear* sign of this selfrestraint is his mastery over the octosyllable couplet, a metre which in less skilful hands so readily becomes diffuse and wearisome.

Marvell writes love poems, but he is not essentially a love poet. He sings beautifully to Juliana and Chlora, but they themselves are only accidents in his song. His real passion—a most uncommon one in the seventeenth century—is for nature, exactly as we moderns mean nature, the great spiritual influence which deepens and widens life for us. How should the in-toxication of meadow, and woodland, and garden, be better expressed than in these two lines [in 'The Garden']:

> Stumbling on melons, as I pass,
> Insnared with flowers, I fall on grass.   [39–40]

unless indeed it be here:

> I am the mower Damon . . .   [41–8]

These mower-idylls, never found in the anthologies, are among the most characteristic of Marvell's shorter poems. I cannot forbear to quote two stanzas from 'The Mower to the Glowworms'. [Quotes 1–8.] Observe how Marvell makes of the nightingale a conscious artist, a winged *diva*. Elsewhere he speaks of her as sitting among the 'squatted thorns', in order 'to sing the trials of her voice'.

I must needs see in Marvell something of a nature-philosophy strangely anticipative of George Meredith. For the one, as for the other, complete absorption in nature, the unreserved abandon-ment of self to the skyey influences, is the really true and sanative wisdom. Marvell describes his soul, freed of the body's vesture, perched like a bird upon the garden boughs:

> Annihilating all that's made
> To a green thought in a green shade.

The same idea is to be found in the lines 'Upon Appleton House', a poem which will repay careful study from all who wish to get at the secret of Marvell's genius. It shows him at his best—and at his worst, in the protracted conceit, whereby a garden, its flowers and its bees, are likened to a fort with a garrison. And here I am minded to enter a plea against the indiscriminate condemnation of conceits in poetry. After all, a conceit is only an analogy, a comparison, a revealing of likeness in things dissimilar, and therefore of the very essence of poetic imagination. Often it illumines, and where it fails it is not because it is a conceit, but because it is a bad conceit; because the thing compared is not beautiful in itself, or because the comparison is not flashed upon you, but worked out with such tedious elaboration as to be 'merely fantastical'. Many of Marvell's conceits are, in effect, bad; the well-known poem, 'On a Drop of Dew', redeemed though it is by the last line and a half, affords a terrible example. But others are shining successes. [For example, the conceit] set in a haunting melody, as of Browning [in 'Daphnis and Chloe', 85–8] . . .

Next to green fields, Marvell is perhaps happiest in treating of death. His is the mixed mode of the Christian scholar, not all unpaganised, a lover of heaven, but a lover of the earthly life too. There is the epitaph on a nameless lady, with its splendid close:

> Modest as morn, as mid-day bright,
> Gentle as evening, cool as night:
> 'Tis true: but all too weakly said;
> 'Twas more significant. She's dead.
>
> ['An Epitaph upon—', 17–20]

There is the outburst on the death of the poet's hero, the great Protector:

O human glory vain! O Death! O wings!
O worthless world! O transitory things!   [255–6]

And to crown all, there are [the] lines [in 'To his Coy Mistress,
21–32], which remind me, for their felicities, their quaintness,
and the organ-note in them, of [Sir Thomas Browne's]
Hydriotaphia . . .

> SOURCE: extract from article in *The Academy*, XLII(17
> Sept. 1892), 230–1.

Alice Meynell (1897)

'The Garden Poems'

. . . It is only in those well-known poems, 'The Garden',
translated from his own Latin, and 'The Nymph Complaining of
the Death of Her Fawn', in that less familiar piece 'The Mower
Against Gardens', in 'The Picture of [Little] T.C. in a Prospect of
Flowers', with a few very brief passages in the course of duller
verses, that Marvell comes into veritable possession of his own
more interior powers—at least in the series of his garden lyrics.
The political poems, needless to say, have an excellence of a
different character and a higher degree. They have so much
authentic dignity that 'the glorious name of the British Aristides'
really seems duller when it is conferred as the earnings of the
'Horatian Ode upon Cromwell's Return from Ireland' than
when it inappropriately clings to Andrew Marvell, cherry-
cheeked, caught in the tendrils of his vines and melons. He shall
be, therefore, the British Aristides in those moments of midsum-
mer solitude; at least, the heavy phrase shall then have the smile
it never sought.

Marvell can be tedious in these gardens—tedious with every

ingenuity, refinement, and assiduity of invention. When he intends to flatter the owner of the 'Hill and Grove at Billborow', he is
most deliberately silly, not as the eighteenth century was silly, but
with a peculiar innocence. Unconsciousness there was not,
assuredly, but the artificial phrases of Marvell had never been
used by a Philistine, the artifices are freshly absurd, the
cowardice before the plain face of commonplace is not vulgar,
there is an evident simple pleasure in the successful evasion of
simplicity, and all the anxiety of the poet comes to a happy issue
before our eyes. He commends the Billborow hill because 'the
stiffest compass could not strike' a more symmetrical and equal
semi-circle than its form presents, and he rebukes the absent
mountains because they deform the earth and affright the
heavens. This hill, he says, with a little better fancy, only 'strives
to raise the plain'. Lord Fairfax, to whose glory these virtues of
the soil are dedicated, and whose own merit they illustrate, is
then said to be admirable for the modesty whereby, having a hill,
he has also a clump of trees on the top, wherein to sequester the
honours of eminence. It is not too much to say that the whole of
this poem is untouched by poetry.

So is almost that equally ingenious piece, 'Appleton House',
addressed to the same friend. It chanced that Appleton House
was small, and out of this plain little fact the British Aristides
contrives to turn a sedulous series of compliments with fair success
and with a most guileless face. What natural humility in the
householder who builds in proportion to his body, and is
contented like the tortoise and the bird! Further on, however, it
appears that the admired house had been a convent, and that to
the dispossessed nuns was due the praise of proportion; they do
not get it, in any form, from Marvell. A pretty passage follows, on
the wasting of gardens, and a lament over the passing away of
some earlier England [quotes 331–2, 335–6]. Moreover, there is a
peaceful couplet about the cattle [quotes 463–4]. But nothing
here is of the really fine quality of 'The Picture of T.C.', or 'The
Garden', or 'The Nymph Complaining of the Death of Her
Fawn'.

In those three the presence of a furtive irony of the gentlest
kind is the sure sign that they came of the visitings of the
unlooked-for muse aforesaid. Marvell rallies his own 'Nymph',
rallies his own soul for her clapping of silver wings in the solitude

of summer trees; and more sweetly does he pretend to offer to the little girl 'T.C.' the prophetic homage of the habitual poets [quotes 15–18, 23–4]. Charmingly then he asks the child, where she sits painted in the midst of flowers, to 'reform the errors of the spring', to make that the tulips may have their part of sweetness, 'seeing they are fair'; that violets may have a longer age, and— inevitably—that the roses may be disarmed of thorns. And still more charmingly he warns 'T.C.' to spare the buds in her flower gathering lest an angry Flora, seeing her infants killed, should take the cruel example:

> And, ere we see,
> Nip, in the blossom, all our hopes in thee.   [39–40]

The noble phrase of the 'Horatian Ode' is not recovered again high or low throughout Marvell's book, if we except one single splendid and surpassing passage from 'The Definition of Love'. The hopeless lover speaks:

> Magnanimous despair alone
> Could show me so divine a thing.   [5–6]

'To his Coy Mistress' is the only piece, not already named, altogether fine enough for an anthology. . . .

SOURCE: extract from article in the *Pall Mall Gazette* (1897).

H. C. Beeching (1901)

'Terseness and Sensuousness, Humour, Delicacy and Gusto'

. . . The first quality to strike a reader who takes up Marvell's book is his extraordinary terseness. Look, for example, at the

poem with which the only good modern edition, that of Mr G. A.
Aitken, opens, 'Appleton House'. The poet wishes to praise the
house for not being too big, like most country-houses of the time,
and this is how he does it:

> Within this sober frame expect
> Work of no foreign architect,
> *That unto caves the quarries drew,*
> *And forests did to pastures hew.*

If this were 'transprosed', it would have to run something as
follows: 'Our boasted Italian architects make houses so huge that
by drawing the stone for them they hollow out quarries into
caves, and cut down whole forests for timber so that they become
pastures.' As a part of the same skill it is remarkable in how few
strokes he can paint a picture. In this same poem, describing a
copse, he says:

> Dark all without it knits; within
> It opens passable and thin   [505–6]

which gives exactly the difference of impression from without and
upon entering. A second notable quality in Marvell's verse is its
sensuousness, its wide and deep enjoyment of the world of sense.
'The Garden', which everybody knows, may stand as the best
example of this quality—

> Stumbling on melons, as I pass,
> Ensnared with flowers, I fall on grass   [39–40]

Marvell is the laureate of grass, and of greenery. A third excellent
quality is his humour, . . . sometimes showing itself as intellectual wit, or as irony or sarcasm. Still keeping to 'Appleton
House', one may notice the ingenuity of the suggestion of
Fairfax's generosity:

> A stately frontispiece of *poor*
> Adorns without the open door   [65–6]

or the deprecation of over-large houses:

What need of all this marble crust
To impark the wanton mole [*sic*] of dust;
That thinks by breadth the world to unite,
Tho' the first builders failed in height.   [21–4]

Once or twice the humour runs to coarseness when it allies itself
with the bitter Puritanism of the time, as in the picture of the nuns
defending their house:

Some to the breach against their foes
Their wooden saints in vain oppose;
Another bolder stands at push,
With their old holy-water brush.   [249–52]

But most characteristic of all the qualities of Marvell's verse is
what Lamb well spoke of as his 'witty delicacy'—his delicate
invention. The shining and unapproachable instances of this
delicacy are 'The Nymph Complaining for the Death of Her
Fawn' and 'The Picture of Little T.C.'. The former of these
pieces is often hyperbolic in fancy, but the hyperbole fits the
pastoral remoteness of the setting; the second needs not even this
apology. It is a masterpiece in a *genre* where masterpieces are rare,
though attempts are not infrequent. Prior, Waller, and Sedley
have tried the theme with a certain success, but their pieces lack
the romantic note. 'The Picture of Little T.C.' has this to
perfection; it has not a weak line in it, and moves through its five
stanzas, each more exquisite than the last, to its admirably mock-
serious close [quotes 25–40].

One other quality of Marvell's lyrical writing remains to be
noticed, which is somewhat difficult to fix with a name, unless we
call it *gusto*. We imagine him smiling to himself as he writes,
smiling at his own fancies, or his own sensuousness, or happy
turns. He wrote, we are sure, for his own pleasure quite as much
as for ours. I remember the remark being made to me that 'The
Bermudas', for a religious poem, went pretty far in the way of self-
indulgence. And so it does. Lastly, it cannot fail to be noted that
Marvell was an artist, with an artist's love of making experiments. Perhaps he never attained perfect facility, but he is never
amateurish.

Among the various groups into which his lyrical poetry divides itself, the least satisfactory is that whose theme is love. Marvell's love-poetry has, with the exception of one piece, as little passion as Cowley's, while it is as full of conceits. 'The Unfortunate Lover' is probably the worst love-poem ever written by a man of genius. 'The Definition of Love' is merely a study after Donne's 'Valediction'. Cleverer and more original, and somewhat more successful, is 'The Gallery'. The two opposite sides of one long picture-gallery into which the chambers of his heart have been thrown by breaking down partitions are supposed to be covered with portraits of his lady. On the one side she is drawn in such characters as Aurora and Venus; on the other as an enchanter and a murderess.

Marvell was the friend of Milton, and one conjectures that, like his respected friend, he also may have had theories as to the true relation of these sexes which interfered with the spontaneous expression of feeling. There is, nevertheless, one poem in which passion is allowed to take its most natural path, although even in it one feels that the poet is expressing the passion of the human race rather than his own individual feeling; and the passion being, as often in Marvell, masked and heightened by his wit, the effect is singularly striking: indeed, as a love-poem 'To his Coy Mistress' is unique. It could never be the most popular of Marvell's poems, but for sheer power I should be disposed to rank it higher than anything he ever wrote. He begins with hyperbolical protestations to his mistress of the slow and solemn state with which their wooing should be conducted, if only time and space were their servants and not their masters [quotes 1–10]. Each beauty also of face and feature should have its special and age-long praise:

> *But at my back I always hear*
> *Time's winged chariot hurrying near;*
> And yonder all before us lie
> Deserts of vast eternity.   [21–4]

> The grave's a fine and private place,
> But none I think do there embrace.   [31–2]

A second division of Marvell's lyric poetry has for its subject religion. The most curious of the religious poems are the pastorals

'Clorinda and Damon', and 'Thyrsis and Dorinda'. Despite their obvious artificiality I must confess that these poems give me pleasure, perhaps because religious poetry is apt to be shapeless, and these, in point of form, are admirable. It is matter for regret that in the first of the two Marvell should have made the nymph sensual and the swain pious; but the friend of Milton, as I have already suggested, probably shared his low views of the female sex. And then the conversion of the lady is sudden and leaves something to desire in its motive. In 'Thyrsis and Dorinda' the two young things talk together so sweetly of Elysium that they drink opium in order to lose no time in getting there. More genuine in feeling, and more religious in the ordinary sense of the word, are two dialogues: one between the 'Resolved Soul and Created Pleasure', the other between 'Soul and Body'. The form of the first is noteworthy. The octosyllabic stanzas are alternately unshortened and shortened, the Soul speaking in serious iambics and Pleasure in dancing trochees; and the allurements of sense rise in a well-conceived scale from mere softness through art up to the pleasures of knowledge. The dialogue between Soul and Body is a brilliant duel, each party accusing the other of his proper woes; and except for . . . one terrible line . . . the poem is an excellent piece of writing. But religious passion sounds a higher and less artificial strain in a pair of odes, the one 'On a Drop of Dew', in which the soul is compared to the dewdrop upon a leaf, which reflects heaven and is reluctant to coalesce with its environment; the other called 'The Coronet', an apology for religious poetry on the ground that because it admits art it leaves room for the artist's pride. 'The Coronet' is interesting as a study in Herbert's manner, and contains one line of exquisite modesty:

> Through every garden, every mead,
> I gather flowers (my fruits are only flowers).   [5–6]

But the ode 'On a Drop of Dew' is by far the finer. The ideas are evolved after the manner of Donne, but the rhythm is slower and more contemplative [quotes 1–30].

A third and final division of Marvell's lyrics would comprise his poems upon nature; and here we have Marvell at his best, because here he lets his passion inspire him. Except in Shakespeare, who includes 'all thoughts, all passions, all desires' we have but little passion for nature between Chaucer and Marvell; but in Marvell the love for natural beauty is not short of passion. Of course his love is not for wild nature—a feeling which only dates from Gray and Wordsworth—but for the ordinary country scenes:

> Fragrant gardens, shady woods,
> Deep meadows and transparent floods
> ['Appleton House,' 79–80];

and for these he brings the eye of a genuine lover and, what is more, of a patient observer. The lines upon 'Appleton House' are full of observation. He speaks of the 'shining eye' of the 'hatching throstle', and has a fine imaginative description of the woodpecker [quotes 539–50].

In his poem called 'The Garden' Marvell has sung a palinode that for richness of phrasing in its sheer sensuous love of garden delights is perhaps unmatchable. At the same time the most devout lover of gardens must agree with Marvell that even in a garden the pleasures of the mind are greater than those of the sense. The poet's thought, as he lies in the shade, can create a garden for himself far more splendid and also imperishable; as indeed, in this poem, it has done [quotes 41–56].

Next to 'The Garden' as a descriptive poem must rank the 'Bermudas'. Marvell's 'Bermudas' are not 'still vexed' like Shakespeare's but an earthly paradise. His interest in these islands arose from meeting at Eton, while he was there as tutor to a ward of Cromwell's, a certain John Oxenbridge, who had been one of the exiles thither for conscience sake. The poem is built upon the same plan as 'The Garden'; first, the sensuous delights are described as no one but Marvell could describe them [quotes 17–24]. And then he passes on, though in this case it must be allowed with much less effect, to the spiritual advantages of the place.

Of the patriotic verse, which in its own way is full of interest, it is impossible to speak in this paper; except of the one poem which can claim to be a lyric, the 'Horatian Ode upon Cromwell's Return from Ireland'. . . . [This] ode was first published in Captain Thompson's edition, and so must take its stand as Marvell's only by the weight of internal evidence. But that evidence is conspicuous in every line. The poem runs on in a somewhat meandering and self-indulgent course, like all Marvell's longer poems. But many details are recognisably in Marvell's vein. The stroke of cleverness about King Charles's head being as lucky as that which was found when they were digging the foundations of Rome, and the fun he pokes at the Scotch and Irish are certainly Marvell. So is the view taken that Cromwell made a great sacrifice in renouncing a private life, which we get also in Marvell's prose; so is the touch about Cromwell's garden:

> where
> He lived reserved and austere,
>   (As if his highest plot
>   To plant the bergamot.)   [29–32]

So also is the remarkable detachment from political prejudice, of which the verses prefixed to the cavalier poet Lovelace's [verse-collection] *Lucasta*, about the same date, afford another instance, a detachment that would have been impossible for the author of 'Lycidas'. Even now, in an age which boasts of its tolerant spirit, it gives one a shock to remember that the stanzas about Charles, which present the very image of the cavalier saint and martyr, come in a poem to the honour and glory of the man to whom he owed his death [quotes 57–64]. These two stanzas are now the only part of the ode that is remembered, and with justice; for the rest of the poem, although in form and spirit it is Horatian, yet it has little of the *curiosa felicitas* of Horace's diction to make it memorable. But in these two stanzas the diction has attained to the happiness of consummated simplicity. . . .

SOURCE: extract from article in the *National Review*, XXVII (July 1901).

T. S. Eliot (1921)

'The Modest and Impersonal Virtue'

. . . The seventeenth century sometimes seems for more than a moment to gather up and to digest into its art all the experience of the human mind which (from the same point of view) the later centuries seem to have been partly engaged in repudiating. But Donne would have been an individual at any time and place; Marvell's best verse is the product of European, that is to say Latin, culture.

Out of that high style developed from Marlowe through Jonson (for Shakespeare does not lend himself to these genealogies) the seventeenth century separated two qualities: wit and magniloquence. Neither is as simple or as apprehensible as its name seems to imply, and the two are not in practice antithetical; both are conscious and cultivated, and the mind which cultivates one may cultivate the other. The actual poetry, of Marvell, of Cowley, of Milton, and of others, is a blend in varying proportions. And we must be on guard not to employ the terms with too wide a comprehension; for like the other fluid terms with which literary criticism deals, the meaning alters with the age, and for precision we must rely to some degree upon the literacy and good taste of the reader. The wit of the Caroline poets is not the wit of Shakespeare, and it is not the wit of Dryden, the great master of contempt, or of Pope, the great master of hatred, or of Swift, the great master of disgust. What is meant is some quality which is common to the songs in *Comus* and Cowley's Anacreontics and Marvell's Horatian Ode. It is more than a technical accomplishment, or the vocabulary and syntax of an epoch; it is, what we have designated tentatively as wit, a tough reasonableness beneath the slight lyric grace. . . .

The difference between imagination and fancy, in view of this poetry of wit, is a very narrow one. Obviously, an image which is immediately and unintentionally ridiculous is merely a fancy. In the poem 'Upon Appleton House', Marvell falls in with one of these undesirable images, describing the attitude of the house toward its master:

> Yet thus the leaden [*sic*] house does sweat,
> And scarce endures the master great;
> But, where he comes, the swelling hall
> Stirs, and the square grows spherical;   [49–52]

which, whatever its intention, is more absurd than it was intended to be. Marvell also falls into the even commoner error of images which are over-developed or distracting; which support nothing but their own mishapen bodies:

> And [*sic*] now the salmon-fishers moist
> Their leathern boats begin to hoist;
> And, like Antipodes in shoes,
> Have shod their heads in their canoes.   [769–72]

Of this sort of image a choice collection may be found in Johnson's *Life of Cowley*. But the images in the 'Coy Mistress' are not only witty, but satisfy the elucidation of Imagination given by Coleridge:

This power . . . reveals itself in the balance or reconcilement of opposite or discordant qualities: of sameness, with difference; of the general, with the concrete; the idea with the image; the individual with the representative; the sense of novelty and freshness with old and familiar objects; a more than usual state of emotion with more than usual order; judgement ever awake and steady self-possession with enthusiasm and feeling profound or vehement. . . .

Coleridge's statement applies also to the following verses, which are selected because of their similarity, and because they illustrate the marked caesura which Marvell often introduces in a short line:

The tawny mowers enter next,
Who seem like Israelites to be
Walking on foot through a green sea. . . .
    ['Upon Appleton House', 388–90]

And now the meadows fresher dyed,
Whose grass, with moister colour dashed,
Seems as green silks but newly washed. . . .
    [Ibid., 606–8]

He hangs in shades the orange bright,
Like golden lamps in a green night. . . .
    ['Bermudas', 17–18]

Annihilating all that's made
To a green thought in a green shade. . . .
    ['The Garden', 47–8]

Had it lived long, it would have been
Lilies without, roses within. . . .
    ['The Nymph Complaining . . .', 91–2]

We are baffled in the attempt to translate the quality indicated by the dim and antiquated term wit into the equally unsatisfactory nomenclature of our own time. Even Cowley is only able to define it by negatives:

Comely in thousand shapes appears;
  Yonder we saw it plain; and here 'tis now,
  Like spirits in a place, we know not how.

It has passed out of our critical coinage altogether, and no new term has been struck to replace it; the quality seldom exists, and is never recognised.

In a true piece of Wit all things must be
  Yet all things there agree;
As in the Ark, join'd without force or strife,
All creatures dwelt, all creatures that had life.
  Or as the primitive forms of all

> (If we compare great things with small)
> Which, without discord or confusion, lie
> In that strange mirror of the Deity.

So far Cowley has spoken well. But if we are to attempt even no more than Cowley, we, placed in a retrospective attitude, must risk much more than anxious generalisations. With our eye still on Marvell, we can say that wit is not erudition; it is sometimes stifled by erudition, as in much of Milton. It is not cynicism, though it has a kind of toughness which may be confused with cynicism by the tender-minded. It is confused with erudition because it belongs to an educated mind, rich in generations of experience; and it is confused with cynicism because it implies a constant inspection and criticism of experience. It involves, probably, a recognition, implicit in the expression of every experience, of other kinds of experience which are possible, which we find as clearly in the greatest as in poets like Marvell. Such a general statement may seem to take us a long way from 'The Nymph and the Fawn', or even from the 'Horatian Ode'; but it is perhaps justified by the desire to account for that precise taste of Marvell's which finds for him the proper degree of seriousness for every subject which he treats. His errors of taste, when he trespasses, are not sins against this virtue; they are conceits, distended metaphors and similes, but they never consist in taking a subject too seriously or too lightly. This virtue of wit is not a peculiar quality of minor poets, or of the minor poets of one age or of one school; it is an intellectual quality which perhaps only becomes noticeable by itself, in the work of lesser poets. . . . The quality which Marvell had, this modest and certainly impersonal virtue—whether we call it wit or reason, or even urbanity—we have patently failed to define. By whatever name we call it, and however we define that name, it is something precious and needed and apparently extinct; it is what should preserve the reputation of Marvell. . . .

SOURCE: extracts from article in *Times Literary Supplement* (31 March 1921); reprinted in Eliot's *Selected Essays* (1932); the extracts here are from the text of the 3rd edition (1951), pp. 293, 297–8, 303–4.

PART THREE

Recent Studies

Maren-Sofie Røstvig 'Surprise and Paradox: Perspectives on Marvell's Life and Poetry' (1970)

Andrew Marvell (1621–78) was known to his contemporaries as the Member of Parliament for Kingston-upon-Hull who, after 1667, gained considerable notoriety as the supposed author of anonymous verse satires written against the Court. They had little or no knowledge of the body of poetry published posthumously in 1681, and Marvell therefore continued to be known largely as a patriot and a politician, the first decisive sign of an interest in his lyric verse being revealed by Charles Lamb in 1821 when he quoted five stanzas from 'The Garden' in one of his essays. The real break-through occurred exactly a hundred years later with T. S. Eliot's reassessment of metaphysical poetry in general and that of Andrew Marvell in particular.

During the first phase of the popularity, in this century, of the metaphysical school, the personality of John Donne tended to overshadow those of his followers, but of recent years scholars have distinguished more perceptively between the various metaphysical poets, at the same time that an increased knowledge of Renaissance traditions has revealed the surprising extent to which Marvell was capable of transforming familiar themes and techniques into poems that seem entirely fresh and original. Part of the secret of the attraction of Marvell's verse lies in a certain riddling quality which it possesses as a consequence of this process of transformation. The reader is exposed to a cat-and-mouse technique of such sly subtlety that he is sometimes left completely bewildered, and it is this element of the unresolved which has made the poetry of Andrew Marvell the happy hunting-ground of critics bent on tearing out the heart of his mystery.

Andrew Marvell the man posits a similar puzzle; his friendship, during the sixteen-forties, with Cavalier poets like
Lovelace and Abraham Cowley is a matter of historical fact, but
so is his friendship with John Milton and his allegiance to Oliver
Cromwell. 'To His Noble Friend Mr Richard Lovelace, upon his
Poems' (1649) deplores the degeneracy of the times in a manner
typical of Royalist poets, but only a few years later Marvell wrote
a panegyric on the occasion of the first anniversary of the
government under Oliver Cromwell.

Did Marvell, then, change his mind or even turn his coat with
the times, or is it possible to resolve these as it would seem
conflicting attitudes into some sort of harmonious pattern? This
particular problem is not merely a biographical one, since
Charles as well as Cromwell figure in Marvell's verse, and so does
the famous leader of the Parliamentary forces, Thomas, Lord
Fairfax. It is as though Marvell, ironically aware of the intent
scrutiny of posterity, perversely refused to be docketed and
labelled, and so saw to it that he wrote on incompatible themes or
subjects. Thus he paid homage to earthly as to heavenly love, he
wrote poems praising and condemning gardens, and it is typical
that each of the three poems acclaimed as masterpieces illustrates
a different mode and a different area of human experience. 'An
Horatian Ode upon Cromwell's Return from Ireland' deals with
public issues, 'The Garden' praises complete withdrawal from
the 'busie Companies of Men', while 'To his Coy Mistress'
addresses the lady in a far from traditional manner but very
much for the traditional reason. This great variety suggests a
completely conscious attitude to the art of poetry, and a
technique of writing which is basically dramatic. Indeed, several
of Marvell's poems are dramatic dialogues or monologues, as, for
example, 'A Dialogue between the Soul and Body' or 'The
Mower's Song'. To add to the confusion, there is a sort of
incompatibility embedded in the very web and woof of Marvell's
verse, which combines a Cavalier flippancy with metaphysical
profundity, sweetness and simplicity of form with great semantic
density.

In reading Marvell, therefore, our expectation must be of the
unexpected. If surprise is a major source of delight in poetry, then
Marvell must be considered a past-master in the art of delighting
his readers in this particular manner. More often than not, the

element of surprise derives from a clever use of paradox, and to a casual reader Marvell's relentless pursuit of paradox may, perhaps, seem nothing but a clever mannerism. The rhetoric of paradox, though, may be a technique consciously chosen to do justice to the infinite complexity of life, and it has been so used by philosophers and poets alike since antiquity. The veritable epidemic of paradoxy which occurred during the Renaissance indicates complete familiarity with the classical tradition of the paradox, and proves that the age possessed sufficient intellectual and linguistic agility to exploit this tradition to advantage. As Rosalie L. Colie has put it,[1] paradox demands total control of thought and expression combined with an appearance of easy achievement—a statement which could be used to describe the peculiar quality of Andrew Marvell's verse.

One of the major problems in interpreting Marvell is resolved on considering the tradition of the paradoxical encomium, and this is the troublesome discrepancy so often felt between tone of voice and subject-matter. In 'The Garden', for example, the tone of voice is openly ironical except for one or two stanzas, but the subject is undoubtedly of serious religious import. This counter-pointing of tone of voice and content is the chief technique employed in the paradoxical encomium, which praises what is usually not considered praiseworthy—folly, for example,[2] or complete inactivity. If the subject-matter is a serious one, the author must treat it in a deceptively facetious manner, and the other way round. It follows, therefore, that we must not be deceived by the quality which Pierre Legouis has described as Marvell's 'chatty' tone of voice; we must remember, instead, that the poetic *lusus* or jest, usually in the form of a paradox, has ancient roots in European literature. Indeed, to readers familiar with the Renaissance tradition of paradoxical writing, Marvell's ironical tone of voice combined with his frequent use of compressed verbal paradoxes is the plainest possible indication that his jests serve a serious purpose. From the Romantic period and until fairly recently the European mind has been largely out of sympathy with this tradition, and serious subjects have tended to be given a serious treatment. Earlier periods, however, were keenly aware of the danger of profaning the highest mysteries by presenting them directly, and this is a fear that Marvell himself gave direct expression to in the poem which he wrote 'On

Mr Milton's Paradise lost'. No wonder, therefore, that Marvell preferred a joco-serious approach in so many of his poems and a method involving a maximum of indirection.

Although Marvell uses simple words placed in a simple syntactical pattern, his lines are usually so packed with meaning that it is difficult to supply the necessary explanations without losing sight of the poetry. In the case of a poet like John Donne, readers are aware of the difficulty involved in understanding the text, and the need for annotation is universally accepted and endured. Marvell, however, wears his wisdom with such an air of gaiety that it goes against the grain to submerge his lines in a flood of commentary. The solution adopted here is to select some poems for relatively close study, while the rest will have to be treated in more summary fashion. Some of the concepts referred to in the process of explication will admittedly seem recondite rather than commonplace Renaissance lore, but we must not yield to the temptation of using our own areas of ignorance to decide what may, or may not, have been well known to the seventeenth century. It is, for example, a Renaissance commonplace inherited from antiquity and the Middle Ages that the universe is a finite sphere enclosing a system of spheres, and that each is moved by a soul which inhabits it. The circular shape, moreover, was taken to reflect the nature of the Deity, both being without beginning or end, and the movement of the spheres was attributed to love. All created things, and particularly the angelic spirits, circle around God, as Herrick explains in the epigram defining Paradise ('Paradise is (as from the Learn'd I gather)/*A quire of blest Soules circling in the Father.*'). When Marvell wrote the poem which he entitled 'The Definition of Love', he turned as a matter of course to the structure of the universe for the terms in which he chose to convey his definition. He would also have been bound to think in terms of the most famous definition of love in the history of philosophy, the one given by Plato and so often referred to by English poets from Spenser to Thomas Stanley and Cowley. And according to Platonic thought love is the mutual longing of the two separated halves of a circle; when the two meet, they fall in love and thus the circle is again made complete. The circle is an ancient symbol of perfection, and so is the concept of the androgyne; to Marvell's generation both were familiar symbols of prelapsarian perfection, and this state of perfection was marked by complete union and rest (i.e. absence of striving, or movement), while our fallen state is characterised by discord and division of every kind, and by 'uncessant Labours'; Man is separated from God, the creatures from Man, and male from female.

These concepts were sufficiently familiar to the age to be used by Herrick as well as Marvell; thus Herrick defines love as 'a circle that doth restlesse move/In the same sweet eternity of love' ('Love what it is'), while another of Herrick's poems—'His Age . . .'—defines the union of friends in terms of the circle, and yet another—'The Eye'—compares the universe with its spheres and its straight and oblique lines to Corinna's eye ('Ah! what is then this curious skie,/But onely my *Corinna's* eye?').

It was therefore only to be expected that Marvell's 'The Definition of Love' should make use of much the same cosmic images; the element of surprise resides solely in the use that Marvell makes of them. The first puzzle is created by the title since a definition should be general, and Marvell seems concerned with a single lover's particular misfortune. The problem would be solved if his situation should reflect a universal predicament. That this may indeed be so, is suggested by the fact that it is Fate herself who has intervened between the lover and the achievement of his desire, the reason being that a fulfilment of the lover's wish would entail *her ruin*. To prevent this, Fate has placed the two so that they cannot possibly meet:

The Definition of Love

I

My Love is of a birth as rare
As 'tis for object strange and high:
It was begotten by despair
Upon Impossibility.

II

Magnanimous Despair alone
Could show me so divine a thing,
Where feeble Hope could ne'r have flown
But vainly flapt its Tinsel Wing.

III

And yet I quickly might arrive
Where my extended Soul is fixt,
But Fate does Iron wedges drive,
And alwaies crouds it self betwixt.

IV

For Fate with jealous Eye does see
Two perfect Loves; nor lets them close:
Their union would her ruine be,
And her Tyrannick pow'r depose.

V

And therefore her Decrees of Steel
Us as the distant Poles have plac'd,
(Though Loves whole World on us doth wheel)
Not by themselves to be embrac'd.

VI

Unless the giddy Heaven fall,
And Earth some new Convulsion tear;
And, us to joyn, the World should all
Be cramp'd into a *Planisphere*.

VII

As Lines so Loves *oblique* may well
Themselves in every Angle greet:
But ours so truly *Paralel*,
Though infinite can never meet.

VIII

Therefore the Love which us doth bind,
But Fate so enviously debarrs,
Is the Conjunction of the Mind,
And Opposition of the Stars.

In an age when astrology and astronomy were scarcely to be separated from each other or from religion, Fate was a synonym for the structure of the universe, and if this is the sense in which Marvell uses the word, he is saying that his love is such that its consummation would entail the ruin of the universe. This is a paradox indeed, since the universe is a manifestation and expression of love. The lovers have been placed by Fate as far apart 'as the distant Poles', and ruin would clearly ensue if the spherical universe, to permit a joining of the poles, were crushed flat. But why is fate so opposed to the lover's achievement of his impossible desire for an 'object strange and high'? And what is this object? And what are the curious iron wedges that prevent the poles from meeting, however fast the spherical universe keeps turning, prompted by love? Answers will be found on reading a few chapters in the popular handbook on the structure of the universe written by Sacrobosco or John Holywood, the *Tractatus de Sphaera*.[3] As this handbook explains, the universe is a round sphere and not a flat circle, and the poles of the world terminate the axis of the universe so that 'the world revolves on them', which is what Marvell states in stanza v. Since one of these poles is always visible to us and the other always invisible, nothing could possibly underline the separation of the lovers more strongly than the image which places them 'as the distant Poles'. The mysterious wedges are best explained in terms of one of Sacrobosco's definitions of a celestial sign or constellation; each sign may be viewed as a pyramid 'whose equilateral base is that surface which we call a 'sign' whilst its apex is at the centre of the earth'. Since the signs follow the movement of the sphere it is obvious that they will always keep the poles apart, and it is equally obvious that unless they did this, the universe would be ruined. The poles are at the extreme points of the spherical universe, and it was axiomatic that extremes must pass through a mean before they are capable of meeting; in this case the Equator would be the mean, but here we find the meeting-point only of the Equinoctial line and the Ecliptic, the most famous of all oblique angles. The obliquity of this angle aptly symbolises the hole-and-corner nature of 'oblique' or imperfect love. Since the 'iron wedges' of the celestial signs (the 'Opposition of the Stars' referred to in the last line) make a circling movement useless, what about a departure away from the poles in a straight line?

According to the laws of perspective, parallel lines, when extended, are seen to meet, but this solution is excluded by the fact that their loves are 'so truly *Paralel*' (i.e. equal), that they 'Though infinite can never meet'; hence the lovers must remain content with a 'Conjunction of the Mind'.

The structure of the universe is relevant to that of man since the microcosmos of man reflects the structure of the macrocosmos, and the same is true of society. If one applies cosmic geometry to society, Marvell would seem to argue that the lovers are separated by social distance as effectively as by the extremes of cosmic distance, which explains why they can enjoy a conjunction only of the mind. Such a tame conclusion, however, is an absurd anti-climax after the splendid cosmic imagery, and it would also deny the implications of the title—that the predicament is a universal one. Moreover, it would also align Marvell with that rather tiresome school of Platonics mocked by Suckling as well as Abraham Cowley. As Cowley phrased it: 'So Angels love; so let them love for me;/When I am *all Soul*, such shall *my Love* too be' ('Answer to the Platonicks'). A better solution is found on applying the cosmic images to man, and by positing that the closing of the circle referred to in Marvell's fourth stanza is an allusion to the well-known concept of the hermaphrodite. Edmund Spenser had rebuked lovers for entertaining the impossible notion of a perfect physical union; there can be no lasting union, in this life, between male and female. Nature alone, so Spenser argues, is bi-sexual or capable of containing opposites; in the case of human lovers Concord or Love both joins and separates (*Faerie Queene*, IV 10 34–5, 41). Unless Concord contained 'heaven in his course', binding everything with 'inviolable bands', fire would mix with the air and land with water. It would indeed be a satisfying conclusion to a subtle poem, if Marvell's last stanza is a complaint that the physical union fails to satisfy because it is not complete and cannot ever hope to be complete; the 'iron wedges' of their separate personalities will always prevent the closing of the circle. The separation into male and female is as much a decree of steel as the separation of the poles of the universe, or of air from fire and land from water. Love may effect a temporary conjunction of opposites, but no lasting union. That perfect love should desire perfect union, as in the prelapsarian androgyne, is natural, but

impossible. Francis I of France might have his portrait painted as
an androgyne, half man and half woman[4], but the perfection
symbolised by this union must remain an impossibility as it
transcends the limits imposed by Nature, or Fate. Marvell's
lover, then, realises that his desire 'for object strange and high'—
a desire rightly characterised as 'begotten by despair/Upon
Impossibility'—is rendered impossible by the very terms of our
existence, and so his final statement is an affirmation that a true
union of lovers can be achieved only in the mind, which is a
position as contrary to received opinion as at all possible.

'A Dialogue between the Soul and Body' presents a closely
related aspect of our human predicament. Here the issue is the
conflict in man himself of irreconcilable opposites:

> O who shall, from this Dungeon, raise
> A Soul inslav'd so many wayes?
> With bolts of Bones, that fetter'd stands
> In Feet; and manacled in Hands.
> Here blinded with an Eye; and there
> Deaf with the drumming of an Ear.
> A Soul hung up, as 'twere, in Chains
> Of Nerves, and Arteries, and Veins.

Paradox alone can do justice to our fallen condition: our vision
blinds us, and our hearing makes us deaf. This argument
presumes that ultimate truth cannot be conveyed through the
avenue of the five senses; if the soul inclines too far towards sense
perception, its inner vision will be impaired, and it is the intuitive
powers of the mind (or pure intellect) that provide true
knowledge. After the Fall, however, this inner vision became
largely obscured, as Milton explains in *Paradise Lost* (IX 1051–4,
1121–3; XI 411–20). Marvell's dialogue suggests that the division,
in man, between mind and body is as absolute as the division of
man into male and female; both as an individual and a lover man
is at the mercy of a cosmic joke or paradox imposing division and
preventing union.

By stressing his despair at the separation in such a forcible
manner, Marvell compels us to realise the infinite sadness of our
fallen condition, thus indirectly drawing attention to the nature
of the perfection that was lost. It is interesting that Marvell

should do so in terms of the contrast between discord (or conflict, division) and concord (or union). This way of thinking about the Fall is typical of the syncretistic Neoplatonists of the Renaissance, but Renaissance theologians, like some of the Fathers of our Church, had assimilated so much of this philosophy that it would scarcely have been felt as an alient element. Thus when Herrick defined the number two as the 'lucklesse number of division' ('The Number of two'), the authority which he invokes is, not Pythagoras, Plato, or the Neoplatonists, but 'the Fathers'. Conversely Herrick (like Milton in *Paradise Lost*, VIII 419–26) defines God as 'most One' (in an epigram entitled 'God is One') or as above number: 'Jehovah, as *Boëtius* saith,/No number of the *Plurall* hath.'

In *The Arte of English Poesie* (1589), Puttenham calls the paradox the 'Wondrer', and Marvell certainly wonders ironically at the condition of which he speaks. Although man has fallen away from unity (or God) into multiplicity or discord, he still yearns for unity, but it is his fate to suffer division. No solution is offered, but to a Christian the answer is never in doubt: Christ is the healer of discord, the restorer of our lost perfection as stated by Paul in his epistle to the Ephesians. Christ made 'in himself of twain one new man, so making peace' (*Ephesians*, II 15), and so, through Christ, man may partake of the same peace or union. 'A Dialogue between Thyrsis and Dorinda' states this argument directly, and it does so, appropriately enough, in language indebted to the Song of Solomon, a poem universally interpreted as a description of the union between Christ and the soul. 'Heaven's the Center of the Soul' to which the soul is irresistibly drawn, a point put even more clearly in the lines 'On a Drop of Dew'.

If the strength of this passionate concern with man's fallen condition seems surprising, we must remember the intensity of the religious mood which swept the English nation at this time when even the most moderate of men could be tempted to feel that the Kingdom of Christ was at hand. The Puritans by no means had a monopoly on religious sentiment; those who saw in Cromwell a scourge of God rather than a leader into the Promised Land, often found consolation in profound religious meditations tinged by Neoplatonic thought. It would have been hard to credit a man like Marvell with a share in the Millenarian enthusiasm which fired so many of his contemporaries, if he had not himself given expression to it in 'The First Anniversary of the Government under O.C.' The poet's hope is a tentative one, since the signs provided by the events of the day were capable of various interpretations; all he can say is that 'if these the Times, then this must be the Man'. Yet even this conditional clause today seems quite startling. To Marvell's generation, however, it did not seem at all absurd that England should have assumed the role of God's chosen people, and in innumerable pamphlets and sermons the great national events are persistently referred to in terms of the exodus from Egypt (i.e. the fallen state) and the entry into the Promised Land (i.e. the regenerated state). As Marvell states, if England were God's 'seasonable People' that would bend to Cromwell's as he to Heaven's will, then

> Sure, the mysterious Work, where none withstand,
> Would forthwith finish under such a Hand:
> Fore-shortned Time its useless Course would stay,
> And soon precipitate the latest Day.   (137–40)

Unhappily, though, most men 'Look on, all unconcern'd, or unprepar'd;/And Stars still fall, and still the Dragons Tail/ Swinges the Volumes of its horrid Flail'. The echo from Milton's 'On the Morning of Christ's Nativity' (published in Milton's *Poems*, 1645) is not only a compliment from one poet to another (Marvell's poem also contains two echoes from 'Lycidas'), it also serves to draw attention to the concept of the Last Day when Sin, through the final victory of Christ, shall be no more. But, to quote Milton, this 'must not yet be so'; the time is not ripe for the second coming. Marvell, as was to be expected, explains the situation in terms of a paradox: 'For the great Justice that did first suspend/ The World by Sin, does by the same extend.' In other words, sin—which once caused the complete destruction of the earth through the Flood—now ensures the continuation of human existence in its fallen form because it prevents the regeneration that must precede the coming of Christ.

It is tempting to stress the doubt and despair which filled the English nation at this time at the expense of the high hopes for the regeneration of the individual and the state. But because we know that the end was disillusionment and the merry monarch rather than the *regnum Christi*, that the English, to quote Milton, chose 'a captain back for Egypt', we must not underestimate the effect of the hope, nor must we forget its close connection with Renaissance humanism. The strength of this hope is indicated by the large number of pamphlets, prose treatises and poems dealing with creation, the Fall, and the Scheme of Redemption, and many of these bear directly on the political scene since their concern is with the regeneration not only of the individual, but of the state as well. Ambiguous as man's nature is, he may sink to the level of a beast or rise to that of the second Adam (Christ), and while the Puritans attributed the work of regeneration entirely to the operation of divine grace, many humanists stressed the importance of a conscious choice. Marvell, therefore, is at one with his age in focussing on the conflict between guilt and innocence, the prelapsarian and the postlapsarian state. While 'The Garden' indicates that Paradise may be regained by the individual, 'Upon Appleton House' includes society in its perspective, which takes in the whole scope of the universal history of man through its many references to the chief phases in this history. Others of Marvell's poems merely describe the conflict between the state of innocence and the state of corruption or imperfection, but without resolving the tension. Whatever interpretation is adopted of the allegorical story narrated in 'The Nymph complaining for the death of her Faun', one point, at least, is clear: the lament is spoken by a creature who represents innocence, and the death of the faun is an act of wilful murder on the part of 'wanton Troopers'. The evocation of innocence, in the language and in the description of the delights of the garden, is so successful that readers cannot fail to be moved. It is, perhaps, because their style and manner are so different that the basic kinship between Marvell and Thomas Traherne has gone unnoticed.

If it is conceded that the larger part of the English nation was committed to a religious view of history, the curious passivity of many Royalists at the time of the execution of King Charles I is more easily understood. A religiously motivated loyalism to the man in power as the leader appointed by God, would explain the ambiguity in Marvell's attitude towards Charles and Cromwell in 'An Horatian Ode upon Cromwell's Return from Ireland'. As soon as their side was favoured by the events of the war, the

Parliamentarians were quick to argue that a divine judgment
had been passed through trial by battle, and many men of
moderation must have shared the sentiments of Thomas, Lord
Fairfax, when he wrote the following lines on the issue of the
execution:

> But if the Power devine permited this
> His Will's the Law & ours must acquiesse.[5]

This is the tenor of many Civil War pamphlets, and this is what
Marvell, too, states in his Horatian ode:

> 'Tis Madness to resist or blame
> The force of angry Heavens flame . . .

The very fact that victory 'his Crest does plume' proclaims
Cromwell the divinely appointed ruler—whether as a scourge for
sinners or saintly leader the future only would reveal. As John M.
Wallace has argued, the delicate balance struck by Marvell in
this ode is not unique, although the splendid phrasing may create
this impression. Marvell's description of the execution suggests
that he was a loyalist; Charles is presented as submitting meekly
to the will of Heaven and freely giving up his power to God's
chosen instrument:

> *He* nothing common did or mean
> Upon that memorable Scene:
> > But with his keener Eye
> > The Axes edge did try:
>
> Nor call'd the *Gods* with vulgar spight
> To vindicate his helpless Right,
> > But bow'd his comely Head,
> > Down as upon a Bed.
>
> This was that memorable Hour
> Which first assur'd the forced Pow'r.
> > . . .

The slowness of the rhythmical movement reinforces the im-

pression that the poem is a deliberate oration where both sides are
tried. The outcome, though, is not in doubt, since history already
has provided the answer; Cromwell's victories are proof of his
election as leader. Like Cincinnatus, Cromwell was called from
his plough—or at least his garden—to serve the state:

> . . .
>
>   And, if we would speak true,
>   Much to the Man is due.
>
>   Who, from his private Gardens, where
>   He liv'd reserved and austere,
>   As if his highest plot
>   To plant the Bergamot,
>
>   Could by industrious Valour climbe
>   To ruine the great Work of Time,
>   And cast the Kingdome old
>   Into another Mold.

As the context is one of classical allusions, the images, too, are
necessarily classical, so that Cromwell is referred to as 'Wars and
Fortunes Son'. In the two poems dedicated to Cromwell,
however, the language is Biblical and Cromwell is presented as
'Heaven's Favorite':

> What man was ever so in Heav'n obey'd
> Since the commanded sun o're Gibeon stay'd?
>   ('A Poem upon the Death of O.C.', 191–2)

'The First Anniversary of the Government under O.C.' presents
Cromwell as Davidic King, that is, as a ruler appointed by God
and an instrument of Providence. This is largely done through
images presenting Cromwell as the Sun, the greatest cosmic
power, or as the master 'musician' who imposes harmony on the
state in the same manner that God imposed harmony on chaos
through the act of creation. The 'wondrous Order and Consent'
imposed by Cromwell implies regeneration of a spiritual kind,
and in the personal passage where Marvell visualises himself as a

serious poet, he intimates that Cromwell hunts the beast of the
Apocalypse:

> If gracious Heaven to my Life give length,
> Leisure to Time, and my Weakness Strength,
> Then shall I once with graver Accents shake
> Your Regal sloth, and your long Slumbers wake:
> Like the shrill Huntsman that prevents the East,
> Winding his Horn to Kings that chase the Beast.
>   Till then my Muse shall hollow far behind
> Angelique *Cromwell* who outwings the wind;
> And in dark Nights, and in cold Dayes alone
> Persues the Monster thorough every Throne . . .(119–28)

Although octosyllabic couplets were Marvell's favourite verse
form, this poem proves his ability to write memorable heroic
couplets and to balance his lines and half-lines with a skill that
anticipates Dryden. The many references to patriarchs and
prophets indicate that regeneration is again a main issue; thus
Cromwell is compared to Noah's family of eight, 'Left by the
Wars Flood on the Mountains crest', to Elisha and Gideon, and
the circumstance that the timespan involved in these references
extends from the first day to the last strengthens the impression
that Cromwell is seen as an agent of God through whom the
scheme of redemption is gradually extended through the world
and all of time.

The secular and the religious aspects of government cannot
always be kept distinct, and certainly not in the seventeenth
century. Marvell's shift of allegiance, therefore, could also be
taken to imply a recognition that a *de facto* government after a
while tends to be accepted as a government *de jure*. Such a
transition is clearly felt in Shakespeare's history plays, where
Henry IV at first (in *Richard II*) is seen as being to some extent a
usurper, but he appears much less so as he establishes himself as
the accepted ruler in the two Parts of *Henry IV*.

Regeneration of the individual and of society is a major theme
in the poems dedicated to Thomas, Lord Fairfax and presumably
written while Marvell stayed on Fairfax's Yorkshire estate as a
teacher of languages to his daughter. Comparatively little is
known of Marvell's life and career before he became a Member of

Parliament for Hull in 1659; we know that he grew up in Hull where his two sisters married into prominent families, and that he spent seven years at Trinity College, Cambridge, matriculating on 14 December 1633. A letter written by John Milton on 21 February 1653 contains the useful information that Marvell had just left the employ of the Lord General, and that Marvell, prior to his stay with Fairfax, had spent four years abroad in Holland, France, Italy, and Spain 'to very good purpose' and 'the gaining of these four languages'. The sequence, then, is one of seven years at Cambridge, four years abroad, possibly in the capacity of tutor, a few years in London before and after this grand tour, and an unspecified period in Fairfax's household after June 1650 (when Fairfax retired) up to the beginning of 1653. Before he became a Member for Hull in 1659, Marvell was the tutor of Cromwell's ward, William Dutton, and after 2 September 1657 he became Latin secretary, a post he had applied for in vain in 1653.

This brief sketch shows that Marvell was a competent classical scholar who had added modern languages to his stock of Latin and Greek, and his years at Cambridge would have exposed him to the double impact of its religious piety and its Platonism. The Cambridge Platonists, like Ficino and Pico della Mirandola, were syncretists in the sense that they believed that Plato and the other ancient philosophers had been given the same revelation as Moses, so that Plato was Moses Atticus. If Marvell did, in fact, share this syncretistic attitude, Fairfax would have found him a congenial companion, since the Lord General devoted much of his spare time during his retirement (and he retired at 38) to making an English translation of a French commentary on the Hermetic dialogues published by François de Foix in 1579. The reason why the dialogues attributed to Hermes Trismegistus enjoyed such a vogue during the Renaissance is stated by de Foix, who believed that Hermes, like Plato, revealed all the mysteries of our Christian faith concerning creation, the Fall, and the Scheme of Redemption.

Many of Marvell's images, like those of Spenser and Milton, assume familiarity with this syncretistic way of thinking about divine revelation, according to which the same truths may be discovered everywhere—in Nature (the Book of God's Works), in pagan myth and philosophy when properly interpreted, and in the Bible (the Book of God's Words). The interchangeability of the two Books is a basic assumption in Marvell's longest poem, 'Upon Appleton House, to my Lord Fairfax', while a study of syncretistic thought provides the best context for the images and paradoxes crammed into the nine short stanzas of 'The Garden'. But Marvell's praise of his 'delicious Solitude' must be connected with two powerful literary traditions as well, one stemming from the classical praise of the happiness of rural retirement, the other from the religious praise of the mystical or spiritual Garden of Eden reached through solitary contemplation. There is a large area of common ground between the two in that both attribute innocence to the rural scene, and theologians had underlined this similarity by introducing references to the Horatian and Virgilian praise of the husbandman in their comments on *Genesis*, II 8. There are many examples, in English literature, of poets and prose writers who combined the classical praise of country life with religious themes before Marvell did so in his poetic tributes to Lord Fairfax—Ben Jonson, William Habington, John Milton, and Robert Herrick come readily to mind.

Although 'The Garden' is not dedicated to Fairfax, it connects formally and thematically with those poems that are. The many bantering phrases used, and the ironical tone of voice, suggest that this poem may have been conceived as a paradoxical encomium of complete inactivity:

> How vainly men themselves amaze
> To win the Palm, the Oke, or Bayes;
> And their uncessant Labours see
> Crown'd from some single Herb or Tree.
> Whose short and narrow verged Shade
> Does prudently their Toyles upbraid;
> While all Flow'rs and all Trees do close
> To weave the Garlands of repose.
>
> Fair quiet, have I found thee here,
> And Innocence thy Sister dear!
> Mistaken long, I sought you then
> In busie Companies of Men.
> Your sacred Plants, if here below,
> Only among the Plants will grow.
> Society is all but rude,
> To this delicious Solitude.

Repose is a key concept, strongly contrasted with 'uncessant Labours' and 'busie Companies of Men'. Complete repose is praised at the expense of action, solitude is preferred to society, single life, even, to wedded bliss. And repose is praised because it represents the most intense creative activity, solitude because it is more refined than society, the single state because it fuses two paradises in one—whatever that may mean ('Two Paradises 'twere in one/To live in Paradise alone.'). The epithets *rude* and *delicious* have a paradoxical relationship to the nouns they qualify—Society and Solitude—and their effect is such that both seem ludicrous. And 'Garlands of repose' is a contradiction in terms, since repose scarcely can lead to any kind of victory. The air of mockery is intensified in the third stanza, where the beauty of women is slighted in favour of 'this lovely green'. Certainly the 'green' is lovely, as any garden enthusiast will readily affirm, but why should it be more *amorous* than women? This absurd proposition is then used to explain the hot pursuit of Daphne by Apollo and of Syrinx by Pan; the gods *desired* their metamorphosis. They wanted Syrinx to turn into a reed and Daphne into a laurel tree.

The statement, in stanza 4, that 'When we have run our Passions heat,/Love hither makes his best retreat', would seem to connect the garden with heavenly love in sharp contrast to mere earthly, sensual love. It is therefore confusing to discover, in the next stanza, that the amorousness of 'this lovely green' copies the erotic abandon of those 'Fond Lovers' so roundly denounced in the preceding stanza.

To understand this basic paradox it is useful again to remember the Renaissance tendency to reconcile the Platonic or Hermetic account of creation and the Fall with the Mosaic account, this reconciliation being the main purpose of the commentary on the Hermetic dialogues that Fairfax tried his best to translate. However, equally useful sources for this syncretistic vision are the prose and verse of Giordano Bruno, or Pico della Mirandola's famous *Oration on the Dignity of Man*. These and similar works describe the metamorphosis of man from his fallen state to a regenerated, higher state through a contemplative withdrawal from the sphere of matter (defined in terms of movement and number) into that of pure mind (defined as complete bodily repose and a return from multiplicity to unity through contemplation of the One). The theme of Marvell's poem, therefore, has the closest possible affinity with well-known concepts propounded by the syncretistic Neoplatonists of the Renaissance, and these are also the men who recommended a jocoserious approach in order to exclude readers incapable of a proper understanding. Fairfax, presumably, would be one of the few capable of penetrating to the core of the poetic fable by virtue of his professional concern with the Hermetic dialogues.

If we define the theme of 'The Garden' as metamorphosis achieved through repose, the metamorphosis being from a state of discord and division to one marked by harmony and union, then the fifth stanza must be taken to describe the loving union between man and all created things, a union which marked the prelapsarian state according to the Hermetic dialogues. The stanza, then, describes, not luxurious enjoyment of sensual pleasures, but a divine plenitude which implies unity through love.

Ben Jonson's 'To Penshurst' shows that a similar plenitude could be attributed to the rural scene in poems based on the classical theme of the happiness of country life. Ben Jonson describes an estate and a family where innocence prevails to such an extent that the effect of the Fall is virtually annulled, so that the creatures pay their homage to man as they once did to Adam; the very carp and pike 'leape on land,/Before the fisher, or into his hand.' The popular neo-Latin poet, Casimire Sarbiewski, similarly merged the concept of the Horatian Sabine farm with that of the Garden of Eden or the *hortus conclusus* (garden enclosed) of Solomon.[6]

The most important point made about the 'happy Garden-state' in stanza 8 is Adam's initial happy solitude. Paradise could be used in the Renaissance as a metaphor for the sexual organs,[7] and it is likely that this usage prompted Marvell's line about two paradises in one. The theory that man at first was an androgyne (i.e. a person with two 'paradises' in one) was so well known in the Renaissance that such an allusion would be no more learned than Marvell's references to classical myth. And, as we have seen, a number of poems were written at this time not only about Platonic love, but about hermaphrodites as well. The Hermetic context explains why Adam is referred to as an androgyne by Marvell; the Hermetic dialogues identify the Fall with the division into two sexes—an act which put man under the necessity of incessantly striving instead of enjoying complete repose, like God.

Stanzas 6 and 7 describe the union, not between man and the rest of creation, but between man and God. This union is achieved through a withdrawal from the lesser pleasures of the garden and by means of a concentration of the powers of the mind (the lines 'Mean while the Mind, from pleasure less,/ Withdraws into its happiness' can be taken to convey both meanings). This withdrawal and concentration is the first stage towards the release of the soul from the body described in stanza 7. The mind is the image of God in man, since God is pure mind, and the mind is accommodated in the body by being joined to the soul, the soul in its turn being directly connected with the body through the avenues of the five senses, as the Hermetic dialogues explain. Marvell uses the two terms—soul and mind—with great precision. The mind can be released only at death (the 'longer flight'); in this life, however, the soul may achieve a momentary release from the body, and since the soul was believed to have fire for its body (fire being the purest and most celestial of the elements), one understands why it 'Waves in its Plumes the various Light'. The fruit tree is a familiar symbol for Christ, the *nova poma* (new apple) hanging on the Tree of the Cross and freely offering himself to all who will accept the gift of redemption. Again it must be stressed that this juxtaposition of Christian with Platonic and Hermetic concepts should be viewed as evidence of a syncretistic bias of the kind that must be attributed to Marvell's patron, Lord Fairfax.

The concluding stanza returns the reader to the 'milder Sun' of the created universe, the Sun being the shadow of God according to Ficino and the Neoplatonists. The reference to the Sun and the zodiac forms a most appropriate conclusion, since the great circle of the Sun combines movement with repose, and since the movement of the stars enables us to compute time, and, as Plato tells us in the *Timaeus*, the computation of time is the beginning of wisdom. This is so because it enables man to reproduce in himself 'the perfectly unerring course of the sun' as Plato puts it, and so 'reduce to settled order the wandering motions in himself', and this is, of course, the purpose of the poet's retreat into his garden.

In 'The Mower against Gardens', '*Damon* the Mower', and the other poems where this fully dramatised character speaks, Marvell's attitude seems suddenly reversed in that it is now the garden which represents corruption. This is logical enough, however, as Marvell is intent on exploiting the paradox that now, after the Fall, gardens are a source of corruption because man has made them so. Only areas untouched by man have retained their innocence.

The praise of a patron's estate is a type of poem often based on the classical theme of the happiness of rural life; Ben Jonson's homage to Sir Robert Wroth, or Casimire Sarbiewski's to the Duke of Bracciano (Epode 1) are good examples of the tradition within which Marvell worked when he wrote 'Upon Appleton House' and 'Upon the Hill and Grove at Bill-borow'. Fairfax himself is never treated ironically, but he is part of a world which is by definition paradoxical. Fairfax's command of this world seems absolute; thus he solves the most stubborn of all mathematical paradoxes, the squaring of the circle, by subjecting his bodily passions (symbolised by the square) to his immortal mind (symbolised by the circle), and on his entrance into his house the building imitates these 'holy Mathematicks': 'But where he comes the swelling Hall/Stirs, and the *Square* grows *Spherical*'. This is more than a witty allusion to the fact that the square hall was topped by a cupola; what is involved, is man's mastery over matter, and the love which matter feels for man as the image of God—a basic point in those Hermetic dialogues that interested Fairfax so profoundly.

'Upon Appleton House' firmly connects perfection with humility and deformity with pride, and since pride was the cause of the Fall, Marvell is once more caught up by his vision of Paradise lost and regained, and it is typical of Marvell that he projects this vision into the scene itself. Marvell begins by tracing the history of Nunappleton, and it was inevitable that a Protestant poet should characterise the period when the estate was a nunnery as a period of corruption, so that it was only when the house was turned to secular uses that it became truly religious ('Though many a *Nun* there made her Vow,/'Twas no *Religious House* till now.'). With stanza 47 Marvell turns to the landscape, where the paradoxical reversal of the traditional scale warns us that more is meant than meets the eye:

> And now to the Abyss I pass
> Of that unfathomable Grass,
> Where Men like Grashoppers appear,
> But Grashoppers are Gyants there:

More illusions follow. The cattle and the meadow 'seem within the polisht Grass/A Landskip drawen in Looking-Glass', and in this looking-glass world they resemble spots placed on faces (according to the fashion of the day), while conversely the tiny seems very great indeed when fleas, viewed through 'Multiplying Glasses', appear like slowly moving celestial constellations.

Marvell's presentation of these marvels of Nature, whereby the deceptiveness of sense perception is proved, is clearly indebted to contemporary experiments with mirrors and other distorting devices. As Rosalie L. Colie has argued, these experiments are an exact parallel, in natural philosophy, to the verbal paradox of contradiction. Marvell plays around with both types of paradox (verbal and scientific), and to all this he adds a number of geometrical and logical paradoxes. The squaring of the circle already referred to is a paradox in geometry, the paradox being that two such different shapes can become one. Yet another type of paradox is exploited when Marvell praises Chance at the expense of Wit or rational inquiry in stanza 74: 'Chance's better Wit' takes him straight to the truth, thus making a study of '*Nature's mystick Book*' superfluous. Before Chance provides this moment of sudden illumination, however, the landscape has served as a kind of stage upon which is acted, as in a masque, the universal history of man ('No Scene that turns with Engines strange/Does oftener than these Meadows change'). The mowers appear like Israelites crossing the Red Sea ('To them the Grassy Deeps divide/And crowd a Lane to either Side') or again as wandering through the wilderness where 'Rails rain for Quails, for Manna Dew.' When the meadow turns into a sea because 'The River in it self is drown'd', the poet retreats from the Flood to seek sanctuary in the wood. 'And, while it lasts, myself imbark/In this yet green, yet growing Ark'. Marvell's references to the chief Old Testament events are too explicit to be ignored; this is clearly the story, told in the jocoserious manner of the paradoxist and by means of Old Testament types, of the fall of man and the scheme of redemption. The Ark of Noah is a type of the church of Christ through whose agency fallen man is redeemed from the flood of sin, as Augustine explains.[8] The Lord, so Augustine writes, 'inhabits the flood of this world by His presence in the saints whom He keeps safe within the Church as in an ark.' Both Marvell and Augustine associate the Bible with trees, the connecting link being the pun on leaves. Augustine even speaks of 'browsing' in the pastures of the divine books, and Marvell similarly requests to be staked down (as an animal tethered to a stake?) in the meadow, presumably in order to 'browse' in the Augustinian sense. Because of the strong feeling that the two 'books' of revelation are parallel texts, it was possible to speak of Nature in terms of the Bible and the other way round.

As soon as the poet retreats into his 'yet green, yet growing Ark', his regenerated state is indicated when he begins to understand the language of the birds, like Adam before the Fall. In the leaves of the forest the poet reads 'What *Rome, Greece, Palestine*, ere said', but Chance proves a better guide than Wit when he discovers that he is dressed like a priest:

> The Oak-Leaves me embroyder all,
> Between which Caterpillars crawl:
> And Ivy, with familiar trails,
> Me licks, and clasps, and curles, and hales.
> Under this *antick Cope* I move
> Like some great *Prelate of the Grove* . . .

Chance, then, has shown that man is the Priest of Nature, mediating between all created things and God. Stanzas 77–78 describe an *imitatio Christi* whereby the Old Adam is crucified and the new man born through the spiritual baptism typified in the Old Testament by the crossing of the Red Sea. The 'crucifixion' is effected by the plants intimately connected with the effect of the Fall: 'Do you, *O Brambles*, chain me too,/And courteous *Briars* nail me through'. Nature shares in this process of regeneration: the very grass seems like 'Green Silks but newly washt', and the great enemy, Satan, has been overcome: 'No *Serpent* new nor *Crocodile*/Remains behind our little *Nile*'. Such is the purity of the new creation that the Sun pines for its own reflection in the crystal mirror of the river.

'Upon Appleton House' concludes with a passage devoted to

praise of Fairfax's daughter Maria. The extravagant nature of this praise is entirely traditional, the person being presented in his or her ideal form so that the praise becomes an exhortation. Maria is more than beauty embodied, she is the idea of beauty in the divine mind so that it is she who bestows beauty on the world: "'Tis *She* that to these Gardens gave/That wondrous Beauty which they have'. While the world has been chaotic ever since the Fall, the lesser world of man is still capable of order. In a truly innocent person we shall still find '*Heaven's Center, Nature's Lap,/ And Paradice's only Map*'. Like Milton, therefore, Marvell concludes by placing the stress entirely on the Paradise within—that is, on the regenerated state.

A survey of Marvell's more traditional love poems would have to focus on 'To his Coy Mistress', a lyric based on the great paradox of Time. The problem is whether Time causes growth or decay, a point debated by philosophers and paradoxists with considerable fervour and ingenuity. Thus David Person stated, in his *Varieties* (1636), that if Time causes sublunary bodies to experience a 'rising, increase or growing', then love, too, when exposed to Time, would experience a similar growth. Marvell's poem, therefore, begins as a mock encomium of coyness, the argument being that since coyness means postponement, and since more time means more growth, then 'My vegetable Love should grow/Vaster than Empires, and more slow.' The time-span envisaged encompasses all of human history, as the lover would begin 'ten years before the Flood' (i.e. in the year 1646 Anno Mundi, the Flood having occurred 1656 years after time began) and the lady would be permitted to 'refuse/Till the Conversion of the *Jews*'. This takes us up to the very end of Time, the conversion of the Jews being one of the signs that the Kingdom of Christ is at hand.

The counter-argument, that Time causes decay rather than growth, begins with a heavily stressed *but*:

> But at my back I alwaies hear
> Times winged Chariot hurrying near:
> And yonder all before us lye
> Desarts of vast Eternity.

The Psalmist had asked, ironically, 'Shall the dust praise thee?'

and 'in the grave who shall give thee thanks?'[9] Marvell's rhetoric
is just as forceful:

> Thy Beauty shall no more be found;
> Nor, in thy marble Vault, shall sound
> My echoing Song: then Worms shall try
> That long preserv'd Virginity:
> And your quaint Honour turn to dust;
> And into ashes all my Lust.
> The Grave's a fine and private place,
> But none I think do there embrace.

The solution is given in the third and last section, the swiftness
and assurance of which is a matter partly of syntax and partly of
imagery. All but the last couplet consist of a quickly-moving,
long-sustained period presenting a string of images whose climax
is reached with the following lines:

> Let us roll all our Strength, and all
> Our sweetness, up into one Ball:
> And tear our Pleasures with rough strife,
> Thorough the Iron gates of Life.

Despite the overtly sexual nature of the consummation described
in this concluding section, the 'Ball' and the 'gates of Life' must
not be taken to carry on the description of the amorous sport. The
epithet 'iron' and the roughness of the sound pattern indicate
that this cannot be an image of consummation. The exploding
cannon-ball was a familiar Renaissance emblem illustrating the
ancient paradox that we must learn to hurry slowly (*festina lente*).
As Edgar Wind informs us, in his study of *Pagan Mysteries in the
Renaissance*, the paradox had been invested with a profound
significance because of a supposed connection with Platonic
thought. Its true meaning was taken to be that man must learn to
harness his own forces, or those of Nature, and then release them
suddenly, in just the right place and moment. If he did this,
miraculous effects could be achieved. Marvell's argument about
Love and Time, therefore, concludes with a reconciliation
between the seemingly irreconcilable aspects of Time. And a
final turn of the ironical screw is achieved when it is remembered

that the cannon-ball and its motto represented *prudence* or *wisdom*—which means that the advice to abandon coyness and instead behave with the utmost abandon, is couched in terms of an image usually taken to symbolise prudence in its most elevated aspect.

'Daphnis and Chloe' discusses love in terms that are distinctly cynical. Daphnis discovers, to his great mortification, that the moment he abandons the siege, the fair one is willing to yield. Such is his pride that he refuses to owe to his departure what his presence was unable to win:

> Rather I away will pine
> In a manly stubborness
> Than be fatted up express
> For the *Canibal* to dine.

The discovery has killed his love, so that a consummation 'But the ravishment would prove/Of a Body dead while warm.' The beauty of the lines almost hides the grossness they reveal, but the story ends in pure farce when Daphnis, out of peeved vanity rather than 'manly stubborness', every night sleeps with a different woman:

> Yet he does himself excuse;
> Nor indeed without a Cause.
> For, according to the Lawes,
> Why did *Chloe* once refuse?

What laws? Obviously of man, and equally obviously fallen man. The poem comments ironically not only on the fallen state of man, but on the pastoral genre indicated by the title. Here is a poem whose title suggests the innocence associated with pastoral, but whose contents reveal the very accents of corruption.

Interestingly enough, one of Marvell's poems depicts or enacts the metamorphosis of the pastoral from a corrupt to an innocent genre. In 'Clorinda and Damon' Clorinda's attempted seduction of Damon is foiled and she is converted, instead, to his profoundly religious view of life. The poem ends by showing how the two join in offering praise to him whose words 'transcend poor Shepherds skill'. . . .

SOURCE: extract from 'Andrew Marvell and the Caroline Poets', in C. Ricks (ed.), *English Poetry and Prose, 1540–1674* (London, 1970), pp. 220–43.

NOTES

1. R. L. Colie, 'Some Paradoxes in the Language of Things', in J. A. Mazzeo (ed.), *Reason and the Imagination* (New York and London, 1962), pp. 93–128.

2. The most famous example is the *Praise of Folly* by Erasmus, originally written in Latin (*Moriae Encomium*) and translated into English in 1549.

3. See the chapters included in English translation in J. J. Bagley and P. B. Rowley, *A Documentary History of England*; I, *1066–1540* (Harmondsworth, 1966), pp. 138–51.

4. Edgar Wind reproduces this painting on plate 80 in his *Pagan Mysteries in the Renaissance* (London, 1958; 1967).

5. Quoted by John M. Wallace, *Destiny His Choice: The Loyalism of Andrew Marvell* (Cambridge, 1968) p. 68.

6. Matthias Casimire Sarbiewski, *The Odes of Casimire* (1646), Augustan Reprint Society, publication no. 44 (Los Angeles, 1953). The following odes are based on the Song of Solomon: II, 19 and 25; IV, 19 and 21. The last-cited ode is particularly relevant.

7. See, for example, John Ford, *'Tis Pity She's a Whore* (II, i 42–9).

8. See Augustine's discourse on Psalm 28 in *St Augustine on the Psalms*, trans Dame Scholastica Hebgin and Dame Felicitas Corrigan (London, 1960), i, 288.

9. Psalms VI 5 and XXX 9. J. B. Leishman (in his British Academy lecture, 1961) invoked an epigram by Asclepiades in the Greek Anthology (V 85):

Hoarding your maidenhood—and why? For not when to Hades
    You've gone down shall you find, maiden, the lover you lack.
Only among the alive are the joys of Cypris, and only,
    Maiden, as bones and dust shall we in Acheron lie.

[Leishman's lecture is reproduced immediately below—Ed.]

J. B. Leishman   Some Themes and Variations in Marvell's Poetry (1961)

THE small collection of Marvell's pre-Restoration poetry, most of which was probably seen by only a few of his intimate friends and which has reached us almost by accident, is perhaps the most remarkable example we have of the interaction between what Mr Eliot, in a famous phrase, called Tradition and the Individual Talent. For, although Marvell's poetry is highly original and, at its best, unmistakably his own and no one else's, he is almost always acting upon hints and suggestions provided by earlier poets, and almost never writing entirely, as children would say, out of his own head. When he returned from his foreign travels in (as is probable) 1646, he seems to have bought and read attentively many of those notable volumes of verse by living or recently deceased poets which, from 1640 onwards, appeared in such rapid succession, often from the press of that most enterprising of publishers Humphrey Moseley. Particular borrowings or imitations prove that he had read (I mention them in order of publication) Carew's *Poems* (1640, 1642, 1651), Waller's *Poems* (1645), *The Poems of Mr John Milton* (1645), Crashaw's *Steps to the Temple* (1646, 1648), Cowley's *The Mistress* (1647), Cleveland's *Poems* (1647 and 1651), Lovelace's *Lucasta* (1649), and Davenant's *Gondibert* (1651). These and other poets, including the Ancients, were continually suggesting to Marvell new and amusing things to do. And how remarkable, considering the comparatively small number of his poems, is their variety! There is something in almost every one of them that recalls some other seventeenth-century poet, and yet perhaps no single one of them is really like a poem by anyone else. Marvell, in fact, is the most representative of all those fine amateur poets of the earlier seventeenth century who wrote mainly for their own pleasure

and that of a few friends. It would be going too far to say that
whatever any other seventeenth-century poet has done well
Marvell has done better. In the art of making the purest poetry
out of almost pure abstractions not even Donne has surpassed
Marvell's 'Definition of Love', but Marvell has nothing comparable with that tenderness which is no less characteristic of
Donne's poetry than its wit: nothing like

> I wonder by my troth, what thou and I
> Did, till we lov'd?

or

> All other things, to their destruction draw,
>   Only our love hath no decay;

or

> So, so breake off this last lamenting kisse.

Marvell's moralising 'On a Drop of Dew' is no less beautiful than
Vaughan's moralising on 'The Water-fall', but he has nothing
comparable with the intense vision of 'The World' or the white
ecstasy of 'The Retreate'. Some of Marvell's descriptions and
images have both the colour and the crystalline purity of
Crashaw's, but, although he is free from Crashaw's not infrequent mawkishness and sentimentality, he also lacks both
Crashaw's child-like tenderness and his rapture. And, although
he often equals George Herbert in structure, he has none of his
passionate personal drama. Nevertheless, although Marvell
cannot equal any of the poets I have mentioned in their special
intensities, he can surpass each and all of them in variety and
breadth. This is partly because he is, in comparison with them,
singularly uncommitted. His poetry is, so to speak, the poetry of a
temperament rather than of any urgent personal experience, but
of a temperament in which nearly all the most attractive virtues
of the earlier seventeenth century seem to be combined.

   To attempt to review, with something more than superficiality, all Marvell's most notable poems would be impossible in a single lecture; one would have to take account of so many other seventeenth-century poets and poems that such a 'project' (as our American friends call it) could only be realised in a sizable book, such as that on which I have myself been for several years intermittently engaged. All I am now going to attempt is to suggest something of the ways in which tradition and originality are combined in a few representative poems, with, I hope, not more illustrative detail than can be comfortably assimilated from a spoken discourse.

How did Marvell begin? There are a few commendatory, elegiac, satirical, and political poems, all of them, except the great Cromwell ode, in the heroic couplet, and all of them, except for that ode, of small intrinsic importance, which can be assigned, because of their allusions to public events, to various dates between 1646 and 1650. When, though, we come to the unpublic, the lyrical, reflective, or descriptive poems, we have almost no external evidence to help us. A recently discovered manuscript proves that the pastoral 'Dialogue between Thyrsis and Dorinda' must have been written before September 1645, and therefore probably before Marvell set out on his foreign travels in or about 1642. It is impossible not to suppose that the poems 'Upon the Hill and Grove at Bill-borow' and 'Upon Appleton House', both dedicated 'To the Lord Fairfax', and 'Musicks Empire', in which Fairfax is evoked in the last stanza, were written during the two years, 1651 to 1653, which Marvell spent with the retired Lord General at his estate of Nun-Appleton in Yorkshire, as tutor to his young daughter Mary. And it seems reasonable to suppose that the poem 'Bermudas' was written some time after July 1653, when Marvell, together with his pupil, Cromwell's ward William Dutton, began his residence with John Oxenbridge, Fellow of Eton College, who had twice visited those islands. These, I think, are the only private poems for whose dates there is any kind of external evidence. I myself am inclined to believe that nearly all the best of what it seems convenient to call Marvell's private poems were written during those two years at Nun-Appleton, when he had infinite leisure and the society of a friend and patron who was both a lover of poetry and, in a small way, a poet himself. The affinity between 'The Garden' and the poem on Appleton House is obvious, and it is difficult not to associate the predominantly pastoral or descriptive element in many other poems with Marvell's residence at Nun-Appleton: more important, though, as a common characteristic is that maturity and security which is equally apparent in poems otherwise so different as the Cromwell ode, 'The Definition of Love', 'To his Coy Mistress', 'The Picture of little T.C. in a Prospect of Flowers', the Mower poems, 'On a Drop of Dew'. I need not prolong the list: apart from certain careless amateurishnesses—an excessive use of inversion for the sake of rhyme, and excessive use of expletives such as 'do', 'did', and 'doth' to supply syllables—of which he never rid himself, one feels that in all these poems, and in those which seem to belong with them, Marvell knew exactly what he wanted to say before he began to write, and that in each poem he has completely realised his intention. I myself seem to be aware almost of a difference in kind between their assuredness, their maturity and security, and what, in comparison, seem the uncertainty, inequality, and sometimes laboured ingenuity of six poems which stand rather apart from the rest. Three of these—'The Match', 'The Unfortunate Lover', 'The Gallery'—are predominantly and sometimes grotesquely emblematical or allegorical, and three of them—'Mourning', 'Eyes and Tears', 'The Fair Singer'—have a more obvious affinity with certain kinds of Renaissance Latin epigram than we find in Marvell's more characteristic poems. Were these Marvell's earliest surviving poems, his beginnings, or were they simply lapses—experiments, contemporary with the more characteristic poems, of a kind which he decided not to pursue? Three of them, I said, were predominantly allegorical, but then so too is 'Musicks Empire', which must have been written at Nun Appleton, since it concludes with a compliment to the Lord General. It is not, indeed, like 'The Match' and 'The Unfortunate Lover', grotesquely allegorical, and it contains the unforgettable phrase, a phrase one might have expected to find rather in Rilke than in Marvell, 'Musick, the Mosaique of the Air'; nevertheless, if one examines it carefully, one finds that the correspondence between the literal and the metaphorical (so exquisitely preserved in 'On a Drop of Dew') is continually breaking down.

'On a Drop of Dew': my parenthetical mention of this, one of Marvell's most perfect poems, may remind us of the fact that, even after he had achieved stylistic assurance, he never lost his taste for allegory in the medieval sense of extended metaphor, for the elaborate comparison or series of comparisons, running through an entire poem, and that this kind of writing is (despite popular notions to the contrary) quite uncharacteristic of Donne. If, then, which is by no means certain, 'The Match' and 'The Unfortunate Lover'[1] are early poems, they are not like Donne, and Marvell did not begin as a disciple of Donne. It would be more possible to maintain that he began as a disciple of Crashaw and of those neo-Latin epigrammatists whom Crashaw often imitated. Consider for a moment the poem 'Eyes and Tears'. It was almost certainly suggested by Crashaw's 'The Weeper', and the fourteen stanzas into which its fifty-six octosyllabic couplets are divided are as loosely connected and as transposable as those of Crashaw's poem, each of them developing, more cerebrally and definingly and less pictorially than Crashaw, some ingenious metaphor or simile to express the superiority of tears to any other terrestrial sight and of sorrow to any other human emotion: laughter turns to tears; the sun, after distilling the world all day, is left with nothing but moisture, which he rains back in pity; stars appear beautiful only as the tears of light, and so on. The eighth stanza,

> So *Magdalen*, in Tears more wise
> Dissolv'd those captivating Eyes,
> Whose liquid Chaines could flowing meet
> To fetter her Redeemers feet,

might almost be regarded as a complimentary allusion to Crashaw's weeping Magdalene, and at the end of his poem Marvell has added a translation of this stanza into Latin elegiacs which would not have been out of place in *Epigrammata Sacra*, the little collection of Latin epigrams on sacred subjects which Crashaw published in 1634. The poem 'Mourning', which, in nine octosyllabic quatrains, attempts to say, by means of ingenious similes and metaphors, what Chlora's tears are, recalls, more immediately than do any of Marvell's more individual and characteristic poems, various things in the enormous and enormously popular collections of Renaissance Latin epigrams. Étienne Pasquier (1529–1615), for example, has a poem entitled

'De Amœna Vidua', 'On Amœna,* having lost her husband', which contains the lines:

> His tamen in lachrimis nihil est ornatius illa,
> > Perpetuusque subest eius in ore nitor.
> Siccine, defunctum quae deperit orba maritum,
> > Semper aget viduo fœmina mæsta thoro?
> Quae flet culta, suum non luget, Amœna, maritum;
> > Quid facit ergo? alium quaerit Amœna virum.

(Yet, amid these tears, nothing could be handsomer than she, and there lurks a perpetual brightness in her face. Will she, who pines in her bereavement for her dead husband, always be thus enacting the mourner on a widowed bed? One, Amœna, who weeps with elegance is not mourning her husband. What, then, is she doing? Amœna, she's looking for another.)[2]

It was at any rate somewhat in this manner, if not actually with these lines in his memory, that Marvell wrote:

> Her Eyes, confus'd and doubled ore
> With Tears suspended ere they flow,
> Seem bending upwards, to restore
> To Heaven, whence it came, their Woe,
>
> When, molding of the watry Sphears,
> Slow drops unty themselves away;
> As if she, with those precious Tears,
> Would strow the ground where *Strephon* lay.
>
> Yet some affirm, pretending Art,
> Her Eyes have so her Bosome drown'd,
> Only to soften near her Heart
> A place to fix another Wound;
>
> And, while vain Pomp does her restrain
> Within her solitary Bowr,
> She courts her self in am'rous Rain,
> Her self both *Danae* and the Showr.

---

*Pasquier is using the adjective *amœna* ('lovely', 'charming') as a proper noun.

Nay others, bolder, hence esteem
Joy now so much her Master grown,
That whatsoever does but seem
Like Grief, is from her Windows thrown;

Nor that she payes, while she survives,
To her dead Love this Tribute due,
But casts abroad these Donatives*
At the installing of a new . . .

I yet my silent Judgment keep,
Disputing not what they believe:
But sure as oft as Women weep,
It is to be suppos'd they grieve.[3]

The cynical notion of grief as something deliberately assumed by
a woman in order to increase her attractiveness is the sort of thing
we scarcely find in English poetry before about 1630. Such
notions, such 'conceits', had for long been 'thought up' by
continental Latin poets, searching for subjects on which they
could write wittily and antithetically, but when the English poets
at last 'got around' to them, they often, as Marvell has done here,
treated them with far greater subtlety and elaboration; and it is
this, I suppose, that has led us to acquiesce too readily in the
application of the term 'metaphysical' to their development of
such conceits. I hasten to assure you that I am not now proposing
to argue about that term. Professor Robert Ellrodt of the
Sorbonne has recently argued at length, and, on the whole,
convincingly, that Donne and George Herbert are the only poets
who are metaphysical; if, then, to write metaphysically means to
write like Donne, Marvell here is not being metaphysical, for he
is certainly not writing like Donne. Also entirely within the
tradition of the neo-classical epigram, although—I think one can
say it without fearing any accusation of insularity—with characteristically English pre-eminence, is that beautiful poem 'The
Fair Singer'. Characteristically English, but less individually
Marvellian, less unmistakably his own, than are most of

---

* 'A donation, gift, present; *esp.* one given formally or officially, as a largess or
bounty' (*O.E.D.*).

Marvell's best poems; for, if none of his contemporaries wrote one quite so good as this, several of them wrote charming epigrammatic poems on similar themes, although, since it is easier to describe sights than sounds, they generally performed some variation on the theme of 'Seeing her Walking' (in the Snow, in the Rain, on the Grass, in the Park, &c.).

> I could have fled from One but singly fair:
> My dis-intangled Soul it self might save,
> Breaking the curled trammels of her hair.
> But how should I avoid to be her Slave,
> Whose subtile Art invisibly can wreath
> My Fetters of the very Air I breath?

It would not have been at all surprising had Marvell appended a translation of this exquisite second stanza into Latin elegiacs. One recalls (although their wit is of a different and less pleasing kind) the three Latin epigrams 'Ad Leonoram Romae canentem' which Milton, during his stay in Rome in the winter of 1638–9, addressed to the famous singer Leonora Baroni. To Donne such a topic would have seemed far too established and conventional, too little of his own choosing and devising, too much of an initial advantage, too much a topic on which some far lesser intellect might conceivably write a not wholly despicable poem. It was not for the likes of him to be just one more encomiast of some Leonora Baroni.

Is Marvell ever really like Donne? His 'Definition of Love',[4] although its last stanza, almost certainly the germ from which the whole poem sprang, was suggested by the third stanza of a not very good poem in Cowley's *The Mistress* entitled 'Impossibilities'—his 'Definition of Love' is, as many readers must have felt, more like Donne's 'A Valediction: forbidding mourning' than perhaps any other single seventeenth-century poem is like any one of Donne's *Songs and Sonets*: 'like', not as a deliberate and inferior imitation, as are so many of the poems in Cowley's *Mistress*, but like with the likeness of a peer. Certainly, without the example of Donne's 'Valediction' I doubt whether Marvell's poem could have been what it is. In what might be called (though I do not much like the phrase) its concrete intellectuality, the way in which it intellectualises feeling or sensation into conceptions, into more or less abstract ideas, which still retain the vividness of perceptions, the style of Marvell's poem strikingly resembles Donne's; and yet, below the surface, is there not a fundamental difference? Let us place three stanzas from each poem side by side.

> Dull sublunary lovers love
>   (Whose soule is sense) cannot admit
> Absence, because it doth remove
>   Those things which elemented it.

> But we by a love, so much refin'd,
>   That our selves know not what it is,
> Inter-assured of the mind,
>   Care lesse, eyes, lips, and hands to misse.

> Our two soules therefore, which are one,
>   Though I must goe, endure not yet
> A breach, but an expansion,
>   Like gold to ayery thinnesse beate.

Donne, as in nearly all the more serious of the *Songs and Sonets*, is here analysing his immediate experience of a particular situation, real or imagined, and developing the paradox that for true lovers absence is not incompatible with presence. Now listen to Marvell:

> For Fate with jealous Eyes does see
> Two perfect Loves; nor lets them close:
> Their union would her ruine be,
> And her Tyrannick pow'r depose.

> And therefore her Decrees of Steel
> Us as the distant Poles have plac'd,
> (Though Loves whole World on us doth wheel)
> Not by themselves to be embrac'd,

> Unless the giddy Heaven fall,
> And Earth some new Convulsion tear;
> And, us to joyn, the World should all
> Be cramp'd into a *Planisphere.**

Marvell is not starting from the immediate experience of a particular situation, is not really being analytic and psychological and paradoxical like Donne, but is simply performing, with characteristically seventeenth-century intellectuality, ingenuity, hyperbole, and antithesis, an elaborate series of variations on the ancient theme of star-crossed lovers. While Donne, not merely in the stanzas I quoted but throughout his poem, is developing an argument ('Even though physically parted, we can remain spiritually united'), Marvell is simply saying over and over again, in various ingenious ways, 'we can never meet'. He is not really, like Donne, being paradoxical: what at first sight looks like paradox appears, when we examine it more closely, to be merely antithesis:

> Their union would her ruine be,
> And her Tyrannick pow'r depose.

And that characteristically exhilarating piece of semi-burlesque hyperbole, that the poles-apart lovers could only be joined if the world were 'cramp'd into a *Planisphere*'—what is it but our old friend the catalogue of impossibilities, ἀδύνατα ('till oaks sweat honey', 'till fish scale the mountains', &c.), so familiar in Greek and Roman poetry, brought up to date? This is one of the great differences between Donne and Marvell: while Donne, one might almost say, devised entirely new ways of saying entirely new things, Marvell assimilated, recombined, and perfected from his contemporaries various new ways of saying old ones.

In what, after the Cromwell ode, is perhaps Marvell's finest single poem, 'To his Coy Mistress', it can be shown that throughout he is doing very old and traditional things in a new way, and that he is only being very superficially like Donne. The

---

* A map or chart formed by the projection of a sphere, or part of one, on a plane. *O.E.D.* quotes from Thomas Blundeville's *Exercises* (1594): 'Astrolabe . . . is called of some a Planispheare, because it is both flat and round, representing the Globe or Spheare, having both his Poles clapt flat together.'

poem is indeed, like many of Donne's and unlike 'The Definition of Love', a continuous argument, and even a more rigidly syllogistic argument than I think we shall find in any of the more serious of the *Songs and Sonets*, where Donne is usually concerned with analysis rather than with demonstration.

If we had infinite time, I should be happy to court you at leisure;
But our life lasts only for a moment:
Therefore, in order to live, we must seize the moment as it flies.

It is only, I think, in such fundamentally unserious poems as 'The Will' that we shall find Donne being as neatly syllogistic as this. Where this poem most resembles Donne, and is perhaps more fundamentally indebted to his example than any other of Marvell's poems, is in its essentially dramatic tone (more dramatic than in any other of Marvell's poems), in the way in which it makes us feel that we are overhearing one of the speakers in a dialogue. But, before proceeding, let us make sure that we have the poem vividly in our minds:

> Had we but World enough, and Time,
> This coyness Lady were no crime.
> We would sit down, and think which way
> To walk, and pass our long Loves Day.
> Thou by the *Indian Ganges* side
> Should'st Rubies find: I by the Tide
> Of *Humber* would complain. I would
> Love you ten years before the Flood:
> And you should if you please refuse
> Till the Conversion of the *Jews*.
> My vegetable Love should grow
> Vaster than Empires, and more slow.
> An hundred years should go to praise
> Thine Eyes, and on thy Forehead Gaze.
> Two hundred to adore each Breast:
> But thirty thousand to the rest.
> An Age at least to every part,
> And the last Age should show your Heart.
> For Lady you deserve this State;
> Nor would I love at lower rate.

> But at my back I alwaies hear
> Times winged Charriot hurrying near:
> And yonder all before us lye
> Desarts of vast Eternity.
> Thy Beauty shall no more be found;
> Nor, in thy marble Vault, shall sound
> My ecchoing Song: then Worms shall try
> That long preserv'd Virginity:
> And your quaint Honour turn to dust;
> And into ashes all my Lust.
> The Grave's a fine and private place,
> But none I think do there embrace.
>   Now therefore—

and Marvell reaches the conclusion of his semi-syllogistic argument, and, after some lines which are poetically rather below the general level of his poem, magnificently concludes:

> Let us roll all our Strength, and all
> Our sweetness, up into one Ball:
> And tear our Pleasures with rough strife,
> Thorough the Iron gates of Life.
> Thus, though we cannot make our Sun
> Stand still, yet we will make him run.

The tempo, *allegro molto* at least, is much faster than that of any of the more serious of Donne's *Songs and Sonets*, and, both in its speed, its mock-serious argument and its witty hyperbole, the poem might seem to have some affinity with Donne's tone and manner in some of his more exuberant elegies. The hyperbole, though—often, like that in 'A Definition of Love', approaching burlesque—is not, as I shall try to show later, really like Donne's, and the argument, although I have called it 'mock-serious', is really more serious, less paradoxical, than the sort of argument Donne conducts in the Elegies. It is also, I think, an argument which Donne would have regarded as too traditional and literary—the argument of Catullus'

> Vivamus, mea Lesbia, atque amemus . . .
> Soles occidere et redire possunt:
> nobis cum semel occidit brevis lux,
> nox est perpetua una dormienda,

which Ben Jonson so delightfully paraphrased as:

> Come my CELIA, let us proue,
> While we may, the sports of loue;
> Time will not be ours for euer:
> He, at length, our good will seuer.
>
> Spend not then his guifts in vaine.
> Sunnes, that set, may rise againe:
> But if once we loose this light,
> 'Tis, with vs, perpetuall night.

On this ancient theme Marvell has executed a series of brilliant seventeenth-century variations, which were partly suggested to him by the last stanza of a poem in Cowley's *The Mistress* entitled 'My Dyet', a stanza from which Marvell has borrowed and made unforgettable the phrase 'vast Eternity'[5]:

> On'a *Sigh* of Pity I a year can live,
>   One *Tear* will keep me twenty 'at least,
>   Fifty a gentle *Look* will give:
> An hundred years on one *kind word* I'll feast:
>   A thousand more will added be,
>   If you an *Inclination* have for me;
>   And all beyond is vast *Eternitie*.

Cowley was by no means the first to introduce arithmetic into love-poetry, but he has here exploited its possibilities in a way that seems to be original. The earliest of these arithmetical amorists, so far as I know, was an anonymous Alexandrian imitator of Anacreon, who, anticipating Leporello's catalogue of his master's conquests in Mozart's *Don Giovanni*, wrote a poem which begins: 'If you can count the leaves of all trees and the waves of the whole ocean, then I will make you sole reckoner of my loves. First set down twenty from Athens and add to them fifteen. Then set down whole chains of loves from Corinth, for it is in Achaea, where women are beautiful.'[6] Catullus, at the conclusion of 'Vivamus mea Lesbia', seems to have been the first poet to write arithmetically of kisses:

> Da mi basia mille, deinde centum,
> dein mille altera, dein secunda centum—

in Ben Jonson's paraphrase:

> Kisse againe: no creature comes.
> Kisse, and score up wealthy summes
> On my lips, thus hardly sundred,
> While you breath. First giue a hundred,
> Then a thousand, then another
> Hundred, then vnto the tother
> Adde a thousand, and so more:
> Till you equall with the store,
> All the grasse that *Rumney* yields
> Or the sands in *Chelsey* fields,
> Or the drops in siluer *Thames*,
> Or the starres, that guild his streames.

Like Johannes Secundus[7] before him, the French Renaissance Latin poet Etienne Pasquier, whom I have already quoted on the subject of a lovely widow, combined, in a poem 'Ad Sabinam', this osculatory arithmetic, or arithmetical osculation, with one of the most popular themes of classical and Renaissance love-poetry, the catalogue of a mistress's charms, declaring that he would print a thousand kisses on every part of Sabina's body:

> Quid reniteris? obstinatiora
> Carpo basia mille singulatim.
> Labris millia, millia en ocellis,
> Genis millia, millia en papillis,
> Obsignabo, licet puella nolit.[8]

(Why do you resist? I snatch my kisses all the more resolutely, a thousand at a time. Thousands on lips, thousands on eyes, thousands on

.s, thousands on breasts I will implant—unwilling though the girl
be.)

. hroughout the first twenty lines of his poem Marvell is making a
brilliantly original use of the time-measuring arithmetic in that
stanza of Cowley's from which he borrowed the phrase 'vast
Eternity'. In the passage beginning

> An hundred years should go to praise
> Thine Eyes, and on thy Forehead Gaze,

he has applied it to that traditional and popular topic, the
catalogue of a mistress's charms—a novel combination, I think,
although it may have been suggested to him by Pasquier's
combination of that traditional catalogue with the osculatory
arithmetic of Catullus. In the exuberant hyperbole and antithesis
of his opening lines, declaring that, had they but world enough
and time, he would be willing to court her and be refused by her
from ten years before the Flood until the conversion of the Jews,
Marvell is not only being original, but writing in a manner in
which no poets except those of the English seventeenth century
ever wrote. When ancient poets handled the topics of *carpe diem*
and *carpe florem*, when they pointed to the contrast between the
returning anise and parsley, the returning seasons, the returning
sun and moon and the unreturning lives of men, or when they
exhorted some unresponsive girl or boy to learn a lesson from the
withering and neglected rose, they nearly always wrote with an
undiluted pathos and seriousness and even solemnity; or, if any
trace of a smile was there, it was a sad one. And the Renaissance
Italian and French poets, when they handled these topics, nearly
always preserved a similar tone. It was only certain English poets
of the earlier seventeenth century who expanded and varied
these and other traditional topics with the witty, elaborate, and
sometimes positively hilarious ingenuity of Marvell in this
poem.

This does not mean that Marvell's poem is, in comparison,
slight or unserious or superficial, for in its central section it sounds
notes as deep as those of any ancient poetry on the topics of *carpe
diem* and *carpe florem*.

> But at my back I alwaies hear
> Times winged Charriot hurrying near:
> And yonder all before us lye
> Desarts of vast Eternity.
> Thy Beauty shall no more be found;
> Nor, in thy marble Vault, shall sound
> My ecchoing Song: then Worms shall try
> That long preserv'd Virginity:
> And your quaint Honour turn to dust;
> And into ashes all my Lust.
> The Grave's a fine and private place,
> But none I think do there embrace.

'Your quaint Honour': that indeed is a characteristically post-classical conception, with a faint echo of the *Roman de la Rose* and a much stronger one of a famous chorus in Tasso's pastoral drama *Aminta*, celebrating that *bel età del oro* when *il gigante Onor* was unknown. But behind the rest of this passage lies, I feel almost sure, either directly or indirectly (for it was imitated by several Renaissance poets, both Latin and vernacular), something much more ancient: an epigram by Asclepiades in the Greek Anthology (v 85):

> Φείδη παρθενίης· καὶ τί πλέον; οὐ γὰρ ἐς Ἀδην
> ἐλθοῦσ' εὑρήσεις τὸν φιλέοντα, κόρη.
> ἐν ζωοῖσι τὰ τερπνὰ τὰ Κύπριδος· ἐν δ' Ἀχέροντι
> ὀστέα καὶ σποδιή, παρθένε, κεισόμεθα.*

Here, as so often, out of something old Marvell has made something entirely new—or, what amounts to the same thing, something that gives impression of being entirely new.

> ἐν δ' Ἀχέροντι
> ὀστέα καὶ σποδιή, παρθένε, κεισόμεθα

> The Grave's a fine and private place,
> But none I think do there embrace.

Had he not known that epigram of Asclepiades, I doubt whether Marvell would, or perhaps could, have written those lines; and

---

*For a verse translation, see Note 9 in the study by Røstvig, above.

yet their irony, their concentration, their colloquial vigour are
absolutely Marvellian and absolutely seventeenth-century: they
could have been written at no other period, and probably by no
other poet. How pale and thin and unmemorable in comparison
(to mention two of the most famous poets of the preceding
century) is Johannes Secundus's imitation of this epigram in one
of his Elegies (IV) and Ronsard's imitation of Secundus's
imitation in his 'Ode à sa maîtresse'![9] While Marvell remains
absolutely contemporary, Ronsard brings in Pluto and Charon's
skiff:

> Pour qui gardes-tu tes yeux,
> Et ton sein délicieux,
> Ta joue et ta bouche belle?
> En veux-tu baiser Pluton,
> Là-bas, après que Caron
> T'aura mise en sa nacelle?

While Ronsard's lines are no more than an agreeable example of
neo-classic imitation, such as any other member of the Pléiade
could have produced, what Marvell has given us is not so much
an imitation as a transmutation. And, indeed, his whole poem is a
superb example of what I meant when I said that his poetry,
although in the highest degree original, would have been
impossible without the numerous literary sources from which he
derived inspiration, stimulation, and suggestion. A stanza of
Cowley's, a poem of Catullus, a Greek epigram, possibly a neo-
Latin one—we can see how they all played an essential part in the
genesis of Marvell's poem, and yet, at the same time, we can also
see that he has transmuted them into something unmistakably
his own. This is indeed originality, but it is a different kind of
originality from that which Donne wanted to achieve.

Nor is it only in what, comparatively speaking, may be called
its literariness and traditionality that Marvell's manner in this
poem differs from Donne's.

>   I would
> Love you ten years before the Flood:
> And you should if you please refuse
> Till the Conversion of the *Jews*.

> My vegetable Love should grow
> Vaster than Empires, and more slow.

Here we have not merely what seems to be an entirely original
use of the well-established topic, or trope, of amatory arithmetic;
we have also, as in 'The Definition of Love', our old classical
friend, the catalogue of impossibilities, ἀδύνατα, brought up to
date. But the manner in which it is brought up to date is not, I
think, a manner which Marvell learnt from Donne. Donne, it is
true, excelled in witty hyperbole, but these lines are not merely
hyperbolical, they are almost burlesque—or, at any rate, they
have a touch of that burlesque extravagance and hilarity which
Marvell, I am convinced, learnt from that enormously popular
contemporary poet John Cleveland and practised extensively in
the Billborough and Appleton House poems and even, to some
extent, in 'The Garden' and the 'Dialogue between the Soul and
Body'. Consider, for example, the third stanza of Cleveland's 'To
the State of Love; or, the Senses' Festival', first printed in the
1651 edition of his poems:

> My sight took say,* but (thank my charms!)
> I now impale her in my arms;
> (Love's compasses confining you,
> Good angels, to a circle too.)
> Is not the universe strait-laced
> When I can clasp it in the waist?
> My amorous folds about thee hurled,
> Like Drake I girdle in the world;[10]
> I hoop the firmament, and make
> This, my embrace, the zodiac.
>   How would thy centre take my sense
>   When admiration doth commence
>   At the extreme circumference?

It was Cleveland too, who, in his poem 'Upon Phillis Walking in a
Morning before Sun-rising', consummated, in a manner which

---

* Made trial: see *O.E.D.*, *say*, sb.² (an aphetic form of *assay*), sense 6, 'a trial of food
by taste or smell'. *O.E.D.* quotes Cooper, *Thesaurus* (1565) '*Degusto* . . . to taste: to take a
little saye.'

inspired many passages in Marvell's 'Appleton House', a characteristic seventeenth-century development of what, since it occurs in pastorals of Theocritus and Virgil, I have been accustomed to call the 'pastoral hyperbole', and which in those two poets amounted to little more than saying that all things flourished in the presence of the beloved and withered at her (or his) departure. It seems likely that the attention of our seventeenth-century poets was first directed to the possibilities of witty elaboration in this topic by that enormously popular poem of Strode's 'On Chloris walking in the Snow', itself inspired by a poem of Tasso's,[11] in whose *Rime* there are many elegant variations on this topic, most of them rather pale and anaemic in comparison with those of our own poets.[12] Even after the topic had been so often handled as to excite Suckling to something like parody,[13] Waller seems to have given a new lease of life to it with one of his Sacharissa poems, 'At Penshurst',[14] first printed in the 1645 edition of his *Poems*, a poem from which I think it can be shown that both Cleveland and Marvell took hints. But while Waller and his predecessors, though bolder and more vigorous than Tasso, had still kept their personifications within more or less decorous and classical bounds, Cleveland in this poem, printed in his first volume of 1647, lets himself go with a riotous and hilarious extravagance that approaches burlesque.

> The sluggish morn as yet undressed,
> My Phillis brake from out her East,
> As if she'd made a match to run
> With Venus, usher to the sun.
> The trees, like yeomen of her guard,
> Serving more for pomp than ward,
> Ranked on each side, with loyal duty
> Weave branches to enclose her beauty.
> The plants, whose luxury was lopped,
> Or age with crutches underpropped,
> Whose wooden carcasses are grown
> To be but coffins of their own,
> Revive, and at her general dole
> Each receives his ancient soul.
> The winged choiristers began
> To chirp their matins, and the fan

Of whistling winds like organs played,
Until their voluntaries made
The wakened East in odours rise
To be her morning sacrifice.

I have only time to place side by side with this a few lines from
that passage towards the end of 'Appleton House' where Nature
pays her respect to the 'young Maria', but they should be
sufficient to demonstrate that this way of writing, which we have
come to regard as so characteristic of him, was suggested to
Marvell by Cleveland:

See how loose Nature, in respect,
To her, it self doth recollect;
And every thing so whisht and fine,
Starts forth with to its *Bonne Mine.*
The *Sun* himself, of *Her* aware,
Seems to descend with greater Care;
And lest *She* see him go to Bed,
In blushing Clouds conceales his Head.   (st. LXXXIII)

'Tis *She* that to these Gardens gave
That wondrous Beauty which they have.   (st. LXXXVII)

Therefore what first *She* on them spent,
They gratefully again present.
The Meadow Carpets where to tread;
The Garden Flow'rs to Crown *Her* Head;
And for a Glass the limpid Brook,
Where *She* may all *her* Beautyes look;
But, since *She* would not have them seen,
The Wood about *her* draws a Skreen.   (st. LXXXVIII)

. . . I have been able to do little more than scratch the surface of
this fascinating subject. Except in my incidental allusion to what
I have called the 'pastoral hyperbole', I have said nothing about
Marvell's happy acquiescence in various characteristic
seventeenth-century developments of the pastoral tradition and
of what, including therein both Marlowe's 'Passionate Shepherd'
and Milton's 'L'Allegro' and 'Il Penseroso', might be called the

'catalogue of delights'. While Donne seems to have scornfully rejected all topics and subjects that might tempt readers to admire him for anything but his sheer poetic skill, anything, such as descriptions of things obviously beautiful or attractive, which stimulated what modern critics have called the 'stock response', Marvell's originality was of a much more tolerant and un-ambitious kind. He was ready, one might almost say, to accept, to exploit, and to recombine, to Marvellise and seventeenth-centurify, anything that had ever made poetry enjoyable.

SOURCE: *Proceedings of the British Academy*, XLVII (1961).

NOTES

1. The first two lines of the last stanza of this poem,

This is the only *Banneret*
That ever Love created yet,

were certainly suggested, as H. M. Margoliouth indicated in a note, by two lines in the poem 'Dialogue—Lucasta, Alexis' in Lovelace's *Lucasta* (1649) a volume to which Marvell contributed some commendatory verses:

Love nee're his Standard when his Hoste he sets,
Creates alone fresh-bleeding Bannerets.

Lucasta was licensed on 4 February 1647-8, and if lines 21–32 of Marvell's commendatory verses are taken to mean that the book had not yet been licensed, we may assume that Marvell wrote them at some time *before* that date and *after* his return from his travels in 1646 (see *Poems and Letters*, ed. Margoliouth, I 216). Is it, though, absolutely necessary to suppose that Marvell had read all the poems in the book before he commended it?

2. *Deliciae C[entum] Poetarum Gallorum*, ed. R. Gherus (1609) II 875.

3. I have omitted the first and eighth stanzas and have made various necessary changes in the punctuation.

4. In what I have to say about this poem I am greatly indebted to some remarks by Professor R. Ellrodt, *Les Poètes métaphysiques anglais*, part I, vol. II (1960) 123 and 148.

5. Cowley, too, evidently thought the phrase a good one, for he used it again in the penultimate line of his ode 'Sitting and Drinking in the Chair made out of the Reliques of Sir *Francis Drake's* Ship', first printed in *Verses lately written upon several Occasions* (1663):

> The streits of time too narrow are for thee,
> Launch forth into an indiscovered Sea,
> And steer the endless course of vast Eternity,
> Take for thy Sail this Verse, and for thy Pilot Me.

6. *Anacreontea* 14, Εἰ φύλλα πάντα δένδρων.

7. *Basia*, VII.

8. *Deliciae C[entum] Poetarum Gallorum*, ed. R. Gherus (1609) II 1000.

9. In his *Poèmes* of 1569 Ronsard published an undistinguished translation of this epigram of Asclepiades, beginning 'Dame au gros cœur, pourquoy t'espargnes-tu?,' and a not much more distinguished expansion of it into a sonnet, beginning 'Douce beauté, meudrière de ma vie'.

10. In Geoffrey Whitney's *A Choice of Emblemes and other Devises* (1586) there is an emblem—reproduced in Rosemary Freeman's *English Emblem Books* (1948) p. 56—representing a freely suspended globe, on the top of which is poised Drake's ship. In the top left-hand corner the hand of Providence, outstretched from a cloud, grasps one end of a girdle which hangs in a loop around the suspended globe, its other end being attached to Drake's ship.

11. *Ritorno di Madonna in tempo di neve* ('La terra si copria d'orrido velo'), in *Rime*, ed. Solerti, II 61. Tasso also has a similar poem entitled *Vista impedita della neve* ('Negro era intorno, e in bianche falde il cielo'), op. cit. 331, together with many less specialised developments of the 'pastoral hyperbole', among the more notable of which are 'Or che riede Madonna al bel soggiorno' (p. 232) and 'Or che l'aura mia dolce altrove spira' (p. 258). See also pp. 216, 222, 224, & c.

12. Strode's poem was first printed in 1632, in W. Porter's *Madrigals and Airs*. Among the 'Excellent Poems . . . by other Gentlemen' in Benson's edition of Shakespeare's *Poems* (1640) are 'Lavinia Walking in a frosty Morning' (L6ᵛ) and 'Vpon a Gentlewoman walking on the Grasse' (M2ᵛ). In the same year appeared as no. 126 in the first edition of *Wits Recreations* (Camden Hotten reprint of *Musarum Deliciae*, & c., II 17) a poem, perhaps more obviously inspired by Strode's, beginning 'I saw faire *Flora* take the aire'.

13. In the dialogue-poem between himself ('J. S.') and Carew

('T. C.') 'Vpon my Lady Carliles walking in Hampton-Court garden', which must have been written before Carew's death in 1640 and Suckling's in 1642.

14. 'Had Sacharissa (1645: 'Dorothea') lived when mortals made', in *Poems*, ed. Thorn-Drury (Muses Library, 1891) 146. Waller seems to have begun paying his addresses to Lady Dorothy Sidney ('Sacharissa') towards the end of 1635, and presumably ceased to address poems to her after her marriage in 1639.

A. Alvarez   The Poetry of Judgement
(1960)

In all the diverse talent of the School of Donne, Richard Crashaw and Andrew Marvell are the two poets most wholly opposed. With Crashaw the recurrent question is why, given that power and fertility, he was not a greater poet. It is as though he had in him the essential stuff of great poetry, but frittered it away. Marvell, on the other hand, produced some of the most perfect poems in the language and yet is, for all that, somehow not a 'major poet'. Dr Leavis once wrote of Dryden: 'He may be a greater poet than Marvell, but he did not write any poetry as indubitably great as Marvell's best.' The corollary is also true: Marvell may have written a few great poems but he was not a great poet.

He has done very well in this century. Eliot, Leavis and Empson, for example, have been prompted by him to some of their finest criticism. So his excellence is firmly established. I merely want to suggest here why, for all the subtlety and accomplishment of his writing, Marvell was essentially one of the last products of a school, but still too much part of it to be quite able to go forward to the next.

He is, in a way, the School of Donne in miniature, working in all the variations of the style: in 'To his Coy Mistress', 'The

Definition of Love' and, in another way, 'On a Drop of Dew', he writes like Donne; in 'The Coronet' and 'Eyes and Tears' he is largely a follower of Herbert; 'The Match', 'The Fair Singer' and 'The Picture of little T. C.' are like Carew and Lovelace; 'Upon Appleton House' is heavily influenced by Cleveland; 'A Dialogue between the Resolved Soul, and Created Pleasure' has something of the formal stance of Cowley; his pastoral poems have behind them an Elizabethan and continental tradition which descended through poets like Aurelian Townshend; 'The Nymph complaining for the death of her Faun' sounds like a kind of pastoral-classical Crashaw; he went on to write political satires in rhymed couplets. In none of these poems was he a mere imitator; he always rehandled his themes and styles in a peculiarly original way. But the variety and varied perfection of his work show that, despite his correct, almost sedate, career—gentleman tutor, government official, MP—he was, in terms of technical accomplishment, the most professional of that extraordinary group of amateurs that made up the School of Donne. He was, in short, 'literary' where Crashaw, with his religious-heroic style, his inventive enthusiasm and his Baroque principle of sensuous substitution, was the most 'rhetorical'. The difference is between a poet whose intelligence worked *on* literature, critically and analytically, and a poet who needed a great deal of artifice in order to express his intelligence at all.

The main element in Marvell's poetry is its balance, its pervading sense of intelligent proportion. He is, I think, the foremost poet of judgement in the English language, and 'An Horatian Ode' is his foremost poem. By *judgement* I mean a quality which presents, balances and evaluates a whole situation, seeing all the implications and never attempting to simplify them. The poet's whole effort is directed towards a full and delicate sanity, so that what he finally achieves is a kind of personal impersonality. For example:

> 'Tis Madness to resist or blame
> The force of angry Heavens flame:
>   And, if we would speak true,
>   Much to the Man is due.

The poem gets its effect by the certainty with which it balances

the large religious and political context—in the first couplet—
against a personal judgement, so that both appear necessary
parts of a whole understanding of the situation.
   Again:

> [Who] Could by industrious Valour climbe
> To ruine the great Work of Time,
>   And cast the Kingdome old
>   Into another Mold.
>
> Though Justice against Fate complain,
> And plead the antient Rights in vain:
>   But those do hold or break
>   As Men are strong or weak.
>
> Nature that hateth emptiness,
> Allows of penetration less:
>   And therefore must make room
>   Where greater Spirits come.

I have seen the lines used as an example of political slipperiness, as
though Marvell were praising Cromwell whilst fundamentally
supporting the King. But what in fact is so impressive in the poem
is the sureness with which the poet separates out the various
threads so that he can proceed without disorder in the full
knowledge of what his feelings on the subject really are. Personal
preferences and natural sanity hold each other in check. His
distaste for that kind of hard-working ambition, particularly
when it sets itself up against the tested sanctities of tradition, sway
the balance one way. His acknowledgement of the natural and
rational laws of power sway it back the other. This manner of
opposing two ways of thinking and feeling is, of course, typical of
a good deal of Metaphysical poetry. But elsewhere, in, say,
Herbert's 'The Collar' or 'Affliction (i)', the turnabout always
follows some peculiarly intricate dialectic by which the poet
argues himself into accepting his full responsibilities. He presents
the whole process of understanding: the knot, the gradual
untying and the final ordering of the threads. In Marvell's
poetry, on the other hand, the personal balance is already
achieved before the poem begins. He approaches his subjects

fully aware of his personal bias. The result is that he always has the air of a man dealing with something outside him, rather than with what at least began as an unresolved complex of emotions. It is this impression of the mind detachedly at play over a number of possible choices that earns Marvell the title of poet of judgement. Another way of putting it would be to call him a political poet. Certainly, 'An Horatian Ode' is one of the two finest political poems in the language; the other is *Coriolanus*. As a political poet he works analytically, resolving at every point personal choice into a larger context of general or social responsibilities. In this sense, Marvell is closer to Dryden and Pope than he is to Donne.

This habit of always leaving himself the elbow-room of impersonality—whether it is called judgement, a political trick of the mind, or a peculiar intensity of civilisation—has saved him from the excesses of his interpreters. There is, for example, an aura of suggestiveness about a great deal of his work that can, with a little effort, be translated into symbolism of a kind. But the fact that Marvell disliked violence—which we know from comments not in his poems—appreciated the peace and quiet of gardens as a relief from the turbulence of the Civil War, and so wrote eloquently, in one disguise or another, on the subject of Eden, does not make him a Quietist, nor does it illuminate his poetry with flashes of mystical insight *à propos* of God or Nature. The strangeness of a poem like 'The Nymph complaining for the death of her Faun', or of that unexpected couplet in 'Bermudas':

> But Apples plants of such a price,
> No tree could ever bear them twice

is no evidence of any specific, extendable religious symbolism in Marvell's verse, nor of any plan to take his readers in by writing charmingly about what was really very serious. Marvell's use of religion seems to be much the same as his classicism. The subtlety of some of the nymph's complaints for her faun:

> Had it liv'd long, it would have been
> Lillies without, Roses within

or

> There is not such another in
> The World, to offer for their Sin

is no greater nor less than that of:

> The brotherless *heliades*
> Melt in such Amber Tears as these.

Empson once wrote of this last couplet: 'It is tactful, when making an obscure reference, to arrange that the verse should be intelligible even when the verse is not understood . . . If you had forgotten, as I had myself, who their brother was, and look it up, the poetry will scarcely seem more beautiful; such of the myth as is wanted is implied.' The Biblical echoes are tantalising and evocative in precisely the same way: they lend the poem weight and seriousness. But they do not restrict the area of its action to their own special realm. The Bible came more naturally to the seventeenth century than to our day; it did not demand any peculiarly specialised effort of attention. For Marvell, as for every other educated man of his time, the Bible, like the classics, was a dimension of his extraordinarily civilised sensibility, and was controlled by it.

It is this that makes him such a deliberate, literary and decorous poet, particularly in his conceits. *Pace* Eliot, I cannot see that Marvell was ever carried away by his ingenuity with metaphors. But he came, as I said, at the end of the School of Donne and so could judge the technical means both for its vitality and in its corruption. And the corrupt conceit had effects very different from Donne's. In short, Marvell had read and taken good account of Cleveland; which meant he knew how to play the game of wit when it suited him. It was this element that Eliot missed when he accused Marvell's figure of the '*Antipodes* in Shoes' of being one of those 'images which are overdeveloped or distracting; which support nothing but their own misshappen bodies'. There is a side to Marvell's wit less serious than the one Eliot wished to emphasise. You can see it directly the conceit is put in its full context:

> But now the *Salmon-Fishers* moist
> Their *Leathern Boats* begin to hoist;
> And, like *Antipodes* in Shoes,
> Have shod their *Heads* in their *Canoos.*
> How *Tortoise like*, but not so slow,

> These rational *Amphibii* go?
> Let's in: for the dark *Hemisphere*
> Does now like one of them appear.

Marvell's concept of wit was flexible enough to include the kind of deliberate playfulness that is found only in light verse, and, if Eliot's *Old Possum* poems are typical, not often in that. The '*Antipodes* in Shoes', in fact, is not so much a conceit as a joke. And Marvell works for it deliberately. There is a preparatory pun in the preceding line—'*Leathern Boats*' suggests 'boots' and so makes way for the 'shoes'—a solemn pedantry in the couplet following and a final piece of absurdity—the comparison of the dark coming down over the hemisphere with the coracles over the heads of the fishermen. They all have the same effect, and the effect is deliberately comic. 'Deliberately', since it is unlikely that a poet as skilful as Marvell would have lapsed so absurdly at the end of a long poem without knowing why. I suggest he has two reasons: the first has to do with the occasion of the poem, the second with its literary means.

The absurd solemnity of that closing stanza may be more extreme than anything that has gone before in the poem but it is the same in kind. The poem is dedicated to Lord Fairfax, whose child, Mary, Marvell was then tutoring. All through the poem Marvell has treated the conventional occasions for conventionally exaggerated praise with a polite mock-seriousness, using conceits that are too conceited, too extreme. This does not hinder him from being very serious indeed in praising what he really admires in Fairfax, the political moderation and the firm desire for peace. But he writes with such delicate control that he can change from the fanciful to the profound without any clashing of gears. The whole effort presumes on a kind of formal intimacy between the poet and his audience: Marvell can be witty with his conventional praise because it is understood that his patron has qualities rarer and finer. In that sense it is a family poem; it would not be in good taste to be fulsome where fulsomeness is to be expected from everyone.

It is also a family poem in that the fancy is supposed to be amusing. And not only, I suggest, to Lord Fairfax. Compare, for example, those infamous Antipodes with a far more successful passage:

And now to the Abbyss I pass
Of that unfathomable Grass,
Where Men like Grashoppers appear,
But Grashoppers are Gyants there:
They, in their squeking Laugh, contemn
Us as we walk more low then them:
And, from the Precipices tall
Of the green spir's, to us do call.

This is a conceit, but it is hardly Metaphysical. It is, instead,
nearer the wit of Lewis Carroll. The conceit, that is, is a matter of
sharply refocusing the scene until it is adjusted to a child's vision:
the hay tall enough to drown in and the grasshoppers gigantic,
threatening presences. There was nothing in the detached
elegance of the wit at Marvell's command which barred him
from writing vivid, adult poetry which might also amuse a child.
The tradition of an exclusively patronizing children's verse did
not seem to have existed in the seventeenth century; perhaps it
did not begin until Isaac Watts stooped to conquer. Marvell's
conceit is no less successful because, like the elaborate pedantry of
the '*Antipodes* in Shoes', it has behind it a faint nonsense air.

I am far from accusing Marvell of quaintness or suggesting
that his poetry was, in any way, kid's stuff. On the contrary,
Marvell's ability to blend this kind of fanciful exaggeration with
a far more serious wit, and to give both an equivalent, if not an
equal, subtlety, is a measure of his sophistication. It is pre-
eminently a literary sophistication. Far from being victimised by
the style, the poet seems perfectly aware of what the exaggerated
conceit is and is not good for. It is, in fact, possible that by using
this kind of witty playfulness to amuse the daughter of the house
he is even taking the measure of the corrupt Metaphysical style.
The most elaborate conceits begin when Mary Fairfax enters the
poem, and this coincides with an obvious and deliberate echo of
Cleveland. Marvell has:

See how the Flow'rs, as at *Parade*,
Under their *Colours* stand displaid:
Each *Regiment* in order grows,
That of the Tulip Pinke and Rose . . .

Cleveland wrote:

> The trees, like yeomen of her guard,
> Serving more for pomp than ward,
> Ranked on each side, with loyal duty
> Weave branches to enclose her beauty . . .

I am not pretending that Marvell's poem is really an elaborate critical parody of Cleveland; but it does seem that when he played Cleveland's game of wit to amuse his patron and his pupil, he was showing that he knew its precise range and value. Instead of being occasionally the victim of false wit, Marvell used it for his own ends.

I have defended at length some not very distinguished lines in order to point up a vital aspect of the poetry of judgement: its peculiarly literary control in the choice and manipulation of special effects. If these are an index of poetic achievement, then Marvell is a master. But when compared with Donne, it seems that what Marvell gained in control he lost in pressure. He rarely, if at all, lapses as Donne did at times. But then he hasn't the excuse. He was never as original; his poetic discoveries were within already charted poetic forms. His first desire in verse was, I think, to do it perfectly. And he gained this perfection by keeping away from insistently personal situations and absorbing all his energies in the literary form and process. He rarely has that air of creative improvisation, of having to invent a new form for a unique occasion. Instead, each poem seems to start from a peculiarly sensitive critical analysis of the particular genre.

Consider, for instance, 'The Definition of Love'. [For text, see Røstvig's article, above—Ed.] It is based on a single aspect of some of Donne's love poems: his habit of bolstering up a feeling with abstract and scientific imagery until it can bear the weight of his complex logic. But Marvell presses this logical abstraction so hard that the feeling which justifies it seems to refine away to nothing. This is apparent in the imagery. The poem begins with three-dimensional allegorical figures—Despair, Hope, Fate—with tinsel wings, iron wedges and decrees of steel, who control 'Loves whole World'. It is all hard, solid and definite. The substantial globe, however, is then reduced to a two-dimensional model, the planisphere, and that, in turn, is reduced to the mere lines of a geometrical figure. Marvell's conclusion about the abstract refinement of their love—'the Conjunction of the Mind'—is borne out by the steady abstraction of the imagery. The poem is less of a love poem than an essay in abstraction. The poet, presumably, meant something of this kind when he called it 'The Definition of Love'. He is not to be criticized for failing to write a poem he never intended. But perhaps the piece is more formally perfect and neat than most of Donne's because Marvell has only the formal aspects to bother about. His stake in the thing seems first and foremost craftsmanly.

Marvell's practice in 'The Definition of Love' is the rule for his work, not the exception. There is not one of his love poems which, when set next to any of Donne's, seems more than an exercise in the poetic kind. This holds even for one of his most perfect poems, 'To his Coy Mistress'. I cannot believe that, in terms of the poem—the biography, in these matters, being neither here nor there—the mistress ever existed. She is merely part of the poem's traditional occasion. She is of course wooed with wit and some admirable ironical flourishes. But the irony is largely at Marvell's own expense:

> Thou by the *Indian Ganges* side
> Should'st Rubies find: I by the Tide
> Of *Humber* would complain . . .

She is to do exotic things in exotic surroundings, while he is left to scribble away at his complaints on the dreary banks of the Humber, which flows through his native city, Hull. Even the brilliant conceit of his 'vegetable Love' gains an extra dimension of irony when you remember his 'green thought in a green shade' and all those innocent, Eden-like gardens to which Marvell wrote so many love poems of another kind. As for his mistress and his ideal love-making:

> An hundred years should go to praise
> Thine Eyes, and on thy Forehead Gaze . . .

That, and such physical detail as appears, is, as the editors have pointed out, founded on a turn of wit that Marvell took from Cowley. But the tone of the verse deepens and the rhythm becomes more charged when in the section beginning 'But at my back I alwaies hear . . .' the subject changes from the girl to death. It is this sudden quickening of the witty detachment into something distinctly more sharply felt that makes me certain that Marvell is addressing himself rather than any supposed mistress. The real and moving poem is about time, death, waste and the *need* to love, rather than about love itself. Whatever of its power does not come from this source comes from the perfection of the performance: from the inevitable syllogistic progression (by which, incidentally, Marvell argues himself into accepting images of violence and war that go flatly against the current of all his other poetry), and, as Eliot said, from the weight behind the verse of the whole tradition of European love poetry.

One of the main differences between Marvell and Donne was not in the sophistication of their wit, which was where most of the other late Metaphysicals fell down, but in the uses their wit was put to. Donne's was exploratory; it brought whole and un-expected areas of awareness into the service of his single, immediate situation; and in doing so he changed the whole language of poetry. By accommodating it to the extraordinary range of his intelligence and to the kind of sceptical intensity of feeling of which he was master, he introduced into poetry a wholly new standard of realism. Marvell's wit, on the other hand, worked in literary forms already to hand and perfected them; it was a force that restrained, controlled and impersonalised.

But there are moments, admittedly rare, when this emphasis on civilised control and artistic impersonality lapses into what might, in a poet less skilled, be vulgar indifference:

> How wide they dream! The *Indian* Slaves
> That sink for Pearl through Seas profound,
> Would find her Tears yet deeper Waves
> And not of one the bottom sound.
>
> I yet my silent Judgement keep,
> Disputing not what they believe:
> But sure as oft as Women weep,
> It is to be suppos'd they grieve.
>> ['Mourning', 29–36]

The first stanza is one of the most allusive Marvell ever wrote, and he always wrote well on tears. Rhythmically, I think, it is based on Donne:

> O wrangling schooles, that search what fire
> Shall burne this world, had none the wit
> Unto this knowledge to aspire,
> That this her feaver might be it?

But Marvell's stanza has undergone a distancing typical of his work; it is something more than merely changing 'wrangling' to 'dreaming'. The slight roughness of Donne's verse has wholly disappeared: for example, the repetition of 'That' and 'this' so close together, which gives the lines their colloquial directness and which depends upon the personal cadence of the speaking voice to carry them off. Gone, too, is the reference to a lively contemporary issue—the Schoolmen at that time were very much under attack. The essence of Marvell's conceit is a certain exoticism; he uses all the technical skill he can muster to build up the strangeness and grandeur of the weeping woman: the alliteration of consonants and vowels, for example, which makes the second and third lines echo on themselves. But having built up his effects with such imaginative strength, Marvell seems able to reassert his 'silent Judgement' only by a final gesture of lame cynicism. Admittedly, the last stanza is more in keeping with the tone of the rest of the poem than is that oddly rich conceit; but the renewed cynicism is so sudden and extreme that it makes me suspect that that beautiful detachment of Marvell's was, at times, defensive. If Donne is also guilty at times of sudden lapses into cynicism, the occasions are always a matter of too much assertion, never of too delicate a withdrawal.

With the exception of George Herbert, Marvell is the most considerable of Donne's followers. But his strength is quite different. He is, as I suggested, far more carefully and absorbedly a craftsman in poetry; and this went with a different poetic stance. It matters not a jot that his love poems are thin in comparison with Donne's; there is, after all, little outside Shakespeare's sonnets that can stand that comparison. The difference is between kinds of poets: between the poet whose first concern is to judge and the poet who, above all, synthesises. The vitality of Donne's poetry depends on his knack of taking on everything that comes with the same immediacy, accuracy and full, tough intelligence. At the end of any of Donne's poems the forces have been resolved and ordered in such a way as to make you believe that a similar readjustment of the feelings has taken place in the poet himself. It is, in a sense, a poetry of action. Marvell, however, is always a little further outside his subjects. His extraordinarily civilised sophistication is a fixed quantity. With it he weighs and judges his material with such dispassionate fairness as to leave you, as a final and lasting taste, with the mature subtlety of his judgement. Unlike Donne and Herbert, he never writes a poem which shows him in the process of attaining this maturity. It is, rather, a quality without which he would not have been able to begin to write. Marvell's detached and sophisticated wit may be infinitely more subtle and less ste-reotyped than that of the Augustan Man of Sense, but it is of essentially the same kind. In achievement, if not chronologically, he is the last of the School of Donne.

SOURCE: article in *Hudson Review*, XIII (1960); reprinted as ch. 5 in Alvarez's *The School of Donne* (London, 1961).

E. W. Tayler   Marvell's Garden of the Mind (1964)

THE significance of Andrew Marvell's experiments in the pastoral genre must be carefully assessed if we are to understand the emotional and intellectual concerns that give purpose and weight to his finest lyrics. For Marvell was not much given to direct statement, his considerable virtues being of an ironic, allusive kind. As a consequence his poems, taken singly and without regard for the conventions of their genre, are more open to appreciation than analysis,

> Annihilating all that's made
> To a green Thought in a green Shade.

Although the body of his lyric verse is small, attempts to discern continuity and regularity, to define basic assumptions and deep commitments, have been frustrated by his reliance on a semi-private vocabulary, by his attitude of urbane detachment, and by a group of brilliant but apparently random poetic experiments. In his pastoral poems, however, Marvell for once explored the possibilities in a particular genre and developed the implications of a single theme: it is here, revealed by his modifications of the pastoral *kind* and by his personal response to the paired terms of Nature and Art, that we possess the clearest indication of attitudes elsewhere concealed by ironic wit.

Marvell wrote a number of poems that are clearly a part of the pastoral tradition, and there is considerable variation in his treatment of them within the genre. Variety has always been characteristic of the genre itself; despite—perhaps even because of—its stereotyped conventions, the form has lent itself to a remarkably wide range of poetic and other intentions. Marvell's use of the genre is no exception, although some of his experiments, such as 'Two Songs at the Marriage of the Lord Fauconberg and the Lady Mary Cromwell', remain comparatively uninteresting, not only because of their occasional nature, but also because the simple Hobbinols and rustic Thomalins are vehicles for little more than courtly compliment.

Marvell's best pastorals, however, depart radically from such relatively unambitious themes and purposes: situations are no longer simple, man is no longer artless, and feelings become quite complicated. The traditional lover of pastoral is replaced by the Mower, a figure at once cheerfully ingenious and darkly mysterious, whose relationship to Nature seems complex and ambiguous and who suffers strangely at the hands of an unusual shepherdess. In short, Marvell's intentions become much more ambitious, growing in both scope and intensity, but the pastoral *kind* remains to provide a form in which the maturer interests may be expressed.

'Ametas and Thestylis making Hay Ropes' and 'Daphnis and Chloe' are possibly among the first of Marvell's pastoral experiments; at least they show no hint of his more serious concerns. Possibly among the first . . . There is no way of determining exactly when most of the *Miscellaneous Poems* were written.[1] In any case, precise knowledge of chronological order would have absolute value only if we could depend on a poet to exhibit straight-line progress toward a particular goal. But success may be lost as well as found, and poets, like other men, commit themselves to a variety of ends, sometimes returning with new understanding to an old problem only after a number of years, so that later work may bear the sediment of early efforts. If 'Ametas and Thestylis' and 'Daphnis and Chloe' are not chronologically early, they are nevertheless experiments that did not lead to additional poems of the same type. They are poems of the fashionable world in the tradition of the love-debate *pastourelle*. Marvell adopts the ethics of this tradition, probably influenced by the French *libertins* of the seventeenth century, and attempts to make the pastoral form sustain some fairly sophisticated arguments about love.

   In 'Ametas and Thestylis' the witty debate closes quickly with the usual gesture:

> Then let's both lay by our Rope,
> And go kiss within the Hay.

In 'Daphnis and Chloe', where a similar theme is attenuated through approximately eight times as many lines, Marvell may have realised that he had extended himself in this direction about as far as he could go. Although there is no doubt that the shepherdess this time remains virtuous, the last stanzas show that the two poems exhibit essentially the same attitude:

> But hence Virgins all beware.
> Last night he with *Phlogis* slept;
> This night for *Dorinda* kept;
> And but rid to take the Air.

> Yet he does himself excuse;
> Nor indeed without a Cause.
> For, according to the Lawes,
> Why did *Chloe* once refuse?

These are obviously poems addressed to something very like Court society, perhaps the small circle of literati at Appleton House, who might be relied upon to appreciate both the wit and the delicious excitement of the naturalistic ethics. To Marvell at this time, as to Tasso in *Aminta*, it seems that 'what pleased was proper', according 'to the Lawes' of *libertin* naturalism.

'Clorinda and Damon' and 'A Dialogue between Thyrsis and Dorinda' may be viewed as transitional poems. Although Marvell's most central and characteristic preoccupations do not yet appear, the poems imply movements in the direction of the best pastorals through their explicit rejection of 'naturalistic' or *libertin* ethics. What pleases is no longer necessarily proper; Marvell even begins to use the pastoral form to discuss religious matters. Such a use was of course not all uncommon, either in the Middle Ages or in the Renaissance. We have seen that it had behind it the putative foreshadowing of Christ in Vergil's Fourth or Messianic Eclogue, the mystical glosses on the pastoral Song of Songs, the shepherds of the Gospels, the medieval uses of the genre, and numerous Renaissance 'imitations', so that Sidney could assert confidently in his *Apologie for Poetrie* that the genre, 'under the prettie tales of Wolves and Sheepe, can include the whole considerations of wrong dooing'.[2] Puttenham similarly emphasises that the genre does not simply attempt to 'represent the rustical manner of loues and communication: but vnder the vaile of homely persons, and in rude speeches to insinuate and glaunce at greater matters'.[3] But the poetical and critical traditions notwithstanding, Marvell apparently at first found it hard to 'insinuate and glaunce at greater matters'.

Marvell's problem was one of technique: How is it possible to write on complex, civilised themes while still retaining all the baggage of traditional pastoral? The answer lies in the allegorical potentialities of the form. Puttenham alludes to this solution with the words 'insinuate and glaunce', but Marvell in 'Thyrsis and Dorinda' attempts to discuss 'greater matters' more or less directly. The speakers are therefore so ingenuous in relation to the subject-matter that even rustic charm cannot save the piece. Although Dorinda has reservations about Death, being unsure where she will 'go', Thyrsis assures her it merely means a new home in Elizium. Dorinda remains only partially satisfied, and presents her swain with a question he could not hope to answer directly and still retain his rustic character:

> But in Elizium how do they
> Pass Eternity away?

Thyrsis' rejoinder conflates planetary music, English sheep dogs, and allusions to the Golden Age in an attempt to reassure the shepherd lass:

> Oh, ther's, neither hope nor fear
> Ther's no Wolf, no Fox, nor Bear.
> No need of Dog to fetch our stray,
> Our Lightfoot we may give away;
> No Oat-pipe's needfull, there thine Ears
> May feast with Musick of the Spheres.

This answer so intrigues Dorinda that she persuades her swain to share 'poppies' with her, thus 'smoothly pass away in sleep', and arrive in Elizium ahead of schedule.

Is the poem a religious allegory? Perhaps. Elizium is a land of 'Everlasting day', the inevitable resting place of the 'Chast Soul': 'Heaven's the Center of the Soul'. But these religious allusions do not form a consistent pattern, nor are they meaningful additions to the dramatic situation of this dialogue between a shepherd and his lass. The subject seems to be, ultimately, the attractiveness of heaven, but if the pastoral is Christian in this sense, its message— that one may anticipate the joys of heaven with a suicidal 'poppy'—is distinctly un-Christian. If the poem is allegorical, its dark conceit leaves a reader in obscurity. Since Marvell was a sophisticated man, an urban wit, he could not have found the convention—admittedly often broken—of rustic speakers and rude diction entirely to his taste; and he had apparently not yet learned to use the pastoral form successfully to hint at complicated notions, to 'insinuate and glaunce at greater matters'.

Marvell himself wrote a kind of poetic commentary on the difficulty of expressing complex matters through the simple diction of unsophisticated shepherds and shepherdesses. 'Clorinda and Damon' resembles 'Thyrsis and Dorinda' in its concern with Christian rather than 'naturalistic' values, but in

'Clorinda and Damon' the rejection of *libertin* ethics has become the main dramatic issue of the poem. It is more successful poetry than 'Thyrsis and Dorinda', mainly because its religious burden nowhere conflicts with the pastoral situation and vocabulary; the pastoral form has become a vehicle for 'greater matters' that deepen without distorting the literal meaning of the pastoral dialogue. Clorinda represents the *libertine* shepherdess, dedicated to natural pleasure on the nearest 'grassy Scutcheon', but Damon, mysteriously armed against her Marlovian blandishments, declines to live with her and be her love:

> *C.* Seize the short Joyes then, ere they vade.
>   Seest thou that unfrequented Cave?
> *D.* That den? *C.* Loves Shrine. *D.* But Virtue's Grave.
> *C.* In whose cool bosome we may lye
>   Safe from the Sun. *D.* not Heaven's Eye.
> *C.* Near this, a Fountaines liquid Bell
>   Tinkles within the concave Shell.
> *D.* Might a Soul bath there and be clean,
>   Or slake its Drought?

Damon explains that 'Pastures, Caves, and Springs' no longer entice him, for the 'other day' he encountered Pan:

> *C.* What did great *Pan* say?
> *D.* Words that transcend poor Shepherds skill,
>   But He ere since my Songs does fill.

Not the Pan of woodland and stream, of riggish dance and goatish desire, but the Great Pan of *The Shepheardes Calender* and 'The Nativitie Ode' whose ethics and words indeed 'transcend poor Shepherds skill'. This Pan is Christ, and thus what began as a relatively slight pastoral lyric has become the vehicle for a weighty event in scriptural history: the impact of Christ's Revelation on natural man. And Marvell has been notably successful in communicating these 'greater matters' without using 'Words that transcend poor Shepherds skill'.

Presumably a man of Marvell's ironic disposition would find techniques of indirection and allusion particularly congenial, but there are obvious dangers in the use of such methods. Most obviously, there is the possibility that readers may misinterpret, or even entirely overlook, the significance of a reference such as that to 'great Pan'. The word, after all, is the same; it is the meaning that has changed. Less obviously, and perhaps for that reason more common, there is the danger of misunderstanding what the poet intends to accomplish through the use of particular allusion at a particular time: a single allusion, however suggestive, does not invariably mean that the poem is a detailed allegory. It is this last danger that seems to have complicated exegesis of 'The Nymph complaining for the death of her Faun' where the Faun—to mention only one of the controversial figures—may be presumed to represent everything from Christ to the Church of England.[4]

'The Nymph complaining' is admittedly thick with classical and Christian allusions, and they lend an effect of depth and solidity to a work that could otherwise have been maudlin and melodramatic in tone. But it will not do to mistake the function of these allusions.

The Nymph's Garden can hardly fail to suggest the Garden of Eden, and the Faun itself—'Lillies without, Roses within'— clearly stands for a kind of Edenic harmony with Nature, the original purity and innocence. Difficulties appear, however, when the reader tries to anchor such symbolic overtones to a detailed, inclusive interpretation. Consider the lines in which the Nymph accuses the 'wanton Troopers' of their crime:

> Though they should wash their guilty hands
> In this warm life-blood, which doth part
> From thine, and wound me to the Heart,
> Yet could they not be clean: their Stain
> Is dy'd in such a Purple Grain.

I think it is safe to say that Marvell nowhere wrote a sentimental line, but there is in the Nymph's words an emotional excess that lies just this side of the maudlin—until suddenly in the following two lines it is channeled into a spiritual context in which such language is entirely appropriate to its object, the Crucifixion:

There is not such another in
The World, to offer for their Sin.

If we now felt inclined, we might possibly see the poem in the
following way: the Faun is Christ, the Nymph is the Virgin Mary,
Sylvio is the God alienated by the Fall, the Garden is Eden, and
what is really a very fine poem has become absurd. There is no
doubt that this exegetical activity 'enriches' one's experience of
the poem, but surely it does the work a disservice to see a simple
equation in such consciously oblique references. We are not
dealing with one-to-one allegory but a technique of allusion
almost random in nature:

> O help! O help! I see it faint:
> And dye as calmely as a Saint.
> See how it weeps. The Tears do come
> Sad, slowly dropping like a Gumme.
> So weeps the wounded Balsome: so
> The holy Frankincense doth flow.
> The brotherless *Heliades*
> Melt in such Amber Tears as these.

By establishing connections, at strategic points, between the
simple dramatic situation and scriptural or other history, Marvell
has transformed the traditional pastoral epicedium into an
intense experience; and although its intensity cannot be ade-
quately accounted for in terms of the death of a faun, it seems
equally clear that the poem is not to be read as a detailed
allegory.

For the moment, however, reading 'The Nymph complaining'
is perhaps less interesting than the difficulties in reading it.
Marvell was to make use of this technique of allusion in his most
unusual group of poems, those concerned with that strange figure
the Mower. Reminiscences of classical and Christian literature
everywhere deepen the texture of these poems, yet the function of
Marvell's oblique references remains obscure. And their obscurity assumes greater importance in connection with the
Mower, for the poems in which he appears offer problems even
on the literal level, problems that seem to require an allegorical
solution. In the Mower episode of 'Upon Appleton House, to my

Lord Fairfax' the reader finds himself beset by difficulties resembling those in 'The Nymph complaining'. There is, however, this difference: the literal action, the basic dramatic situation, of the Mower episode seems completely intelligible only through reference to another level of meaning.

In the Mower episode[5] the traditional shepherd is replaced by the Mower, a figure who reflects something of the pastoral convention and something of what his name suggests. On the one hand, the Mowers exhibit the usual idyllic charm of rural life; from their sea of 'unfathomable Grass' they 'bring up Flow'rs', and their dances illustrate their simple, close relationship with Nature:

> Where every Mowers wholesome Heat
> Smells like an *Alexanders sweat*.
> Their Females fragrant as the Mead
> Which they in *Fairy Circles* tread:
> When at their Dances End they kiss,
> Their new-made Hay not sweeter is.   (427–32)

Yet their idyllic harmony with Nature may be shattered with incredible rapidity:

> With whistling Sithe, and Elbow strong,
> These Massacre the Grass along:
> While one, unknowing, carves the *Rail*,
> Whose yet unfeather'd Quils her fail.
> The Edge all bloody from its Breast
> He draws, and does his stroke detest;
> Fearing the Flesh untimely mow'd
> To him a Fate as black forebode.   (393–400)

Viewed against the usual sentiments of the pastoral tradition, the incident is quite extraordinary: the moment of violence suddenly obliterates the mood of pastoral calm.

Thestylis, conventionally the simple shepherdess (often the simple shepherd!), is referred to as 'bloody', her actions vulture-like: 'Greedy as Kites has trust it up.' 'Death-Trumpets creak' in the throats of the parent birds, and the meadows suddenly become a 'Camp of Battail', 'quilted ore with Bodies slain'. The entire incident has occupied only four stanzas (L–LIII), but the reader acquainted with pastoral conventions will want to know why it is there at all. What are we to make of it? The language is too forceful and violent to be dismissed as a fanciful conceit provoked by the sight of a few hayricks: the accident of the 'bloody . . . stroke' seems to possess some significance above and beyond the literal level of the action. Unlike 'The Nymph complaining', however, this episode does not seem to allude to an area of experience in which the appropriateness of the violent language may be appreciated.

Of course, there are in the episode, as elsewhere in Marvell, many literary and historical allusions, and yet they seem to illuminate only the passage at hand and not the accident of the 'bloody . . . stroke'. But perhaps the pun on 'Levellers' represents a covert allusion to the Puritans, so that 'the Field' is the field of Civil War, the Mower is Cromwell, and the 'Rail' is Charles? Or maybe the Mower is Fairfax . . . This kind of reading, though variations of it have appeared persuasively in print, seems to me to depend primarily on rare ingenuity and a real ability to confuse vehicle and tenor; it also requires a reader to attend to one system of allusions while resolutely refusing to think about others. What does one do with the reference to 'Roman Camps', 'Desert Memphis Sand', 'Pyramids', 'Manna', 'Marriners', and 'Israalites'? Is Marvell warning his countrymen against the menace of Israeli seamen operating out of Egypt? Note what happens when we actually *pursue* an allusion—those 'Levellers', for example. In Stanza LVI the 'levell'd space' after the harvest is described in a highly suggestive conceit:

> The World when first created sure
> Was such a Table rase and pure.

But if we are disposed to view this comparison as an attempt to make the meadows symbolize the world at a certain moment in history, we are quickly disabused in the next two lines where Marvell draws on his knowledge of bullfighting to find a more apt simile:

> Or rather such is the *Toril*
> Ere the Bulls enter at Madril.

Like the Nymph's Faun the Mower reveals a capacity for
harmony with nature, but as always in Marvell the relationship
of man and Nature is precarious, liable to be lost in a moment.
This double attitude will be familiar to readers of 'The Picture of
little T.C. in a Prospect of Flowers', where the Nymph 'reforms'
the 'errours of the Spring', but is warned that an offense against
course of *kind* will shatter the idyllic relationship:

> But O young beauty of the Woods,
> Whom Nature courts with fruits and flow'rs,
> Gather the Flow'rs, but spare the Buds;
> Lest *Flora* angry at thy crime,
> To kill her Infants in their prime,
> Do quickly make th' Example Yours;
> And, ere we see,
> Nip in the blossome all our hopes and Thee.

Such hints as this of darker depths in Nature are focused in the
Mower, where they form a strong contrast to the more conventional tone of traditional pastoral.

Although the allusions in 'Upon Appleton House' offer
perhaps even more difficulties than those of 'The Nymph
complaining', it at least seems clear that the accident of the
'bloody . . . stroke' possesses considerable emotional significance for Marvell. Indeed, in 'Damon the Mower' the 'bloody'
interlude is repeated, this time within the convention of the
pastoral love complaint. Damon, pining for the love of Juliana,
reflects on his harmony with nature:

> And, if at Noon my toil me heat,
> The Sun himself licks off my Sweat.
> While, going home, the Ev'ning sweet
> In cowslip-water bathes my feet.

But Juliana is the source of 'unusual Heats', all Nature wilts, and
the 'Massacre' of 'Upon Appleton House' reappears with more
serious consequences. Again all grass is flesh:

> While thus he threw his Elbow round,
> Depopulating all the Ground,

> And, with his whistling Sythe, does cut
> Each stroke between the Earth and Root,
> The edged Stele by careless chance
> Did into his own Ankle glance;
> And there among the Grass fell down,
> By his own Sythe, the Mower mown.

Again the reader of 'decorative' pastoral is unprepared for the sharply detailed, realistic moment of violence, and again he does not quite know what to make of it. Although the commonplaces of pastoral hyperbole have become strangely serious, there is no real explanation for the darker implications of the piece, suggested but undefined:

> Only for him no Cure is found,
> Whom *Julianas* Eyes do wound.
> 'Tis death alone that this must do:
> For Death thou art a Mower too.

Surely the significance of the Mower would have been clear to Fairfax's circle at Appleton House, but to the modern reader there may seem to be a lack of awareness on Marvell's part that in the Mower he has created an ambiguous figure. At least, in contrast to 'The Nymph complaining', there is no technique to show the reader, more or less precisely, what the ambiguity means. Although it is evident that the Mower possesses considerable emotional meaning for Marvell, above and beyond the figure's literal significance, there is no context in which the 'bloody' incidents are seen as purposeful excess, in which the force of the language is justified, or in which the capacity of the Mower for both harmony and conflict with Nature is resolved. The central tenet of pastoral verse, the idyllic correspondence between man and Nature known as the pathetic fallacy, has apparently been deliberately violated, and yet there is no overt explanation of why Marvell departed so radically from the pattern of traditional pastoral. The significance of these departures can be appreciated fully only in the context of the other Mower poems, only as we compare context with context in order to make private meanings public.

'The Mower to the Glo-Worms' is a pretty little lyric that has no obscurities for someone not overcurious about the last stanza. The first three stanzas invoke the Glo-Worms, whose function it is to guide the 'wandring Mowers'. In the fourth and last stanza the 'unusual' Juliana reappears, the Mower's harmony with Nature is again lost, and the whole affair is given an intellectual emphasis oddly at variance with the conventions of pastoral love lyrics:

> Your courteous Lights in vain you wast,
> Since *Juliana* here is come,
> For She my Mind hath so displac'd
> That I shall never find my home.

By ignoring the other Mower poems we could probably find a place for this lyric in the tradition of the pastoral love complaint – even though love is not explicitly mentioned in the poem. Certainly this 'displacement' of the mind seems to be far less serious than the accident of the 'bloody . . . stroke'. And yet another poem in the series, 'The Mower's Song', suggests that Marvell's use of the word 'Mind' was anything but casual.

'The Mower's Song' also concerns Juliana and the mind, and again Marvell adventures from the pastoral theme of harmony with Nature:

> My Mind was once the true survey
> Of all these Medows fresh and gay;
> And in the greenness of the Grass
> Did see its Hopes as in a Glass;
> When *Juliana* came, and She
> What I do to the Grass, does to my Thoughts and Me.

The pastoral harmony between the Mower and Nature no longer exists; the correspondence is in the past tense. As in 'The Mower to the Glo-Worms', moreover, Marvell sees lost harmony, the 'true survey', as having had its basis in a particular condition of the mind, now lost with the coming of Juliana. Her presence— the word 'love' is again absent from the poem—has dark implications for the Mower. The refrain,

> When *Juliana* came, and She
> What I do to the Grass, does to my Thoughts and Me,

recalls the violence of the 'bloody . . . stroke' and once again demonstrates an imaginative refashioning of Isaiah's proposition: for the Mower all flesh is grass, all grass flesh.

Stanza II emphasises the Mower's alienation from Nature and explicitly jettisons the convention of attributing human emotions to Nature by exactly reversing the terms of the pathetic fallacy:

> But these, while I with Sorrow pine,
> Grew more luxuriant still and fine;
> That not one Blade of Grass you spy'd,
> But had a Flower on either side.

The word 'luxuriant', because of the ambiguous antecedent of 'these', may be read as a significant pun: if the antecedent of 'these' is taken to be 'Medows', as the context requires, then 'luxuriant' simply denotes exuberant growth; if, however, 'these' is taken to refer to 'Thoughts', its immediate grammatical antecedent, 'luxuriant', then includes a pun on its old meaning of 'lascivious'. For it will presently appear that this poem and also the next to be considered—'The Mower against Gardens', beginning 'Luxurious Man, to bring his Vice in use'—are about how man gets and employs his lascivious thoughts.

In Stanza III the Mower reproaches the 'Unthankful Medows' that could a 'fellowship so true forego', and then, in the next stanza, he turns to threats of 'luxuriant' proportions:

> But what you in Compassion ought,
> Shall now by my Revenge be wrought:
> And Flow'rs, and Grass, and I and all,
> Will in one common Ruine fall.
> For *Juliana* comes, and She
> What I do to the Grass, does to my Thoughts and Me.

Ostensibly, the Mower's motive for revenge is the betrayal of the meadows that meet in their 'gawdy May-games' while he and his 'Thoughts' suffer from Juliana.

Although such an explanation seems more satisfactory than

any derived from the literal action of 'Upon Appleton House' or 'Damon the Mower', it still fails to account for the darker undertones of the whole poem or the emotional metre and diction of this stanza, especially in the refrain, and in the third and fourth lines whose three commas and repeated connectives accentuate the slow, impressive movement of a heroic style. Granted that the intensity of such threats is common, if not to real lovers, then at least to their literary counterparts, it remains difficult to find a place for the Mower's threat in the pastoral tradition. Not only has the original correspondence between the Mower and Nature been lost, but now the Mower seems determined to contribute to his own alienation from the 'true survey'. Pastoral harmony has become pastoral discord.

But if we pause for a moment to examine the poem in more abstract terms, the situation may be summed up in such a way as to explain Marvell's modifications of the pastoral *kind* and to provide some answers to the questions I have been raising throughout. Man once existed in an ideal correspondence and harmony with Nature: the appearance of woman resulted in the loss of the ideal state, in the awareness of mortality, in the inclination to sin. This is, of course, the Christian story of the Fall of Man from the pastoral harmony of Eden.

The Mower, to be sure, is not Adam nor is Juliana Eve; the poem must be read with at least as much literary tact as is required by 'The Nymph complaining'. It is not accurate to say that 'The Mower's Song' is an allegory of the Fall of Man, but neither is it sufficient to plead that this is a very complex poem that new critics (from Puttenham on) should be assiduous to read on a minimum of two levels. The reader has been led to consider a pastoral love complaint in relation to an event in scriptural history, but the exact poise or balance that Marvell has achieved remains hard to state explicitly: genre becomes trope.

In 'The Mower's Song' Marvell has avoided the limitations of conventional pastoral almost entirely, and avoided them successfully, despite the fact that he is perhaps most oblique and indirect here. Since the poem is more subtle and carefully articulated than the Mower episode of 'Upon Appleton House' or 'Damon the Mower', a reader appreciates the significance of another area of experience, one that 'transcend[s] poor Shepherds skill', without being confused by suggestive but irrelevant, or only momentarily relevant, terms; that is, by allusions and comparisons which, while they may throw light on the passage at hand, yet fail to form a consistent group amongst themselves.

There is in 'The Mower's Song' a simultaneous blending of kinds of experience as Marvell accommodates the literary technique of pastoral to scriptural history. With the exception of one key word—'fall'—he does not even use terms ambiguously suggestive of scriptural events. Instead, he has made the plot or action of the poem significant in itself; the organisation of the action and the relationship of the Mower to Nature are in themselves expressive of the Fall of Man. Even though the Fall is barely suggested by the plot, the diffuse connection established in the reader's mind is enough to provide an explanation of the characterisation of Juliana and to reveal the basis for the Mower's ambiguous relationship with Nature. Genre has merged with scriptural history, as indeed it often had before during the Middle Ages and Renaissance. The genre that had always described *an* Eden here describes *the* Eden, the theological 'home' of 'The Mower to the Glo-Worms', from which man lapsed with the coming of woman: 'For She my Mind hath so displac'd. . . .'

As Golding's Ovid has it,

> Moreouer by the golden age what other thing is ment,
> Than Adams tyme in Paradyse.[6]

Which is not to imply that Marvell is 'traditional' in any restricted sense; he draws on earlier pastoral, but he is not indistinguishable from the tradition. By manipulating the traditional form of the pastoral, Marvell has managed to make it an adequate vehicle for his own attitudes toward Christian history, for clearly he has not limited himself to a simple retelling of the story of the Fall.

Marvell sees the Fall primarily as a change that occurred in the mind of man, as a change in the way man looks at or thinks about Nature, because he carefully distinguishes between 'Thoughts and Me' and takes pains to emphasise the role of the mind: 'My Mind was once the true survey. . . .' The fifth and last stanza of 'The Mower's Song' illustrates the attitude:

And thus, ye Meadows, which have been
Companions of my thoughts more green,
Shall now the Heraldry become
With which I shall adorn my Tomb;
For *Juliana* comes, and She
What I do to the Grass, does to my Thoughts and Me.

The grammatical structure of the refrain refuses to let the reader regard man's experience with Nature and man's experience of himself and his 'Thoughts' as separate or unconnected. The Fall is seen as a change in the response of the mind to Nature: 'Companions of my thoughts more green'. Man's present spiritual condition is a tomb with Nature figuring as its decorative heraldry. Thus man's inability to think 'thoughts more green' corresponds to his alienation from the 'true survey' of Nature that he formerly enjoyed, from the Edenlike state of mind that allowed him to exist in harmony with a 'companionable' and 'compassionate' Nature.

The remaining poem in this group, 'The Mower against Gardens', reinforces the conclusions derived from 'The Mower's Song', and provides even more explicit statements of Marvell's attitude toward the mind of man, the Fall, and Nature—all of which permit us to see that Marvell was engaged in the traditional Nature—Art controversy.[7] The lapsed, corrupted mind of man is the subject of the poem, the theological time is post-Fall:

Luxurious Man, to bring his Vice in use,
Did after him the World seduce.

Although the poem bristles with horticultural puns and theological allusions, the main theme is clear: Man, through the activities of his 'double . . . Mind', corrupts the meadows—'Where Nature was most plain and pure'—and fulfils the threat of 'The Mower's Song' ('Will in one common Ruine fall'). Theologically speaking, the fallen mind possesses for most religious thinkers some knowledge of good as well as evil, but here Marvell restricts himself to man in his knowledge of evil. He is represented as having overreached his natural limits and succumbed to the medieval vice of *curiositas*:

> And yet these Rarities might be allow'd,
> To Man, that sov'raign thing and proud;
> Had he not dealt between the Bark and Tree,
> Forbidden mixtures there to see.

Marvell communicates his theme by developing a contrast between the natural, untouched meadows and the artificial garden. The meadows are 'sweet Fields' where Nature is free to impart a 'wild and fragrant Innocence'.[8] On the other hand, the activities involved in making the garden—that 'dead and standing pool of Air'—are expressed in witty vice-metaphors: the bastard plant no longer knows the 'Stock from which it came'; grafting produces an 'uncertain and adult'rate fruit'; the emasculated cherry (stoneless) is induced to 'procreate without a Sex'—for this 'green Seraglio has its Eunuchs too'. Thus two worlds are presented in opposition: one, the world created by man, is expressed in metaphors of 'luxuriant' illegitimacy; the other, a world of fauns and gods, is the preferred state, where 'presence' rather than 'skill' is the ideal agent.

Man's emphasis on 'skill' has led to a corresponding neglect of the innocence to be had from the 'sweet Fields' of Nature. Nature, then, when not deformed by 'Forbidden mixtures', still preserves something of the intercourse between heaven and earth that man forfeited through the Fall. Man's 'double . . . Mind', on the other hand, has attempted to recreate, out of its knowledge of evil, the Garden of Eden—and the result is Acrasia's Bower.[9] Art has corrupted Nature.

I have been trying to define some of Marvell's fundamental commitments by pointing out a development in his thought and literary technique from the highly derivative and naturalistic pastorals of the fashionable world, to a criticism, especially in 'Clorinda and Damon', of *libertin* ethics, and finally to the use of the pastoral form as a vehicle for the expression of his more mature concerns. Marvell was not of course unique in using the pastoral form for Christian ends; in fact, our historical perspective makes such a use seem almost inevitable. Given the 'Christianisation' of Vergil's Fourth Eclogue, the shepherds of the Gospels, the mystical glosses on the Canticles, and the medieval and Renaissance tendency toward allegory, it is hard to see how readers and writers could fail to identify a conception like that of the Golden Age, where a bountiful, beneficent Nature literally dropped food into men's laps, with the Christian idea of the Garden of Eden. Nor was Marvell unique in using pastoral as a way of responding to the division between Nature and Art. Given our knowledge of the tradition, such a use, again, seems almost inevitable. But if Marvell's use of pastoral is not unusual, his particular modifications of the tradition are, and it is here that the poet reveals himself and his philosophy of man most clearly.

The way Marvell manipulates the most venerable pastoral convention, that of man in idyllic sympathy with Nature, leaves no doubt that he was deeply preoccupied with man's double estate—his capacity both for harmony with, and alienation from, Nature. This attitude towards man in relation to Nature is, moreover, not simply a matter of temperament; it has a firm, precise theological basis in the scriptural fact of the Fall from Eden and the consequences that may be supposed to have proceeded from it.

Thus three main traditions are necessary for an understanding of Marvell's poetry: the literary tradition of pastoral; the philosophical tradition of Nature and Art that has always been associated with pastoral; and the Christian tradition, which gives a particular shape and meaning to the other two. In the more poetic (and private) terms with which I have been working, Marvell sees the Fall as having produced a 'double . . . Mind ', one that possesses both the Mower's capacity for the harmony of the 'true survey' and the alienation of the 'bloody . . . stroke'; for Innocence and Vice; for Nature and Art.

Art or 'skill' is the immoral activity of a 'double . . . Mind' as it deals in 'Forbidden mixtures'. Marvell makes the matter most explicit in 'Upon Appleton House', where the activities of 'Man unrul'd' contrast unfavourably with the instinctively good behavior of birds and beasts (stanza II). Stated in the conceptual terms with which we are familiar:

> But Nature here hath been so free
> As if she said leave this to me.
> Art would more neatly have defac'd
> What she had laid so sweetly wast;
> In fragrant Gardens, shaddy Woods,
> Deep Meadows, and transparent Floods.   (st. x)

Nature, 'orderly and near' (IV), produces Fairfax's garden, which is not artful but nevertheless 'in order grows' (XXXIX). For Marvell the *locus amoenus* is, like Milton's Eden, the result not of 'nice Art' but 'Nature boon'. Art is, in short, a principle of corruption, of false rather than true order, the instrument of man's further alienation from Nature and hence from God, whose Book of the Creatures human Art has deformed.

The Mower in these terms becomes a much more comprehensible figure. Clearly he is Marvell's symbol of fallen man, the lowest of the angels and the highest of the beasts, made in the image of his God and yet capable of the depths of depravity. The Bible notes that God made man upright, but he has sought out many devices, like Marvell's 'Luxurious Man' who, 'to bring his Vice in use,/ Did after him the World seduce'. The result is the Mower, the natural man who displays a faculty for both harmony and alienation, a faculty possibly shared by all men in all times in relation to Nature. And yet Marvell's Nature is not Wordsworth's, because the one is ordered where the other is spontaneous. Similarly, the Mower is symbolic but not Symbolist, for the meanings clustered around Marvell's mysterious figure, while in the last analysis indefinable, are in an important sense neither vague nor illimitable but retain by association something of the firm outline characteristic of their theological formulation. Nor is the Mower's ambiguous relationship with Nature in any way Empsonian; the ambiguity is limited, defined, by scriptural history, and it may finally be resolved through reference to the theological fact of the Fall.

The themes of harmony and alienation, most clearly articulated in connection with the Mower figure, appear to be similarly, though less obviously, present in the ironic wit of most of Marvell's best lyrics, lending these deceptively casual verses the weight and precision derived from a specific view of man and the universe. There seems to be little doubt, for example, that 'The Picture of little T.C.' would be an extremely slight effort if it were not for the last stanza, where the dark moral undercuts the courtly posturings of the preceding lines. The same is true of the concluding lines of 'A Dialogue between the Soul and Body':

> What but a Soul could have the wit
> To build me up for Sin so fit?
> So Architects do square and hew,
> Green Trees that in the Forest grew.

Here a knowledge of Marvell's general attitude toward Nature and Art permits us to appreciate the full force of the Body's wry comparison; the Soul is like the architect not only in its amoral capacity to 'build' but also in its immoral capacity to use Art to deface 'green' Nature. Marvell's language, perhaps to a greater degree than that of most poets, reveals its full resonance only in relation to the entire body of his lyric verse, which is the reason that T.S. Eliot has done the poet a disservice in suggesting that the critical task in the 'case' of Marvell is 'to squeeze the drops of the essence of two or three poems': 'The fact that of all Marvell's verse, which is itself not a great quantity, the really valuable part consists of a very few poems indicates that the [distinguishing] quality of [his verse] is probably a literary rather than a personal quality.'[10] It has seemed to me, rather, that the literary quality of this individual talent is, despite its traditional elements, highly personal.

Even the more explicitly religious poems are difficult to appreciate in isolation. 'The Coronet', for example, may appear at first glance to be a purely religious meditation, but it is to be read as a pastoral. The 'I' of the poem speaks of his 'Shepherdess', and a whole dimension of the poem vanishes if we are inattentive to what is involved when Marvell represents his 'I' as a singer-shepherd. The poem is a paradigm of conversion, a dramatization, like Herbert's 'The Collar', of the need for Grace through the deliberate cultivation and then rejection of blasphemous or religiously mistaken thoughts. Marvell's shepherd begins by announcing his intention to reform, to replace his Saviour's crown of 'Thorns' with a 'Chaplet' of flowers (his 'fruits are only flow'rs'):[11]

> Dismantling all the fragrant Towers
> That once adorn'd my Shepherdesses head.

But he is forced to reject these thoughts, for he finds that pride, the 'Serpent old', has become part of the 'Chaplet' with 'wreaths of Fame and Interest'. (Chaplet means prayer as well as wreath, and therefore also refers to the song of the shepherd.) The ascent, as St Bernard says, is through humility rather than pride; and thus the shepherd begs God to 'disintangle' the 'winding Snare' of Satan 'Or shatter too with him my curious frame',

> Though set with Skill and chosen out with Care.
> That they, while Thou on both their Spoils dost tread,
> May crown thy Feet, that could not crown thy Head.

The little Augustinian drama is complete, the progress from sinner to saved that so absorbed the seventeenth century ('The Collar', Walton's life of Donne, or Donne's 'If poisonous minerals . . . ') has been re-enacted in the poem with great concentration of meaning. A good example of the concentration possible in this kind of pastoral may be found in the 'curious frame' of line twenty-two: it refers first to the artful chaplet (poem and prayer and wreath) that is 'set with Skill', the 'skill' or Art that deformed the 'Meadows' in 'The Mower against Gardens'; but it also refers to the human being, that overly curious creature whose Art may obscure the divine Nature within; and finally it refers to the poem itself, an object of curious Art that must be 'disintangled' from human 'Fame and Interest' in order to become a pure chaplet or psalm in praise of the 'king of Glory'. By the end of the poem the sinner has been saved, and the pagan shepherd-poet has become a David, that shepherd-poet who danced before the Ark of God.

Even in the poems of human love the theme of alienation from Nature through Art gives Marvell's tone a distinctive toughness, setting such a lyric as 'To his Coy Mistress' clearly apart from others of its kind. Whereas the lovers of Donne's 'The Sunne Rising' are identified, in half-ironic hyperbole, with the universe, the sun being advised to

> Shine here to us, and thou art every where;
> This bed thy center is, these walls, thy sphere,

Marvell's 'am'rous birds of prey' gain our attention through their isolation, their defiant opposition to the world:

> And tear our Pleasures with rough strife,
> Through the Iron gates of Life.
> Thus, though we cannot make our Sun
> Stand still, yet we will make him run.

This attitude of ironic defiance, the tough determination to live
with one's nature though it is somehow out of joint with the
world, has been much admired. Yet we have seen that Marvell's
attitude is only superficially admirable in modern terms, for it
stems not from the metaphysical disillusionment of the twentieth
century, but from the theological conviction that man fell from
the ideal harmony of the Garden of Eden. In contrast to that of
the Underground Man, Marvell's malaise has a cure within the
terms of the system that defines the nature of his illness.

The fact is that Marvell, unlike most of his modern readers,
thought it possible to recover the lost harmony with Nature,
which before the Fall man had possessed in the Garden. There is
more than a hint of the possibility in the ordered innocence of the
Fairfax garden of 'Upon Appleton House', where the recovery is
linked to contemplative retirement. In the 'Horatian Ode'
Cromwell leaves his 'private Gardens' and joins 'wiser Art' to
'Nature', so becoming the union of active and contemplative or
the 'Man . . . that does both act and know'. But the clearest
illustration appears in the contemplative lesson of 'The Garden',
probably Marvell's most famous and variously read poem. The
themes of alienation and harmony, of Art and Nature, are
present in 'The Garden', and probably it could be demonstrated
that they are as sure a guide to the total attitude of the poem as
any of the numerous influences already brought to bear on its
richly suggestive verses. But here my purpose is only to round out
this discussion of Marvell's pastoral experiments, to sketch the
workings of man's 'double . . . Mind' in its knowledge of good
rather than evil. It is in this sense that 'The Garden' offers a
solution to the desperate condition of man implied by 'The
Mower against Gardens' and 'The Mower's Song'.

The speaker of the poem withdraws from the 'busie Companies
of Men' into the solitude and innocence of the garden, finding
there what the reader of pastoral will recognise as an elegant
condensation of the 'soft' primitivism associated with the Golden
Age:

> What wond'rous Life in this I lead!
> Ripe Apples drop about my head;
> The Luscious Clusters of the Vine
> Upon my Mouth do crush their Wine.

Doubtless these lines are sensuous, but sexual, hence sensual, connotations are more easily kept where they belong, in the background, if we remember that this is an account of what Nature really *was* during the Golden Age, animated in Marvell by a Christian Neoplatonism that saw the landscape tremulous with divinity. This garden is neither the Acrasia's Bower of 'The Mower against Gardens' nor the spiritual tomb of 'The Mower's Song'. There Nature had been corrupted by the overcurious Art of man's 'double . . . Mind', but here the intimacy of the speaker with Nature is meant to recall the harmony of the Garden of Eden. Here intimacy precedes the purification of the mind:

> Mean while the Mind, from pleasure less,
> Withdraws into its happiness:
> The Mind, that Ocean where each kind
> Does streight its own resemblance find;
> Yet it creates, transcending these,
> Far other Worlds, and other Seas;
> Annihilating all that's made
> To a green Thought in a green Shade.

The withdrawal of the mind, creating an inner world of Nature and annihilating the outer world corrupted by Art, precedes the illumination of the soul in the next stanza; thus for a moment the poet, translating physical into spiritual geography, recovers the 'true survey' of 'The Mower's Song'.

Through the process of 'annihilation' the speaker has managed to think 'thoughts more green' in a world seduced by the Art of 'Luxurious Man'. Art, or 'all that's made' by the mind of man, has been transformed into Nature, or the 'green Thought in a green Shade'. Within himself the speaker has formed a garden, a paradise notably free of dainty devices: this is the *hortus conclusus* of the mind, established within not by Art but by the other impulse of that 'double . . . Mind', by 'Annihilating all that's made/To a green Thought in a green Shade'. The Mower has, after all, found his 'home', the spiritual residence of Adam's sons located in the dark backward and abysm of theological time, and his return has fulfilled the promise of Milton's angel:

> then wilt thou not be loth
> To leave this Paradise, but shalt possess
> A Paradise within thee, happier far.

To us Marvell's attitude toward Nature and Art perhaps seems primitivist, even rigidly anti-intellectual, and yet his intention probably extended no farther than the effort of the moralist to put matters in proper perspective: so that salvation might be attained, so that the lost pastoral innocence, the paradisiacal integrity of Nature, might be reconstituted with the aid alone of literary Art in the garden of the mind.

SOURCE: extract from *Nature and Art in Renaissance Literature* (New York, 1964), pp. 142–68.

NOTES

[The Notes here are abbreviated from
those in the original version—Ed.]

1. It is possible to use external or direct internal evidence to date a number of Marvell's poems, especially the satires and those few published before 1650. But by far the greater part of his lyric poetry appeared only posthumously in 1681. One may speculate, and speculate quite reasonably, that much of the pastoral verse must have been written in the early 1650s at Nun Appleton, when Marvell was tutor to Mary Fairfax: an earlier Fairfax had translated Tasso; the house and grounds favored contemplation; an audience educated in the subtleties of pastoral literature remained at hand; the pastorals reveal technical accomplishments lacking in the poems before 1650 and show few overt affinities with the later satires; and the long 'Upon Appleton House' betrays many similarities with the short pastoral pieces. But in the absence of further evidence these speculations remain speculations.

2. G. Gregory Smith (ed.), *Elizabethan Critical Essays* (Oxford, 1904) I 175.

3. *The Arte of English Poesie*, ed. G. D. Willcock and Alice Walker (Cambridge, 1936) p. 38. Both Sidney and Puttenham refer to

the 'allegorical' rather than the 'decorative' tradition of pastoral. John Fletcher's definition, on the other hand, refers to the latter tradition: 'Understand, therefore, a pastoral to be a representation of shepherds and shepherdesses with their actions and passions, which must be such as may agree with their natures, at least not exceeding former fictions and vulgar traditions; they are not to be adorned with any art, but such improper ones as nature is said to bestow as singing, and poetry; or such as experience may teach them, as the virtues of herbs and fountains, the ordinary course of the sun, moon, and stars, and such like.' 'To the Reader', *The Faithful Shepherdess*, in *The Works of Francis Beaumont & John Fletcher*, ed. W. W. Greg 1908 III 18.

4. M. C. Bradbrook and M. G. Lloyd Thomas, *Andrew Marvell* (Cambridge, 1940) pp. 49–50, tend to identify the faun with Agnus Dei and see the 'love of the girl for her fawn' as a 'reflection of the love of the Church for Christ'. Everett H. Emerson, 'Andrew Marvell's "The Nymph complaining for the death of her Faun" ', in *Études anglaises*, VIII (April–June 1955) 107–10, argues that while the poem is not an 'allegory', it nevertheless embodies Marvell's emotional response to the Church of England in the 1640s. This poem, like the 'Horatian Ode', has become the occasion for numerous articles; it is an academic *cause célèbre*, plunder in the running battle between Historical Scholar and New Critic. My own feeling is that the poem is best read as a pastoral epicedium on the loss of love, but I do not hazard a full-scale interpretation here because it would not be entirely pertinent to the rest of my argument and because my purpose is not polemical.

5. Only some 64 (stanzas XLIX–LVI) of the 776 lines of 'Upon Appleton House' are devoted to the Mowers as the poet, oscillating between physical and spiritual topography, moves in verse from house to garden to meadow to wood. Courtly compliment to Lord Fairfax is a major theme of this extraordinary work, but Marvell also explores the relation of man to nature and a variety of other important themes. The informing principle of the entire poem lies in an ideal of conduct embodying 'measure' and 'proportion' in the 'vast and all-comprehending Dominions of Nature and Art'.

6. *The .xv. Bookes of P. Ovidius Naso, entytuled Metamorphosis, translated oute of Latin into English meeter* (1575), sig. A7ʳ. Cf *The Shepheardes Calender*, 'June', lines 9–10, *The Complete Poetical Works of Spenser*, ed. R. E. Neil Dodge (Cambridge, Mass., 1936) p. 29.

7. Frank Kermode, whose sensitive, learned criticism is useful in any reading of Marvell, locates the poem within the established terms of the Nature-Art controversy and cites a number of relevant documents outside Marvell; see 'Two Notes on Marvell', in *Notes and Queries*, CXXVII (March 1952), 136–8, and 'The Argument of Marvell's

"Garden" ', in *Essays in Criticism*, II (July 1952) 225–41. [Reprinted in this Casebook—Ed.] A more general view of Marvell in relation to Nature may be found in J. H. Summers, 'Marvell's "Nature" ', in *Journal of English Literary History*, XX (June 1953) 121–35. [Reprinted in this Casebook—Ed.] Summers chooses to emphasise only one aspect of the Mower: 'He symbolises man's alienation from nature.'

8. Like John Rea, who maintains that a 'green Medow is a more delightful object' than the 'Gardens of the new model' because 'there Nature alone, without the aid of Art, spreads her verdant Carpets, spontaneously imbroydered with many pretty plants and pleasing Flowers, far more inviting than such an immured Nothing'— *Flora: seu, De florum cultura. Or, a Complete Florilege* (1665) p. 1.

9. The literary and philosophical contrast between two kinds of gardens is an important theme in medieval and Renaissance literature. Readers of the *Romance of the Rose* will be familiar with the theme, but of course the famous example occurs in Spenser, where the Garden of Adonis in which Art complements Nature is contrasted with the Bower of Bliss in which Art usurps the proper functions of Nature.

10. T. S. Eliot, 'Andrew Marvell', in *Selected Essays*, 3rd ed. (1951) p. 292. [The substance of the essay is reprinted in this Casebook—Ed.]

11. The allusion to Matthew VII 20 ('Wherefore by their fruits ye shall know them') implies the entire poem: flowers must become fruits through the Grace of God.

Rosalie Colie (1970)   Pictorial Traditions

Obviously, figures involve imagery, and imagery has something to do with pictures visible to the eye or the mind. Marvell's use of visual tradition is remarkable, even in an age when 'iconography' was one material reservoir for a poet. Many of the poems he wrote fall into standard forms accommodating ecphrasis, or poetic rendering of a work of art, and follow the Horatian maxim that poetry and painting are alike, *ut pictura poesis*. 'The Gallery' is an obvious example, as are the various Instructions to a Painter, both forms common in late seventeenth century poetry, and both of them dependent upon visual traditions and visual crafts. Into its short length 'The Gallery' compresses the form Marino made famous,[1] though Marino's collection is obviously more various, rambling, and diffuse than Marvell's remarkable exercise in diminution. 'The unfortunate Lover' animates a series of love-emblems to raise for us serious questions about the translation of traditions from one art into another. 'The Picture of little T.C.' is an exact poetic parallel to pictures of children ringed with emblematic flowers indicating the transience both of childhood and beauty; 'On a Drop of Dew' provides in verse the moralising meditation upon a small, commonplace, and—in this case, at least—beautiful object, the descriptive nicety of which is related to the technique of the illustrated emblem. Marvell conspicuously uses art objects as metaphorical elements: Fleckno is 'This *Basso Relievo* of a Man'; 'The Gallery' is about pictures; 'The Nymph complaining' designs her own tomb; 'Upon Appleton House' utilises landscape traditions and emblem traditions with remarkable sophistication and skill. As we might by now come to expect, Marvell's use of visual traditions provides useful hints toward his poetic practice as a whole.

'The Gallery' belongs in a traditional type, dominated by Marino's anthological *La Galeria*, in which it was 'fair' to depict in words real pictures (such as Titian's great 'Maddalena'), conventional pictures on themes so common as to need no particular model, and pictures sheerly imaginary. Marino's gallery was an 'ideal' one, for all its occasional actuality of description; the poems derive as much from the perfecting imagination as from real visual experience, but both rely heavily on visual conventions and traditions. Marvell's 'Gallery' is something else again: it celebrates an act of the imagination, since the poet chooses as a metaphor for his mind, literally preoccupied with his mistress, a gallery of pictures. He makes up an ideal collection, but only for himself—no other man could be expected to value this collection as he did, intent on a particular beloved. Furthermore, his collection is ideal in the literal sense of the word, since it is of his ideas of her, these figured forth as hung on the inside walls of his mind. He 'furnishes' his mind with her; perhaps the poem is a memory-poem, more likely a parodied memory-poem, in which his lady's moods are forever recorded.[2] This is a love poem, extravagant but distant, introspective but unpersuasive; this lover mediates on the facets of his lady's character, as in another poem he meditates on the various aspects of a drop of dew. A love poem, this poem observes and presses various conventions of metaphoric utterance about ladies. Clora is 'a 'Murtheress', killing her lover by tormenting him with her weapons, which are, of course, 'Black Eyes, red Lips, and curled Hair'. At another time, in another mood, she benevolently enchants him, as Aurora, as Venus; then again, she is a witch. She is *la bella dame sans merci* as well as the perfect love-object, naked asleep or naked awake on her shell. Last of all, she is 'a tender Shepherdess', designated as artless, like so many other graceful, disorderly ladies in seventeenth-century poems—Julia, Eve—by her 'Hair . . . loosely playing in the Air'.

The poem is courtly not in its reference to courts (Whitehall and Mantua), but in its deliberate artificiality and sophistication. The poet is up-to-date as a connoisseur; in his interior decoration, tapestries are put away to make room for a display in the modern kind:

> And the great *Arras*-hangings, made
> Of various Faces, by are laid;

to be replaced by

> . . . a Collection choicer far
> Then or *White-hall's*, or *Mantua's* were,

that is, by a display of paintings finer than the King's own, purchased from the Gonzaga cabinet at Mantua. The mental cabinet of the poem manages to be 'choice' by its careful, exclusive concentration on one subject; since all the paintings are of one sitter, they offer a kind of consistency, and since they are all different, they offer variety as well. The 'Inhumane Murtheress', who examines her engines of war and instruments of torture is like an Italian picture of dark gardens and mysterious flickering lights; this one image can be connected to the bizarre, grotesque image of horror common in the work of the French *libertins* to whom Marvell is so often (I think unduly) likened. Here, Clora is

a night-witch. Aurora asleep, in the third stanza, is like the
nymphs of Titian and others, or like Giorgione's sleeping Venus,[3]
with Venus's attributes of doves and roses around her; the ' *Venus*
in her pearly Boat', save perhaps for her posture, is familiar to
everyone, with her airs, halcyons, ambergris and other perfumes
somehow depicted. Marvell solves the problem of sweetness in a
way different Botticelli, but both this stanza and Botticelli's great
picture catch the peculiar freshness of windborne odors.

The first four pictures in this gallery alternate a lovable with a
cruel mistress, a decorous confrontation prescribed in literary
versions of love affairs. This love affair, though, is of the mind and
therefore undramatic; the poet simply surveys Clora's moods or,
rather, her decisions to adopt moods each fixed in a mental
picture. He does not, like the sonnet-lover faced with the same
variation in a lady's behavior, embark upon the tortuous self-
investigation characteristic of more analytical love poetry. The
compliments to this lady increase stanza by stanza, though
hardly the intimacy between poet and lady; in the end, he is as
distant from her as at the beginning. First she is a murderess, then
Aurora, next an enchantress who, however demented, nonetheless gives herself over entirely to pre-occupation with love.
Finally she is Venus, the unspoilt goddess of love rising from the
sea. In all these 'pictures', the lady is promisingly and tantalis-
ingly displayed; the poet has yet to be awarded the full delights of
this mistress, and simply dwells on their possibility. There is a
curiously aseptic quality to this poem, as if the situation were in
fact only mental, as if there were no real lady, no real love affair.
The poet offers no invocation, no plea, no persuasive, as he enjoys
his ideas and his art, his ideas *of* art. There is an affinity between
the connoisseur-speaker in this poem, delighting in his artefacts,
and the Nymph in her poem, delighting in her pretty garden and
her candid statue; both are satisfied with the beautiful, objec-
tified constructs of their own minds.

Even in this poem, there is a pastoral undersong. Against the
manifest artificiality of high art and the grandeurs of two courts,
against the artifices of magicians, against even the superb
stylisations of Aurora and Venus, the poet sets over his preferred picture of his beloved as she seemed when he 'first was
took':

> A tender Shepherdess, whose Hair
> Hangs loosely playing in the Air,
> Transplanting Flow'rs from the green Hill,
> To crown her Head, and Bosome fill.

As in Marvell's other pastoral poems, there is the bulge here of the poet's tongue in his cheek. He recognises that a lady must play roles; he knows what those roles are; by fixing her in them himself, then choosing among them, he can fix her in ways that no flesh and blood lady can be fixed. If she persists in her varying theatricals, then his art can always stay one jump ahead of her imagination:

> These Pictures and a thousand more,
> Of Thee, my Gallery do store;
> In all the Forms thou can'st invent
> Either to please me, or torment:

He can turn her into an object, even if it is an object of art; he can denature her moods, reduce all her emotions, real or acted, to mere pose. In his view of her she is beautiful and rare; but she is not even unique. She is artificial, and she is his artifice. Customary artifice is brought up against the open sublimation of the artist; it doesn't matter who the lady is, or whether she is real or not: the poet's imagination can do without her, can satisfy itself alone. The lady actually is not really 'in' these pictures; rather, at the beginning of the poem, the poet invites her to go around his gallery with him, to appraise his taste; the poet's idealism turns out to be as thin as the lady's poses. This courtship is merely 'courtly', an artefact of the imagination, even down to the suitor's stylised affectation of preference for pastoral innocence.

'The unfortunate Lover' is a different arrangement of tableaux symbolising emotional states. Where the pictures of 'The Gallery' demonstrated the facets of Clora's behavior, however stereotyped, the images so carefully depicted in 'The unfortunate Lover' are all directed to show a single personality. If one can say this of so compulsive a character, the images of this poem are analytic of his psychology. This lover demonstrates the complicated manifestations of a single mode of reaction, a personality emotionally violent and consistently self-frustrating. Clora was

forever being fixed in 'The Gallery'; the unfortunate Lover is
ever in motion, although involuntary motion, it seems. She is
fragmented by the poet's devices; he is given in full, studied from
every side.

At the outset, the Lover is distinguished from those happy pairs
who play so sweetly with one another through the pages of Otto
van Veen's *Amorum Emblemata*[4] or of Herman Hugo's *Pia
Desideria*,[5] or of Quarles's *Emblems*.[6] There, pairs of child-lovers,
sometimes two *amorini*, sometimes an *amorino* with a little girl,
play together, struggle over a palm, diagnose and cure each
other's pains, cover a torch with a barrel or otherwise enjoy their
childhoods together[7] (Figs. 1, 2, 3).*

> Alas, how pleasant are their dayes
> With whom the Infant Love yet playes!
> Sorted by pairs, they still are seen
> By Fountains cool, and Shadows green.

'Alas', so inappropriate to the perfection described in the stanza,
sets the tone for the whole poem, for to our unfortunate Lover
such idylls are denied. This lover's difficult nature is revealed in a
series of emblematic scenes to which parallels and analogues can
be found in the emblem books, especially those dealing with the
subject of love. In this poem, Marvell is up to something quite
complex, attempting a mediation between verbal and visual arts.
Love emblems on the whole derive from literary sources, which
they illustrate, depicting the metaphorical extravagances of the
Anthology, the Latin love lyrics, and the petrarchan tradition. In
many cases, emblems reversed the /*ut pictura poesis*' dictum,
picturing poetical forms, some of them very bizarre, in visual
shapes. In 'The unfortunate Lover', Marvell points to the origins
of emblems by reversing the normal emblematic procedure,
which was to make extravagant pictures form hyperbolical
metaphors. In this poem, he extends the usual range of metaphor
and conceit by borrowing from the extravagant and conceited
pictorial tradition, itself based on figures of speech. This is the
opposite procedure from his demonstration in other poems of

---

* Figure references here and subsequently relate to the illustrations section, pages
159–66 below.

meaning in metaphor by seeming to unmetaphor, to take the metaphors in their own terms. Here, he starts from the heightened fantasy of emblem, to take their overstatements literally, as the 'real' setting of this lover's life.

The lover is a mariner, his life and love likened to a ship. Veen's emblem (Fig. 4) shows an *amorino* gazing after a ship heeling over; the epigram accompanying the picture celebrates the safe return to harbor of the endangered vessel. Born into a tempest and from a 'Shipwrack', his poor mother having

> . . . split against the Stone
> In a *Cesarian Section*.

this lover can only turn out stormy within himself. Our lover does not make port. His love is pointless and futile: the winds of love not only blow this lover, as they do the little love in Veen's picture (Fig. 5), but also they 'become' him. He is a wind and a generator of winds. '*Sunt Lacrimae Testes*', Veen's emblem assures us;[8] this lover is by his own reflective behavior a constant witness to his own internal state:

> The Sea him lent these bitter Tears
> Which at his Eyes he alwaies bears.

He is like Clora in her wicked moods, a night-lover, which is normal enough, according to the emblematist, for lovers take to night;[9] our lover never looks on day unless it is darkened by storms. There is no cure for this lover (stanza 5; Veen, 155); he chooses to prolong his life without repose (Veen, 95), chooses then to remain frenetic.

His upbringing was deficient, too: 'Corm'rants black' attended him, feeding 'him up with Hopes and Air,/Which soon digested to Despair', one bird feeding him while another billed at his heart. This is a version of '*Quod nutrit, exstinguit*,'[10] (Fig. 6) the constant torment of a man kept alive only to go on suffering, as for instance the Body and Soul feel they are, in their 'Dialogue'.

After such a birth and such an education, it is hardly surprising that the lover is thrust upon a life of violence. Veen's '*Fit Amor Violenter Avi*', seems to illustrate the whole of Marvell's poem;[11] other emblems serve to support the same theme: '*Est Miser Omnis*

Amans', for instance, and '*Quod Enim Securus Amavit?*'[12] Cupid piles fire on his own flame (Veen, 143), or is crucified and burnt (Veen, 185, 229); whatever happens, he is always committed to the excruciations of punishment and pain in exchange for loving. As in Alciati's emblem (Fig. 7),[13] our lover is an Ajax, insanely taking on forces no man can withstand and most men do not dare to attack. The naked lover in Alciati's picture 'cuffs' the air, as the heavens rain fire down on his body. Our lover is 'betwixt the Flames and Waves', braving the 'mad Tempest', 'Cuffing the Thunder with one hand' as he clings to his rock with the other. Each wave threatens to dislodge him, and he is 'Torn into Flames, and ragg'd with Wounds'. 'Flames' figure large in love emblems; Veen's *amorini* play with fire, one sustaining the flame that consumes him, another blowing up his candle as it gutters.[14] For another, the wind blows up the fire; another says like the salamander, '*Mea Vita per Ignem*' (Fig. 8).[15] These are emblematic fires, of course: the little lover fans his flame or blows up his candle, but always, because he is only a baby, he does it symbolically. Our lover has poignancy, if no more actuality, because we watch him grow up in years if not in wisdom, watch him suffering for his obsession. Love shoots him through, not once but many times

> And Tyrant Love his brest does ply
> With all his wing'd Artillery.

as Veen shows his little amor shooting at a target fastened to the breast of a man looking hopelessly into the distance out of the picture,[16] and another poor man shot full of arrows, prone on the ground (Fig. 9).[17] This kind of love is too violent to last—even the poet cannot torture the lover past the point of sufficient unreason, and must eventually save his figure by another means. This means is the transformation of the lover into a heraldic device of himself, of his behavior and his temperament, the colors marking him once and for all: 'In a Field *Sable* a Lover *Gules*'.

Marvell plays again and again with artifying nature, and naturalising art; he even turns people into works of art, as particularly illustrated in 'The Gallery'. In 'The Nymph complaining', there are levels of artification: the girl constructs her garden, first, which is given in thoroughly visual terms; the fawn's death has its counterparts in the emblem-literature, as it gently dies, weeping balsam and leaking its life away; white deer, stags, and even unicorns (habitually associated with virgins and the Virgin) appear collared and chained, domesticated in the service of a particular lady, in heraldry, tapestry, and emblem. The final statue, designed by the girl for us, recalls the Niobe story and reverses the Pygmalion one. In Ovid's narrative, the artist's creation became animate; in Marvell's poem, an animate artistic girl opts out of life for the beautiful irresponsibilities of a detached work of art.[18]

'On a Drop of Dew' is another poem of cool self-sufficiency, told in impersonal terms, the only emotion the dewdrop's worried yearning to return to the peaceful, quiet heaven whence it came. 'Dew' is a subject treated in emblems and emblem poems; Marvell lengthens the form, so to speak, in this poem, to unite the visual elements with a religious meditation, extended over considerable time. Noticeably, many visual elements of this poem have their counterparts in still life painting; indeed, the meditation and the still life, in particular that sort called 'Vanitas', share the theme of seeing through the emptiness of materiality into the permanent spiritual meanings of religious value. Dewdrops or drops of water challenged painters' skill, as also the tears to which they are (in this poem, too) inevitably likened. The painter's task is to render the crystalline quality of water-drops against its background of color and form, showing the texture of the background through the surface, at once transparent and reflecting. Marvell's dewdrop lies on a rose leaf, where

> it the purple flow'r does slight,
> Scarce touching where it lyes. . . .

> Restless it roules and unsecure,
> Trembling lest it grow impure:

The play of light and shade on the little globe is precisely explained, and that explanation moralised:

> So the World excluding round,
> Yet receiving in the Day.
> Dark beneath, but bright above:

'Exhaled' from the heavens, the dewdrop remains on earth only for a little while before being returned to the sky by the sun's power; in this, like the Resolved Soul, it yearns for and aspires to its original state. This figure, the dewdrop, is 'right' in form, properly crystalline and clear, properly transparent and translucent, properly spherical. For a moment on earth it captures and recapitulates all the perfections of the sphere whence it descended:

> . . . recollecting its own Light,
> Does, in its pure and circling thoughts, express
> The greater Heaven in an Heaven less.

Its perfect sphericity means that it balances on a point, scarcely touching the rose petals at all:

> How girt and ready to ascend.
> Moving but on a point below,
> It all about does upwards bend.

In this poem the dewdrop maintains its purity, even to the extent of shunning 'the sweat leaves and blossoms green', and 'the World excluding round'. The spherical shape of the dewdrop corresponds to the 'sphere' whence it came, and expresses also the necessary inward attention and self-concentration of pure virtue. It mourns while on earth, is 'its own Tear', keeps itself uncontaminated by the world, even though the world of its environment is so lovely. Its virtue is distilled, white, 'intire', congealed, and chill; world-rejecting and emotion-rejecting, it exists until it can

> . . . dissolving, run
> Into the Glories of th' Almighty Sun.

In some respects the notion on which the poem is built is common-place enough; this is characteristic descent and ascent of the soul, its theme worked out without doctrinal or moral idiosyncrasy. What is impressive is the way in which, circling around his spiritual object-subject, the poet manages to give the impression of the integrity, the totality of this water-drop within the material world. He places his dewdrop between one kind of language—'orient', 'bosom', 'blowing roses'—and another—'white', 'intire', 'congealed', 'still', the languages themselves of psychomachia. The beautiful world is a real threat to this sensitive and scrupulous emblem for the soul; like the Resolved Soul, the dewdrop desiring dissolution must resist the secular preoccupations, even when they are as little 'sinful' as the rose and garden of this poem. In the word 'dissolving', profane and divine love are allowed for a moment to run together, as one realises the likeness between religious and secular rapture. Only to secular suit is the dewdrop 'coy'; it yearns, weeps, waits, hopes for unification with the deity.

Marvell made use of iconic sources open to him, of course adapting them to the poet's general needs and to his own needs in particular. In other cases, he manages to exploit emblematic or graphic traditions: the conceits of 'Eyes and Tears', for instance, the notion of tears as 'Lines and Plummets', or the notion of tears weighed against joy, are illustrated in emblems. In 'The Match', the extended conceit of love's arsenal owes as much to visual as to literary analogues. In both 'The Garden' and 'Upon Appleton House', there are important adaptations from the emblem books; and 'Upon Appleton House' makes complex use of many optical and visual techniques. In the Mower poems, the mower has his symbolisms, and the glowworms theirs, both figures emblematised too; the landscape of 'Upon the Hill and Grove at Bill-borow' is thoroughly emblematised (Fig. 10). One of Marvell's major preoccupations, the garden itself, is an important emblem-topic. One literary picture book, Henry Hawkins's religious meditation on the Virgin, takes a garden as its frame; several elements in that book offer useful comparison to Marvell's techniques.

Hawkins's *Partheneia Sacra* (1633) is a little book of Catholic devotion, and an excellent example of the confluence of the literature of meditation and emblem literature. Generally speaking, it is for the use of 'Parthenes', virgins or nuns, and deals with the *hortus conclusus,* literally and symbolically. Some of the elements of the garden which Hawkins elects to treat are very conventional, others seem more matters of his choice. In structure, each topic or 'Symbol' has several sections, as is characteristic of 'emblem' form—in this case, the 'Devise', a picture; the 'Character', the 'Morals', the 'Essay', the 'Discourse', the 'Poesie' (with a second picture), the 'Theorie', and the 'Apostrophe', or prayer to either the Virgin or to God. In all these, Hawkins manages to say a great deal about his garden, the flowers, the dew, the house, the birds and so forth, that make it up: not surprisingly, some of his elements are like elements in Marvell's verse. Hawkins's 'The Deaw', for instance, has many similarities with Marvell's poem, although a comparison of the two 'dews' serves to show how little theology and doctrine Marvell used in his poem. Hawkins's dew-meditation, like his other meditations, tends toward panegyric of a specifically Catholic kind. Something in Hawkins's language is more akin to Crashaw's usage than to Marvell's, which is to say, not that luxuriance of language is a Roman Catholic stylistic device, but that Marvell's language, even in his most sensuous passages, tends toward the spare. Hawkins's 'Character' of the dew begins:

The *Deawes* are the sugred stillicids of Nature, falling from the Limbeck of the Heavens, as so manie liquid pearls, and everie pearl as precious as the truest Margarits. They are liquifyed Cristal, made into so manie silver-orbs as drops. They are the verie teares of Nature, dissolved and soft through tendernes, to see the Earth so made a Libian Desart, which she supplies a meer compassion with the ruine of herself. . . . They are the *Manna* of Nature, to vye with those Corianders, food of Pilgrims, made by Angels: with this unhappiness, they could not be congealed, to make a food so much for men, as a Nectar for the plants to drink.[19]

In Hawkins's discussion of the dew, he repeats Pliny's remark about its 'compliance' with everything it meets, its manner of 'temporising' with its earthly environment, so that it takes on the character of its background. This is precisely what Marvell's dewdrop does *not* do: for the common-place of the dew's protean, mirroring, rainbow qualities, Marvell substitutes the theme of its integrity, independence, and rejection of all other things in its earthly environment. Marvell's drop is exclusive, self-contained, self-reflecting, an emblem for rejection of *res creatae*. Though Hawkins's passage offers verbal parallels to Marvell's poem—'dissolve', 'recollect', 'congealed'—it points in a different direction. Hawkins's eye and mind wander from the dew to other things; his meditative technique is expansive. Marvell concentrates ever more fully on the single, self-concentrated object;

he narrows his meditation inward. Though certainly very graphic, Hawkins's visual imagery does not compose a single picture, but stresses the different units; the lovely engravings illustrating his book (Fig. 11) are of single elements: one carefully drawn rose or lily, one elegant bee. Marvell keeps our attention on one thing, but all the rest of its environment is depicted in relation to it, the rose leaf, the way the light falls, the motion of the dew on its 'point'. Marvell's meditative way, in this poem, rejects visual *copia*, which so often inspired contemplation and vision, to concentrate on one precise, meaningful object, self-contained but existing in a world of other things. Hawkins gives a more generous universe than Marvell's in this particular poem. In Hawkins's enclosed garden, all things are free and interchangeable; certainly in the poem, this is not so: the poem is about demarcation and separation. The rigor of Marvell's poetic discipline reinforces our sense of the dew's, or the soul's, need for rigor in a world full of distraction and dissipation.

That Marvell's visual imagination could be prodigal also is apparent in 'Upon Appleton House', with its abundant translation of different pictorial conventions, different emblematic modes. There, the poet worked both in the large and in the small, impressionistically and emblematically, fantastically and with a magnifying glass, to give us a world of great visual plurality, a world as wide as imagination can make it. In many ways, 'Upon Appleton House' is the climax of Marvell's experiments in poeticising pictorial modes—but that is another story, told in another place. . . .

SOURCE: extract from chapter 3 in '*My Ecchoing Song*': *Andrew Marvell's Poetry of Criticism* (Princeton, N. J., 1970), pp. 106–17.

NOTES

[These Notes have been abbreviated and renumbered from those in the original version—Ed.]
1. Giambattista Marino, *La Galeria*.

2. For material on memory and mnemonics, see Francis A. Yates, *The Art of Memory* (London and Chicago, 1966).

3. For a useful article on this type, see Millard Meiss, 'Sleep in Venice', *Akten des 21. Internationalen Kongresses für Kunstgeschichte*, at Bonn, 1964 (Berlin, 1967), III, 271–9.

4. Otto van Veen, *Amorum Emblemata* (Antwerp, 1608).

5. Hermann Hugo, *Pia Desideria* (Antwerp, 1624).

6. Francis Quarles, *Emblems* (London, 1635). Quarles took many of his illustrations, with the plates reversed, from Hugo's book.

7. For these particular subjects, see Quarles, III, IV, and Veen, p. 277.

8. Veen, p. 188.

9. Ibid, pp. 112–13.

10. Ibid, pp. 190–1; the English version (trans Richard Verstegan, Antwerp, 1608) gives the following verse:

Quod Nutrit, Extinguit
The torche is by the wax maintayned whyle it burnes,
But turned upsyde-down it straight goes out and dyes,
Right so by Cupid's heat the lover lyves lykewise,
But thereby is hee kill'd, when it contrairie turnes.

See also Andrea Alciati, *Emblematum libellus* (Paris, 1535), p. 32, Prometheus with the eagle; and Geoffrey Whitney, *A Choice of Emblems* (Leyden, 1586), p. 75, same subject.

11. Veen, pp. 224–5.

12. Ibid, pp. 125, 139.

13. Alciati, Emblema CVII; I think this is the picture referred to by J. Max Patrick, *Explicator*, XX (1961–2), item 65.

14. Veen, 139, 137.

15. Ibid, 229; this may relate, too, to 'Th' *Ambhibium* of Life and Death'.

16. Ibid, 153.

17. Ibid, 215.

18. For another lady mourning a slain deer, see J. S. Held, 'Rubens and Virgil: A Self-correction', *Art Bulletin*, XXIX (1947), 125–6: a discussion of an oil sketch showing Sylvia and her stag, with hunters and farmers in combat around her. The Virgilian reference is given in Nicholas Guild, 'Marvell's 'The Nymph Complaining for the Death of her Faun', *MLQ*, XXIX (1968), 385–94.

19. Henry Hawkins, *Partheneia Sacra* (Rouen, 1633), pp. 59–60

LIST OF ILLUSTRATIONS

Figures 1 and 2: in Quarles's *Emblems* (1635), taken from Hermann Hugo, *Pia Desideria* (1624); figures 3–9: in Otto van Veen, *Amorum Emblemata* (1608);

Fig. 10: in Camerarius, *Symbolorum et emblemata . . . centuriae*; fig. 11 in Henry Hawkins, *Partheneia Sacra* (1633).

Fig. 1 Holy Lovers ('The unfortunate Lover')

Fig. 2 Holy Lovers ('The unfortunate Lover')

Fig. 3 Playful Amorini ('The unfortunate Lover')

Fig. 4 The Ship of Love in Travail ('The unfortunate Lover')

Fig. 5 The Lover assailed by the Winds of Love
('The unfortunate Lover')

Fig. 6 The Lover with his self-consuming Torch
('The unfortunate Lover')

EMBLEMATA. 148

Vis Amoris.

EMBLEMA CVII.

A L I G E R V M *fulmen fregit Deus aliger, igne*
Dum demonstras vti est fortior ignis Amor.

EX quatuor Græcorum epigrammaton, quo signi-
ficatur amore strenuo nihil vehementius aut in-
superabilius, adeò vt rebus ipsis quæ violentissimæ
putantur non cedat. Itaque Græcis nominatur
πανδαμάτωρ.

P iiij

Fig. 7 The Lover assailed by Love's Thunder
and Lightning ('The unfortunate Lover')

Fig. 8 Salamander in Love's Fire ('The unfortunate Lover')

Fig. 9 The Lover wounded in the Breast by Love's Arrows ('The unfortunate Lover')

LXXIII.

HVMILIBVS DAT

GRATIAM.

75

l'n faveur est pour ch; humble.

Alia cadunt vitiis, virtutibus infima surgunt.
Hoc te mons sterilis, vallis amæna monet.

le superbe Nuebe, le petit s'éléve
la montaigne est sterile
et la plaine fertile

T 3   *Trifolia*

Fig. 10 The High and the Low, the Great and
the Humble ('The Hill and Grove at
Bill-Borrow')

19

Fig. 11 'Th' industrious Bee' ('The Garden')

J. V. Cunningham   Logic and Lyric: 'To his Coy Mistress' (1953)

In this essay I shall propose the question: May the principal structure of a poem be of a logical rather than of an alogical sort? For example, to confine ouselves to the Old Logic: May a lyric be solely or predominantly the exposition of a syllogism? and may the propositions of the lyric, one by one, be of the sort to be found in a logical syllogism?

The incautious romantic will deny the possibility, and with a repugnance of feeling that would preclude any further discussion. For logic and lyric are generally regarded as opposites, if not as contradictory terms. 'It is a commonplace', says a recent writer on logic, 'that poetry and logic have nothing to do with each other, that they are even opposed to one another.'[1] You will find this explicitly stated, sometimes with the substitution of 'science' for 'logic', in most of the school handbooks on the study of literature, in most of the introductions to poetry. 'The peculiar quality of poetry', we read in one of these, 'can be distinguished from that of prose if one thinks of the creative mind as normally expressing itself in a variety of literary forms ranged along a graduated scale between the two contrasted extremes of scientific exposition and lyrical verse.' And, a little later, '[Poetry] strives for a conviction begotten of the emotions rather than of the reason'. Consequently, we are told, 'The approach of poetry is indirect. It proceeds by means of suggestion, implication, reflection. Its method is largely symbolical. It is more interested in connotations than in denotations.'[2] This is common doctrine. Poetry is in some way concerned with emotion rather than with reason, and its method is imaginative, indirect, implicit rather than explicit, symbolical rather than discursive, concerned with what its terms suggest rather than with what they state. The kind of poetry which most fully possesses and exhibits these concerns, methods, and qualities is generally thought to be the lyric, and hence the lyric, of all poetry, is regarded as the most antithetical to reason, logic, and science.

This was not always the case. In the eighth century, for example, a scholiast of the school of Alcuin regarded not only grammar and rhetoric but dialectic or logic also as the disciplines that nourish and form a poet. In the medieval and Renaissance traditions of commentary on Aristotle's logic, poetic is sometimes regarded as a part, a subdivision, of logic—as, indeed, I consider it myself. So late as the eighteenth century, David Hume writes in an essay 'Of the Standard of Taste': 'Besides, every kind of composition, even the most poetical, is nothing but a chain of propositions and reasonings; not always indeed the justest and most exact, but still plausible and specious, however disguised by the coloring of the imagination.' And even today the writer on logic whom I quoted earlier asserts, in denial of the commonplace: 'Every poem, except in rare extreme cases, contains judgements and implicit propositions, and thus becomes subject to logical analysis.'[3]

But may the chain of propositions and reasonings be not merely plausible and specious but even sufficiently just and exact? May the poem be not merely subject to logical analysis but logical in form? May, to return to our point, the subject and structure of a poem be conceived and expressed syllogistically? Anyone at all acquainted with modern criticism and the poems that are currently in fashion will think in this connection of Marvell's 'To his Coy Mistress'. The apparent structure of that poem is an argumentative syllogism, explicitly stated. 'Had we but world enough, and time', the poet says,

> This coyness, Lady, were no crime . . .
> But at my back I always hear
> Time's winged chariot hurrying near . . .
> Now, therefore . . .
> . . . let us sport us while we may.

If we had all the space and time in the world, we could delay consummation. But we do not. Therefore. The structure is formal. The poet offers to the lady a practical syllogism, and if she assents to it, the appropriate consequence, he hopes, will follow [quotes the whole poem].

The logical nature of the argument . . . has been generally recognised, though often with a certain timidity. Mr Eliot hazards: 'the three strophes of Marvell's poem have something like a syllogistic relation to each other'. [See essay at end of Part Two, above – Ed.] And in a recent scholarly work we read: 'The dialectic of the poem lies not only or chiefly in the formal demonstration explicit in its three stanzas, but in all the contrasts evoked by its images and in the play between the immediately sensed and the intellectually apprehended.' That is, the logic is recognised, but minimised, and our attention is quickly distracted to something more reputable in a poem, the images or the characteristic tension of metaphysical poetry. For Mr Eliot the more important element in this case is a principle of order common in modern poetry and often employed in his own poems. He points out that the theme of Marvell's poem is 'one of the great traditional commonplaces of European literature . . . the theme of . . . "Gather ye rosebuds", of "Go, lovely rose" . . . Where the wit of Marvell', he continues, 'renews the theme is in the variety and order of the images'. The dominant principle of order in the poem, then, is an implicit one rather than the explicit principle of the syllogism, and implicit in the succession of images.

Mr Eliot explains the implicit principle of order in this fashion:

In the first of the three paragraphs Marvell plays with a fancy which begins by pleasing and leads to astonishment. . . . We notice the high speed, the succession of concentrated images, each magnifying the original fancy. When this process has been carried to the end and summed up, the poem turns suddenly with that surprise which has been one of the most important means of poetic effect since Homer:

> But at my back I alwaies hear
> Times winged Charriot hurrying near;
> And yonder all before us lye
> Desarts of vast Eternity.

A whole civilisation resides in these lines:

> Pallida Mors æquo pulsat pede pauperum tabernas
> Regumque turres . . .

. . . A modern poet, had he reached the height, would very likely have closed on this moral reflection.

What is meant by this last observation becomes clear a little later, where it is said that the wit of the poem 'forms the crescendo and diminuendo of a scale of great imaginative power'. The structure of the poem, then, is this: It consists of a succession of images increasing in imaginative power to the sudden turn and surprise of the image of time, and then decreasing to the conclusion. But is there any sudden turn and surprise in the image of time? and does the poem consist of a succession of images?

This talk of images is a little odd, since there seem to be relatively few in the poem if one means by 'image' what people usually do—a descriptive phrase that invites the reader to project a sensory construction. The looming imminence of Time's winged chariot is, no doubt, an image, though not a full-blown one, since there is nothing in the phrasing that properly invites any elaboration of sensory detail. But when Mr Eliot refers to 'successive images' and cites 'my *vegetable* love', with *vegetable* italicised, and 'Till the conversion of the Jews', one suspects that he is provoking images where they do not textually exist. There is about as much of an image in 'Till the conversion of the Jews' as there would be in 'till the cows come home', and it would be a psychiatrically sensitive reader who would immediately visualise the lowing herd winding slowly o'er the lea. But 'my *vegetable* love' will make the point. I have no doubt that Mr Eliot and subsequent readers do find an image here. They envisage some monstrous and expanding cabbage, but they do so in ignorance. *Vegetable* is no vegetable but an abstract and philosophical term, known as such to the educated man of Marvell's day. Its context is the doctrine of the three souls: the rational, which in man subsumes the other two; the sensitive, which men and animals have in common and which is the principle of motion and perception; and, finally, the lowest of the three, the vegetable soul, which is the only one that plants possess and which is the principle of generation and corruption, of augmentation and decay. Marvell says, then, my love, denied the exercise of sense but possessing the power of augmentation, will increase 'Vaster than empires'. It is an intellectual image, and hence no image at all but a conceit. For if one calls any sort of particularity or detail in a poem an 'image', the use of the wrong word will invite the reader to misconstrue his experience in terms of images, to invent sensory constructions and to project them on the poem.

A conceit is not an image. It is a piece of wit. It is, in the tradition in which Marvell was writing, among other possibilities, the discovery of a proposition referring to one field of experience in terms of an intellectual structure derived from another field, and often enough a field of learning, as is the case in 'my vegetable love'. This tradition, though it goes back to the poetry of John Donne, and years before that, was current in Marvell's day. The fashionable poetry at the time he was writing this poem, the poetry comparable to that of Eliot or of Auden in the last two decades, was the poetry of John Cleveland, and the fashionable manner was generally known as 'Clevelandising'. It consisted in the invention of a series of witty hyperbolical conceits, sometimes interspersed with images, and containing a certain amount of roughage in the form of conventional erotic statements:

> Thy beauty shall no more be found,
> Nor in thy marble vault shall sound
> My echoing song. . . .

It was commonly expressed in the octosyllabic couplet. Cleveland, for example, writes 'Upon Phillis Walking in a Morning before Sun-rising':

> The trees, (like yeomen of the guard,
> Serving more for pomp than ward). . . .

The comparison here does not invite visualisation. It would be inappropriate to summon up the colors and serried ranks of the guard. The comparison is made solely with respect to the idea: the trees, like the guard, serve more for pomp than ward. Again:

> The flowers, called out of their beds,
> Start and raise up their drowsy heads,
> And he that for their colour seeks
> May find it vaulting to her cheeks,
> Where roses mix,—no civil war
> Between her York and Lancaster.[4]

One does not here picture in panorama the Wars of the Roses. One sees rather the aptness and the wit of York and Lancaster, the white rose and the red, reconciled in her cheeks, or one rejects it as forced and far-fetched. This is a matter of taste.

But if the poem is not a succession of images, does it exhibit that other principle which Mr Eliot ascribes to it—the turn and surprise which he finds in the abrupt introduction of Time's chariot and which forms a sort of fulcrum on which the poem turns? Subsequent critics have certainly felt that it has. In a current textbook we read:

The poem begins as a conventional love poem in which the lover tries to persuade his mistress to give in to his entreaties. But with the introduction of the image of the chariot in l. 21, the poet becomes obsessed by the terrible onrush of time, and the love theme becomes scarcely more than an illustration of the effect which time has upon human life.[5]

And the leading scholar in the field [Douglas Bush], a man who is generally quite unhappy with Mr Eliot's criticism, nevertheless says:

the poet sees the whole world of space and time as the setting for two lovers. But wit cannot sustain the pretence that youth and beauty and love are immortal, and with a quick change of tone—like Catullus's *nobis cum semel occidit brevis lux* or Horace's *sed Timor et Minae*—the theme of time and death is developed with serious and soaring directness.[6]

These, I believe, are not so much accounts of the poem as accounts of Mr Eliot's reading of the poem. Let us question the fact. Does the idea of time and death come as any surprise in this context? The poem began, 'Had we but world enough and time'. That is, it began with an explicit condition contrary to fact, which, by all grammatical rules, amounts to the assertion that we do not have world enough and time. There is no surprise whatever when the proposition is explicitly made in line 21. It would rather have been surprising if it had not been made. Indeed, the only question we have in this respect, after we have read the first line, is: How many couplets will the poet expend on the ornamental reiteration of the initial proposition before he comes to the expected *but?* The only turn in the poem is the turn which the structure of the syllogism had led us to await.

Mr Eliot compares the turn and surprise which he finds in this poem to a similar turn in an ode of Horace, and the scholars seem to corroborate the comparison. This is the fourth ode of the first book:

> solvitur acris hiems grata vice veris et Favoni,
> trahuntque siccas machinae carinas.

The poem begins with a picture of spring and proceeds by a succession of images, images of the external world and mythological images: '

Sharp winter relaxes with the welcome change to spring and the west wind, and the cables haul the dry keels of ships. The herd no longer takes pleasure in its stalls or the farmer in his fire, and the pastures no longer whiten with hoar frost. Cytherean Venus leads her dancers beneath the overhanging moon, and the beautiful graces and nymphs strike the ground with alternate foot, while blazing Vulcan visits the grim forges of the Cyclops. Now is the time to wind your bright hair with green myrtle or with the flowers that the thawed earth yields. Now is the time to sacrifice to Faunus in the shadowed woods, whether it be a lamp he asks or a kid:

> pallida mores æquo pulsat pede pauperum tabernas
> regumque turres.

Pallid death with indifferent foot strikes the poor man's hut and the palaces of kings. Now, fortunate Sestius, the brief sum of life forbids our opening a long account with hope. Night will soon hem you in, and the fabled ghosts, and Pluto's meager house.[7]

Death occurs in this poem with that suddenness and lack of preparation with which it sometimes occurs in life. The structure of the poem is an imitation of the structure of such experiences in life. And as we often draw a generalisation from such experiences, so Horace, on the sudden realisation of the abruptness and impartiality of death, reflects:

> vitae summa brevis spem nos vetat incohare longam.

(The brief sum of life forbids our opening a long account with hope.)

But the proposition is subsequent to the experience; it does not rule and direct the poem from the outset. And the experience in Horace *is* surprising and furnishes the fulcrum on which the poem turns. It has, in fact, the characteristics which are ascribed to Marvell's poem but which Marvell's poem does not have. The two are two distinct kinds of poetry, located in distinct and almost antithetical traditions; both are valuable and valid methods, but one is not to be construed in terms of the other.

In brief, the general structure of Marvell's poem is syllogistic, and it is located in the Renaissance tradition of formal logic and of rhetoric. The structure exists in its own right and as a kind of expandable filing system. It is a way of disposing of, of making a place for, elements of a different order: in this case, Clevelandising conceits and erotic propositions in the tradition of Jonson and Herrick. These reiterate the propositions of the syllogism. They do not develop the syllogism, and they are not required by the syllogism; they are free and extra. There could be more or less of them, since there is nothing in the structure that determines the number of interpolated couplets. It is a matter of tact and a matter of the appetite of the writer and the reader.

The use of a structure as a kind of expandable filing system is common enough in the Renaissance. The narrative structure of a Shakespearean play can be regarded as a structure of this order. It exists in its own right, of course, but it is also a method for disposing various kinds of material of other orders—a set speech or passion here, an interpolated comic routine in another place. The structure offers a series of hooks upon which different things can be hung. Whether the totality will then form a whole, a unity, is a question of interpretation and a question of value. It is a question, for example, of what sort of unity is demanded and whether there are various sorts.

In Marvell's poem, only the general structure is syllogistic; the detail and development are of another order, and critics have been diligent in assigning the poetic quality of the whole to the non-syllogistic elements. Is it possible, then, to write a lyric that will be wholly or almost wholly syllogistic? It is. There is such a lyric in the *Oxford Book of English Verse*, a lyric of somewhat lesser repute than Marvell's, but still universally praised and universally conceded to possess the true lyrical power. It is Dunbar's 'Lament for the Makaris'.

SOURCE: article in *Modern Philology*, LI (August 1953), 33–81.

NOTES

These Notes have been reorganised and renumbered from those in the original version. For discussion of the argument in Cunningham's essay, see Frank Towne, 'Logic, Lyric and Drama', *Modern Philology*, LII (May 1954), 265–8; and Bruce E. Miller, 'Logic in Marvell's "To his Coy Mistress"', *North Dakota Quarterly*, XXX (1962), 48–9.—Ed.]

1. Richard von Mises, *Positivism* (Cambridge, Mass., 1951), p. 289.

2. Harold R. Walley and J. Harold Wilson, *The Anatomy of Literature* (New York, 1934), pp. 143, 144.

3. Scholiast cited in Otto Bird, 'The Seven Liberal Arts', in Joseph T. Shipley (ed.), *Dictionary of World Literature* (New York, 1943), p. 55; J. E. Spingarn, *A History of Literary Criticism in the Renaissance* (New York, 2nd edn, 1908), pp. 24–7; David Hume, *Philosophical Works* (Edinburgh, 1854), III, 264; von Mises, loc. cit.

4. John M. Berdan (ed.), *The Poems of John Cleveland* (New Haven, 1911), pp. 80–1.

5. Wright Thomas and Stuart Gerry Brown (eds), *Reading Poems* (New York, 1941), p. 702.

6. Douglas Bush, *English Literature in the Earlier Seventeenth Century* (Oxford, 1945), p. 163.

7. My translation, except for 'the brief sum of life forbids our opening a long account with hope', which is Gildersleeve's; see Shorey and Gordon J. Laing, *Odes and Epodes of Horace*, ed. Paul Shorey (Chicago, rev. edn, 1910).

A. J. N. Wilson   On 'An Horatian Ode Upon Cromwell's Return from Ireland' (1969)

Varying, even diametrically opposed, views stand expressed by critics about the 'Horatian Ode', and little progress seems to be made towards resolution of these differences. The cause is plain. Because Marvell is classed among the metaphysical poets, and because the Ode reflects and philosophises, critics have tortured its body, beyond reason, in the hope of extracting somehow a formulable essence: tending to see the burden of the poem as contained mainly in this or that passage or passages, they have tried to accommodate the whole to their pre-judgement. Thus an over-systematised and centralised understanding is presented, which has to be swallowed or rejected more or less whole. Further confrontation of views rendered vain by the very way the views are formed may perhaps be avoided if we will consider how, from stanza to stanza of the Ode, the living whole is created by the poet's daring eloquence. Reading the poem stage by stage, I have tried to take the meaning and tone of each and the 'series iuncturaque' throughout, and have striven to keep back till the end, on each occasion of study, my thoughts about its burden as a whole. In this article (which leaves some minor difficulties and allusive detail aside), I try so to present the phases of the Ode as to elicit definite agreement or definite hostility. Thus clear, but limited contentions will (I hope) make for fruitful argument.

The title already claims for Marvell's poem something of the Roman and panegyric character of the odes by Horace which celebrate Augustus and his greatness with special reference to his military victories. Cromwell will be extolled as the national hero-statesman who, by reconquering Ireland for England, has won for himself and his country surpassing glory; gnomic reflections—

as recurrent and characteristic in Horace—are to be expected on the significance of his career under the higher power ruling our human world. But how far is the 'Horatian Ode' really akin to Horace, and what light does its thought receive from such kinship? That is but one question about this poem, which, along with its highly individual and contemporary features, has various classicising, but not specifically Horatian, aspects.

Taking together the title, the first two stanzas, and the concluding four, I proceed on the reasonable assumption that the Ode was completed between the return of Cromwell from nearly conquered Ireland in late May 1650 and his invasion of Scotland in late July 1650.[1] In June, Cromwell rose from the Lieutenant-Generalship of the Republic's forces to Commander-in-Chief, when Lord Fairfax resigned because he thought, on grounds of political morality, that England should only counter Scottish invasion, not invade Scotland; but the poem's view of invasion of Scotland as imminent does not necessarily link it with that appointment. Already in January, when victories in Ireland had hugely increased Cromwell's power and Scottish war looked certain, it was assumed that the conqueror of the Irish would soon return to take a part against Scotland fitting his military genius and his powerful energies. That genius and those energies had made their deep impression on Marvell; but the Ode, first printed in 1681, does not appear to have been presented to Cromwell (who was apparently unacquainted with the author in 1650), and its circle of readers, then or later, may or may not have been large.[2] We can but guess Marvell's inner thoughts on political issues at the time, and nothing in its known circumstances makes the Ode a political declaration, such as must be defended in resulting argument or controversy, rather than a view of Cromwell appealing to Marvell's thought and imagination as engaged in the making of a *poem*:[3] if one makes this latter assumption about the genesis of the Ode, one will at once recognise the poetic character of the licence, necessary for internal purposes, which it takes with the facts of Cromwell's career.

If absence of contrary indication shows the Ode to have been a private poem, this circumstance will immediately distinguish it from the odes of Horace celebrating Augustus. Those politically important poems were written to be read widely (as wide readership went at the time), and steps to that end were certainly taken.[4] Thus they are encomiastic, or panegyrical, in a proper, if not the primitive, sense. But in a poem apparently never sent to its hero and perhaps read by a few friends only, is not there question, from the start, about the panegyrical element and its intent?

The three great movements of the Ode successively proclaim the fiery purpose of Cromwell in waging war against the King and in compassing his eventual destruction (stanza 3–18); Cromwell's recovery of Ireland for England (stanzas 19–24); his imminent march against the Scots, his victories to come beyond, and the glory therefrom awaiting him and England (25–30); this division leaves aside the equal connection of stanzas 17–18 with the first and with the second movement, and of stanza 24 with the second and the third. Immediately we see, in the advance of the Ode, from 1642, through these three stages, a contrast with the odes of Horace celebrating Augustus; for those might almost have suggested, to later generations, that Augustus was born fully armed like Athena to win, at once, the Actian victory over the forces of oriental evil. But let us now begin with the opening pair of stanzas.

These, in their proclamation of Scottish war as imminent, are external to the chronological sweep of the poem, starting at stanza 3, with 1642. But they are admirable as a lead-in; for they both anticipate the peroration, from stanza 27:

> The *Pict* no shelter now shall find
> Within his party-colour'd Mind

and prepare us for stanza 3 and those that immediately follow. This is done by means of a *Roman colour*, more important than the quasi-Latinisms, as the sense given to 'appear' and to 'cease'.[5]

That colour comes through combined touches. Stanzas 1–2, taking for granted the justice of the war, and exalting the glory attainable in it by an ambitious individual, relatively slight and depreciate the civilized activities of peace, typified in poetic composition and in study; the passage not only adopts the Roman attitude, but, in the second couplet of stanza 1, englishes the common language of Latin speakers and poets. As Roman armies campaigned, summer after summer, in dry and bare lands, 'vita umbratilis', life 'in the shadows', acquired a contemptuous note, harsher than 'sheltered life', and extending beyond the rich, in their cool colonnades or arbours, even to the shepherd, resting or singing out the day's extreme heat in the shade.[6] Such contempt was sharpened by the idea that primacy must be given to the art which, through constant wars, gave Rome her primacy: 'sit in civitate' (Cicero proclaims) 'ea prima res propter quam ipsa est civitas omnium princeps'. Even very civilian Romans, once they enter on the theme of Roman war, slight, together with the *vita umbratilis*, those arts practicable only in a life of that character; though, in other contexts, these are for them a main part of the basis of society. Thus, while Octavian, in *Georgic IV*, towards the close, follows up the defeat of Cleopatra by thundering in war to the Euphrates,

> illo Vergilium me tempore dulcis alebat
> Parthenope, *studiis* florentem *ignobilis oti*[7]

[I (Vergil) was passing the time pleasantly at Naples, prospering in the pursuit of ignoble ease—Ed.]

Marvell, in his turn, adopts the Roman voice, and the implications of Cicero when he pronounces 'cedat forum castris, otium militiae, stilus gladio, umbra soli' [Let the forum give way to the camp, leisure to affairs of war, the pen to the sword, the shade to the sun—Ed.].[8]

> 'Tis time to leave the Books in dust,
> And oyl th'unused Armours rust;
> > Removing from the Wall
> > The Corslet of the Hall.

In an ode standing rather by itself (1 29), Horace addresses Iccius, a professed student of moral philosophy who has become suddenly avid of the glory and prizes of war and is selling his philosophic library to buy armour of Spanish steel. Mocking Iccius for abandonment of his principles from alien motives, Horace inverts, *pro hac vice*, Roman contempt for the *vita umbratilis* and the language in which it was expressed; Marvell cancels the inversion, and uses Horace's language of books and armour in the typical Roman way.

Roman national war, for Latin authors, is, by definition, just and glorious; connected with this attitude are those finding expression in the phrase 'vita umbratilis' and kindred phrases. Marvell's language gives Roman colour to the imminent war, and thus makes it just and glorious. When we pass suddenly, at stanza 3, from the imminent Scottish campaign back to the start of the civil war, all this is resumed by the echo, in the second line, of Vergil's 'ignobilis oti', and the reader is caused to re-act, for a moment, not as to civil, but as to national war. The momentary deception, using Roman colour, helps him accept the radical transition to an un-Roman theme, or rather to a theme to be treated from an un-Roman attitude.

For Latin poets, civil war among Romans is *bellum impium*, as war between kindred worshipping the same gods. Hence the Latin poet must either ascribe utter and equal *furor*—with all the word conveys of infatuation and crime—to each side, *or* exalt one side morally and make the other to blame for the disaster. He cannot view great leadership in civil war in the way Marvell does in stanzas 3–6, in language which speaks wonder and amazement, yet preserves moral neutrality. Lucan's *Pharsalia* I, where the speed and impetus of Caesar are conveyed in arresting terms, has indeed provided phrases which the Ode adapts, perhaps to cast, by oblique allusion, a Caesarian aura around the impetus of Cromwell. But the *condemnation* of Caesar by Lucan has nothing correspondent in Marvell's stanzas, whether one considers tone or particular phrasing; the verbal debt is less important than this essential difference.[9]

In the Lucan passage, Caesar is said 'instare favori numinis', but the idea of 'favor numinis' is not important; in the Ode, Cromwell, without impairment of his vehement individuality, is seen from the start as the instrument of Fate (stanzas 3 and 7); the poem's view is set when we read:

> But through adventrous War
> Urged his active Star.

Here, in the pregnant second line, the idea of a destiny under which all things move to their certain end is combined with the free exercise by Cromwell of his fiery personal will: the combination accords with Vergil, where, in the *Aeneid*, despite emphasis on the obedience to Fate of Aeneas, individuals, including him, can advance or retard particular ends by freely-willed personal conduct. The dual notion is maintained in the next stanza:

> And, like the three-fork'd Lightning, first
> Breaking the Clouds where it was nurst,
>   Did thorough his own Side
>   His fiery way divide.

In the first couplet, the Lightning is, as Jove uses it for his purposes of rule, 'three-fork'd' ('trisulcum')[10]. In the second, is conveyed the personal ambition and energy that enabled Cromwell to break through the body of the Parliamentarians to dominant authority: what lightning is in the *natural* world, that Cromwell is in the *political* world. Inspired, no doubt, by Lucan's comparison of Caesar with lightning, 'expressum ventis per nubila', Marvell uses it to bring out an aspect of *his* Cromwell without counterpart in the Caesar of the passage of Lucan. In the still accepted idea of the generation of lightning (unquestioned, as Aristotelian), an exhalation, arisen from the earth, gets imprisoned in a cloud, and, fighting for escape, breaks into flame through friction, and forces its way out in the form of lightning. Cromwell, imprisoned in the Parliamentary 'Clouds', bursts into flame, and out as lightning.[11] In Marvell, we can hardly surmise whether this stanza endorses the ancient idea of macrocosmic correspondences between the human and the natural world, or is only effective, poetic analogy, playing with that idea. In either case, stanza 4 presents already the particularity of the violent phenomenon which stanza 5 brings under general law.

What these stanzas present with moral neutrality, might seem hardly to differ from the ruinous personal ambition, typical of the late Roman Republic, that Augustus and his poets most discountenanced. Yet this neutrality (if that word may be applied to stanzas speaking wonder and amazement) is remote from the view of the historian. For, in fact, Cromwell's rise to dominance among the Parliamentarians was due (in a way the Ode hardly suggests) in major part to his military efficiency and success, and his political efforts in the first war (though he obviously wanted military scope worthy of his abilities) aimed at the efficiency and success of the whole cause. Again, the contrast is striking between the fact that Cromwell long approved negotiations with Charles, after his capture, about his future status, and the view, given in stanzas 3–14, of the warrior-hero pursuing a personal struggle, in which he long envisages the death of his adversary, and finally brings it to pass:

> And *Caesars* head at last
> Did through his Laurels blast.

In the second line of that arresting couplet, a thought could be missed. Laurels, or things wreathed in laurel, could not, in a Roman belief treated by Pliny, be burned or blasted by lightning, and there is obvious allusion in the couplet to this belief. But every Roman Emperor—every Caesar—had the right, independent of the winning of military victories, to wear the laurel wreath at any time,[12] and, for an Horatian Ode, it is but one step from this to make *Laurels* symbolise that sanctity of the person which should, in the terms of tradition, guard the King, but which availed Charles nothing, since his destruction was determined by Fate:

> 'Tis Madness to resist or blame
> The force of angry Heavens flame.

The tempo of the Ode, which resembles that of the opening stanzas of 'Odi profanum . . .',[13] may seem too slow, in stanzas 3–6 for instance, for celebration of irresistible impetus; yet, this admitted, the measure admirably conveys Cromwell in his other aspect of 'industrious Valour' with all the suggestion thereof steady and methodical advance. Certainly, despite the end-stop or end-pause in each stanza, a strong forward pressure carries the *reader* steadily on, and there is no obtrusive check when the poem, in stanzas 7–8, returns to the point of 3 and takes up the theme again at more length. After stanza 7, looking back with the first couplet and forward with the second, stanza 8:

> Who, from his private Gardens, where
> He liv'd reserved and austere,
>   As if his highest plot
>   To plant the Bergamot,
>
> Could by industrious Valour climbe
>   . . .

embodies the cherished Roman antithesis of *quies/otium* and *industria*, yet gives to Cromwell's *otium* the dignity allowed by the Romans to that life under strict moral-philosophic conditions. Cromwell's pre-war activity from his denunciation of the Bishop of Winchester, in the Parliament of 1628, for 'Popery' to his membership of eighteen Committees in that of 1640, is properly and poetically abolished in the service of this antithesis; yet the antithesis brings out, as nothing else could, the aspect of Marvell's vision of Cromwell belonging most to reality, his 'industrious Valour'. This is the phrase which the historian, Sir Charles Firth, summing up Cromwell's gifts of intellect and character, finds particularly happy: 'if he learnt the lessons of war quicker than other men, it was because he concentrated all his faculties on the task, let no opportunity slip, and made every experience fruitful'.[14]

From initial celebration of Roman *virtus*, stanza 9 runs into an un-Roman course in lines 2–4:

> Could by industrious Valour climbe
> To ruine the great Work of Time,
>   And cast the Kingdome old
>   Into another Mold.

Cromwell, at one moment, is climbing by *virtus*, as the hero in Horace, to Olympian glory;[15] at the next, there is superimposed on that picture the enemy scaling the wall of an ancient city to destroy it. Though the military language, as such, is Roman, and though Cromwell replaces what is destroyed, the lines are un-Roman in so far as the literary Roman mind, though horrified by the *furor* and bloodshed of the age of upheaval, hardly took in the extreme degree in which the Roman 'Work of Time' was ruined and re-cast politically in *their* revolution.

But in the Ode, Fate and Nature demand just this:

> Though Justice against Fate complain,
> And plead the antient Rights in vain:
>> But those do hold or break
>> As Men are strong or weak.
>
> Nature that hateth emptiness,
> Allows of penetration less:[16]
>> And therefore must make room
>> Where greater Spirits come.

The point is that, by the very nature of civil war and the events that followed, no arguments from right by the weaker cause could have effect on the outcome, its defeat and the death of its head. It is not said that the *weaker party only* had just claims; one is to leave aside the question of Parliament's or Cromwell's claims in terms of right, and accept that, in civil war, under the inscrutable power ruling mens' affairs, a cause is not helped at all in virtue of its justice, or hindered on account of its injustice.

Stanzas 12–13 convey, in balanced antithesis, the combination of qualities making Cromwell 'et proelio strenuus et consilio bonus'. It is not pedantry to point out that Cromwell, bravely as he fought in the thick of battle, was seriously wounded only once, for an aspect of the Ode is just such freedom with fact, whether in the rhetorical question, 'What field . . . ' , or in the following six lines, which substitute one single, decisive (and certainly legendary) act of guile by Cromwell for his protracted and agonising deliberations in 1646–9.[17] In the case of *Charles*, stanza 7:

> 'Tis Madness to resist or blame
> The force of angry Heavens Flame

may take in that blindness to reality which made him 'utterly regardless . . . of the resisting forces of those with whom he dealt',[18] and the same sort of tragic blindness may seem suggested in stanza 13. Yet the reader of 1650, having watched the events of 1648–9, or perhaps had some part in them, is left, in stanzas 14–16, to bring together for himself his own idea of tragedy and his view of the fall and death of Charles. In these stanzas, the Ode swerves and changes tone, rather in the manner Horace's Cleopatra Ode swerves and changes tone, where it passes from exaltation over Augustus' victory to admiration for the courage of the defeated Queen.[19] But there follows sudden reversion to the previous temper in two stanzas which yet conclude with presage of the very different second movement.

In the tragic stanzas, the execution was so presented as to excite, or revive, admiration, together with pity, for the King; now it is suddenly and starkly proclaimed not only necessary for the *security* of the new Republic, but an augury of future national greatness of an wholly new kind. Belief in the ultimate sacro-sanctity of the King's office and person, intensely strong in most Englishmen and, it seems, even in many avowed Parliamentarians, produced a profound sense of shock when Charles was executed, and a lasting sense, in some men, of complicity in crime;[20] stanza 17 of the Ode, having starkly asserted the necessity of the execution for the security of the new regime, reaches, in one breath, bolder assertion, in stanza 18. At the beginning of Rome, the 'architects' making Jupiter his first temple, terrified by the omen of a 'bleeding head' produced from the excavations, were assured by the Etruscan seer that the omen was good, and his prophecy was realised by history, which made the place 'caput rerum' or 'Capitolium';[21] so Englishmen, if frighted by the regicide, should see that the Republic, which it has made safe, will lead them to new greatness, comparable with the 'happy Fate' of imperial Rome. The first token of England's 'happy Fate' has already been received, in the recovery of Ireland by Cromwell:

> And now the *Irish* are asham'd
> To see themselves in one Year tam'd.

Now that the Ode comes again to national war, Cromwell is praised in encomiastic vein. Encomium destroys itself, if it is not total, if it does not offer consistent and uniform praise of the character and conduct of the great man. This is quite apart from the desire of men for praise or the hope of others to gain by offering it. Once the encomiastic genre or vein is adopted, even slight allusions to defective or negative qualities must be avoided, since they may stir the latent spirit of doubt that can lead on to

total rejection. That is why, despite the massacres allowed by
Cromwell at Wexford and Drogheda and his extreme severity in
Ireland generally, the second movement begins, in the Irish
stanzas, by putting testimony so unlikely at the time into the
mouths of that people; it cannot begin otherwise, if it is to go on to
the tribute of stanzas 21–24 to the bearing of Cromwell towards
the English Republic. Of course, most Englishmen were then
(and till recently) indifferent to the lot of Irishmen, and
unthinking indifference may have led even an acute man like
Marvell to put absurdly inappropriate language into Irish
mouths; but we know nothing of Marvell's inner mind, and these
stanzas, whatever inner mind they may have sprung from, are
determined by the necessities of the Ode.[22]

In line 80, the attempt is made, in accordance with the needs of
encomium, to identify Cromwell in Ireland and Cromwell in
England; but the attempt is not successful. The Irish (on the
natural construction) admit that Cromwell is fit for 'highest
Trust' *by themselves*; but in the next couplet, the Trust becomes the
office of trust held by Cromwell, *seen as conferred on him by the
English*. Syntactically (as is obvious) lines 81 f. run *forward* to
'How fit . . . ' ; but the difficulty remains. The Ode wants to
reach the formal tribute to Cromwell's bearing towards the new
Republic (stanzas 21–24) in a consistent *laudatio*, and, attempting this, runs into trouble.

Horace, in his poetic and rhetorical language about Augustus,
makes him earthly viceroy for a personal deity presiding over the
whole scheme of things; but the officially encouraged view of the
Princeps as holding his powers in trust from Senate and People is
not even suggested by him, almost as if he wished not to challenge
contradiction. By contrast, the 'Horatian Ode' (whether or not
the poet was aware of difference from Horace) challenges the
disbeliever to contradict, reiterating, in successive stanzas,
Cromwell's Republican deference. This emphatic reiteration has
not been properly appreciated by those who have seen, in lines
81 f., suggestion of doubt as to Cromwell's future obedience;
'nor yet . . .' seems best understood as simply praising something
unusual and contrary to the tendency for men to be corrupted
almost at once by great authority; 'still' means 'consistently'; and
the second couplet of stanza 21, versifying an ancient adage in a
crisp and Horatian way and introducing it at this particular

point, hails as deserved his great and growing influence and authority.[23]

When, from the quiet ending of the second movement, stanza 25 suddenly surges forward, and, at 26, general is followed by specific prediction, one might, thinking back to the *Republican* stanzas (21 ff.), conceive that Cromwell is to liberate states from Kings, and to make them Republics; but it is open to the reader to conceive rather that he will save Protestant peoples and communities from oppressive Catholic rule or persecution. It had been the favourite dream of many English Protestants (not fulfillable under Charles) that England should intervene success-fully in Europe on behalf of the Protestants; even that should not have seemed justification for spreading warfare through the length and breadth of France and Italy soon after the conclusion of the Thirty Years War, and I would like to think that a sane man and admirable poet did not really want a crusade in a form so far-flung and devastating. But again we have no evidence of Marvell's inner mind, and can only note that, in eulogy of any warrior hero, prophecy is conventionally required of *boundless* conquests; in these stanzas, the Ode certainly evokes the imperialist vaticinations of Horace, though not any particular one of the prophecies of conquest by Augustus.[24] Whether Marvell's stanzas should be taken as breathing that confident bellicosity opening the Regulus ode, or are rhetorically hyper-bolical, as the various predictions of far Eastern conquest, I would not like to choose; their Horatianism, in an age that loved self-identification with antiquity, does not make them 'merely conventional'.

Sweeping prediction issues, in the closing stanzas (27 ff.), into prophecy of Cromwell's triumphant leadership in the coming war with Scotland. After the long story of Scottish attempts to force Presbyterianism on England, and various Scottish exploi-tation, in 1646–8, of Parliamentary disunity and the plight of the captive King, the Scottish Presbyterian government had now recognised the future Charles II on the understanding that he would not only respect Presbyterianism in Scotland, but enforce it in England and in Ireland, should he succeed in getting the English throne. Since the Scottish Presbyterians were lording it over Charles, not the reverse, that land would not well rank among 'the states not free'; but their complicated interference in

England is reflected in the first couplet of stanza 27. Coupling the Scots with the repeated urge of the ancient *Picts* to invade the south, with poverty-stricken Pictish barbarism, painted skins, and merely painted protestations of peace and friendship, the Ode sends Cromwell marching against them like an invincible Roman. Only an echo-maniac would insist on an echo of Claudian's 'nec falso nomine Pictos' in what was surely a pun in common circulation;[25] but the common allergy to puns and conceits, where serious matters are being treated, should not distract us from the Roman colour of these stanzas and the peroration of the Ode.

The Horatian claim of the title wins my respect more and more, as the first comparison of Cromwell with a hunter is followed by the Falcon, and the Falcon by the *English Hunter*. That is not because of imitation of Horace in the Cleopatra Ode or in the opening of *Odes* IV 4,[26] but because, in these comparisons, there is a Horatian sense for timing, for compression, and for the telling use of the single word in the proper place. Yet here, in stanzas 27 f., there is, perhaps, suggestion of Hannibal's cry of despair after the death of Hasdrubal at the Metaurus:

> dixitque tandem perfidus Hannibal
> 'cervi, luporum praeda rapacium,
>   sectamur ultro, quos opimus
>   fallere et effugere est triumphus'.[27]

[At length perfidious Hannibal said: 'Like deer, the prey of rapacious wolves, we actually pursue those whom it is the noblest triumph to deceive and escape from'—Ed.].

The very disarray of the Scots ('But . . .' is clearly emphatic) may tempt the conqueror to perilous relaxation of effort, and the 'Fortunae filius' must indefatigably 'urge his . . . Star' to final victory in Scotland:

> And for the last effect
> Still keep thy Sword erect.

The 'Spirits of the shady Night'—the shades of the dead Charles

and of dead enemies—will cry for his blood in vengeance; but
his military might, if not relaxed, will fright even ghostly foes, and
give him safe passage through them, as Aeneas's courage and
drawn sword will give him safe passage, in Vergil, through the
ghosts and the shadowy forms of the Underworld. The evocation
of Iugurtha's angry ghost, in Horace's ode to Pollio, and the
Sibyl's exhortation to Aeneas at the gate of Orcus

> tuque invade viam vaginaque eripe ferrum;
> nunc animis opus, Aenea, nunc pectore firmo[28]

[Stride on your way and snatch your blade from its scabbard; now you
need courage and a stout heart—Ed.].

are both here, in this penultimate couplet; but the conflation is
too strained for imaginative effect, and it is fortunate that the
Ode comes to its conclusion in a highly effective couplet.

Cromwell's authority can be finally secured only by defeat of
the Scots in war; that defeat (for the Pictish stanzas do *not* mean
the Scots will fly from his mere name) will need all the *virtus* and
the *consilium* required for his previous victories; these are the '*Arts*'
of this famous final couplet. I see good reason to prefer this
understanding to a more sinister reading of the lines. If the
couplet is meant to recall Sallust's 'imperium facile iis artibus
retinetur quibus initio partum est' [easy rule is sustained by those
skills by which it was first achieved—Ed.].[29], it is worth noting
that Sallust says '*facile* retinetur', and is arguing only that it
would be much better for imperial peoples, if they and their
leaders regularly showed, in ruling empires, as much courage and
wisdom as they can show in acquiring them. Sallust emphasises
'virtus animi'; and it is a different thought when the ambitious
man is said to be restricted, power now gained, to precisely those
courses, however sinister, by which he gained it. That arguable, if
depressing thought (uttered by many, no doubt, down the
centuries)[30] was applied to Cromwell by some Englishmen in and
around 1650, and the couplet might be recalling remarks such as
that of Anthony Ascham: 'though the usurper thought not of
establishing himself in an absolute Jurisdiction, yet at last he will
find himself oblig'd to secure his conquest by the same means he
obtain'd it'.[31] Yet everything about stanzas 27–30 makes the final

couplet specifically *their* upshot. Though the strong forward movement carries the reader on, *Fortune* may destroy her son, in his hour of triumph, if he relaxes his efforts and vigilance; the *Fortunae filius* [i.e. Fortune's son—Ed.][32] may be in most danger just when danger seems past, and must remember that only his *virtus* and *consilium* can hold what they have gained. If the couplet is read in this way, it neatly seals the third movement and, through it, the Ode. If it versifies the thought expressed by Ascham, it hangs loose to stanzas 27–29, and is alien to the burden of the poem hitherto: for what suggestion has there been that Cromwell's career as national leader is determined, *in this way*, by his career as leader in civil war?

> Each individual seeks a several goal,
> But Heavn's great view is one, and that the whole.

The Ode (as some, in effect, believe) sees its age and Cromwell's impact on it in terms such as these, or as exhibiting what Pope urges in the other eloquent lines of the *Essay on Man:*

> All Nature is but art, unknown to thee,
> All chance, direction which thou canst not see;
> All discord, harmony not understood,
> All partial evil, universal good.

But Pope was seeking an explanation of the evils and discords of the world in terms of a rationally understandable necessity, which should be satisfying to the reasoning theist; although the age was inclined to providential interpretation of history and of the whole *rerum concordia discors*, nothing indicates that Marvell is seeking such an explanation or resolution. The Ode achieves unity, not by 'resolving' the discords of England or Britain, nor by justifying God's ways in using Cromwell or Cromwell's ways under God, but by presenting them successively in language that seizes the mind and carries it along with the march of the stanzas. It condenses Cromwell's career into a myth, a poetic alloy of real and invented constituents. Within that myth, Fate makes poetically acceptable the changed aspect of Cromwell, as we pass from the first movement to the second, not by suggestion of moral argument, but by reference to that inscrutable and baffling power which pagan acceptance (as against Christian hope or the various kinds of 'humanist' optimism) often holds accountable for the sum and outcome of mens' affairs. Thus *Fate*—often, though not always, seen in such terms by Latin authors—is an indispensable part of the neo-Roman colour and eloquence of the Ode. These phrases need no apology. The poetic conceptions of the Ode and the language in which they are cast are *sui generis*, yet they are held together by a stylistic uniformity, which has drawn upon distinct ages of Roman literature and assimilated features from each.

The urgent brevity, the sudden transitions, which overcome us by their suddenness, the bold contrasts, to which fact or probability may be sacrificed, these are reminiscent of authors of the post-Augustan age; of the Horatian features some have been suggested, something in the measure, accentual though it is, the structure, as definite as that of some of Horace's late odes, the poetic analogies and the skill with which they are introduced and kept within proper limit, the sudden reflective or gnomic passages. More important, to me, than any of these stylistic features is what I have called the Roman colour: the compressed allusive phrases of the Ode contribute both to this colour and to the poetic argument. But there is nothing in the poetic argument which requires, at the time of composition, commitment on Marvell's part to Cromwell, or even, as yet, the beginnings of such a commitment; nothing which commands us to regard the Ode as other than a view of Cromwell appealing to the thought and imagination of a man who was still primarily a poet and a scholar.

In early 1649, with Ireland lost to the Republic but for Dublin, and almost certain, as it seemed, to become a springboard for the return to England of the future Charles II, Cromwell spoke, after his nomination to command there, to the Great Council of the Army. 'I confess', he said in the speech, 'I have often had these thoughts with myself which may be carnal and foolish: I had rather be overrun by a Cavalierish interest than a Scotch interest, I had rather be overrun by a Scotch interest than an Irish interest, and I think that of all this is the most dangerous . . . If they shall be able to carry on their work they will make this the most miserable people in the earth, for all the world knows their barbarism . . . It should awaken all Englishmen.'[33] By spring

1650, the back of Irish resistance was broken, and Scotland seemed certain to be defeated, to those, at least, believing in the rightness of the war and Cromwell's star. Objectively, the Ode expresses the confidence of all that class of Englishmen; but (to take only one stanza) do the Scots come as *Picts*—treacherous, dangerous, but quick to fly—more because Marvell, in 1650, disliked and despised them, or because this is a Romanising poem? We cannot solve that question; we can see how the *color Romanus* of the peroration answers that of the opening.

This recurrent *color Romanus* requires us, I think, in stanzas 20–24, to see Cromwell as the servant of a *new* Republic which will be comparable with the *old* Roman Republic at its best; the thought of stanza 18, linking the success of Rome under destiny and England likewise, is carried on, beyond stanzas 19–20, to a comparison of Cromwell with an all-conquering, but disciplined, pro-consul of the state which, in its pristine days gave to after-time the exemplar of disciplined patriotism. Horace on Augustus, however, is not recalled here, and the characterising phrases of stanzas 20–24 (' . . . still in the Republicks hand' is the obvious example) are alien to his language about the *Princeps*; equally unplausible is any attempt to bring into these stanzas Augustus as represented by himself in his *Res Gestae* or by others in the officially encouraged presentation of his rôle after 28/7 B.C. In that presentation, the Roman Republic, threatened by the *furor* of its enemies, was taken by Augustus under his personal protection; then, in 28/7, he 'restored the Republic to the Senate and People', but, by their will, continued his work for the state, as its chief and most influential servant. The *restoration* (in all this) of the Republic was emphasized, and Velleius can exclaim, with apparent seriousness, 'prisca illa et antiqua rei publicae forma revocata' [that venerable and ancient model of the state was restored—Ed.].[34] But did this image of Augustus—hardly acceptable to all his subjects, much less to Tacitus or Cassius Dio— find acceptance in Marvell's day, or with Marvell? For all the evidence to the contrary, his picture of the Princeps may have been *Tacitean*; nor is there real correspondence, in any case, between his stanzas, stressing loyalty to a newly established Republic, and propaganda suggesting the *restoration* of the 'prisca . . . et antiqua rei publicae forma'. But a comparison, not with Augustus, but with any loyal and great proconsul of the pristine Republic, is appropriate to an Ode in many ways reminiscent of Horace, but, in others, not so much Horatian as boldly Roman.[35]

SOURCE: article in *Critical Quarterly*, II, No. 4 (1969), 325–41.

NOTES

1. On the assumption that stanzas 1–2 refer to war against Scotland as inevitable and imminent, stanza 3 says 'As it is proper now for the forward Youth to act, so Cromwell acted in 1642; as he acted then, so the forward Youth should now be acting'. Reference, in stanzas 1–2, to 1642 (which has been thought possible) would make discontinuity between the title and the opening, render this less effective, and deprive 'So' of its emphatic comparative force, characteristic of the Ode (cf. stanzas 17 and 23). Apart from the continuing local resistance of the Irish, the peace of England in summer 1650 was that of a still divided country, which had seen bitter fighting as late as 1648; poetic fiction ignores this, in stanzas 1–2, for the internal purposes of the Ode.

2. When the bulk of Marvell's poems were published soon after his death, as *Miscellaneous Poems . . .* , 'An Horatian Ode' was omitted from all but two of the now extant copies, presumably because authority had taken exception to the praise of Cromwell: see Margoliouth (ed.), *The Poems and Letters of Andrew Marvell*, i, p. 206.

3. There is, to me, something problematic, in one way or another, about the poems sometimes said to show 'Royalist' sentiment in Marvell in 1648–50. Is the irritation of the poem to Lovelace against puritan censorship of good letters (Margoliouth, i p. 3) really *Royalism* in any important sense? Has the sympathy of the elegy on Hastings for aristocratic distinction any clear bearings on Marvell's *political* outlook? Aristocrats and aristocratic attitudes were there among the Parliamentarians too. The Elegy on Lord Francis Villiers is not certainly by Marvell (text and note by Margoliouth, ibid, Appendix). *Tom May's Death* (ibid., p. 90), not quite certainly authentic, may *conceivably* have been written only after the Restoration, and its Royalism is put in the mouth of that great loyalist, Ben Jonson, speaking in the Elysian Fields (see Margoliouth, p. 239f, on the question of the date, and 'Additional Notes' xv, for circumstances bearing on the authenticity of the ascription). These poems and inferences from them need further review.

4. Even after he had published *The First Anniversary of the Government under O.C.* (1655) and other public poems and had drawn nearer to Cromwell, first as tutor to his ward (1653), then as 'second Latin Secretary' (1657), Marvell could not have made a claim comparable to the justified boast of Horace (*Odes.* IV 3 22f.' . . . . monstror digito praetereuntium/*Romanae fidicen lyrae*').

5. The couplet must say Cromwell could not *rest* . . ., not that he could not *leave off*, 'in the inglorious Arts . . .'. That sense, answering to Latin 'cessare', occurs in the period: see *OED.*, 'cease', +2, quoting Stanley, *Hist. Philos.* (1655–60): 'matter . . . will cease if none move it'. 'Appear' is used with sense like that of 'apparere' in Horace' lines, 'cum lamentamur non apparere labores/nostros . . . ' (*Epistles* II 1 224f.) Is this strong sense normal? *OED* 'appear' (5) quotes Shakespeare *Coriolanus* (IV iii 35) for 'appear' 'to make one's mark'; but the words are 'appear well'.

6. For the complex of attitudes conveyed by 'vita umbratilis', see P. L. Smith, in *Phoenix*, XIX (1965), 298ff. Tityrus, in Vergil's first *Eclogue*, sings in the shade 'numbers languishing':

> Tityre, tu patulae recubans sub tegmine fagi
> silvestrem tenui Musam meditaris avena
> . . .
> . . .   tu, Tityre, lentus in umbra
> formosam resonare doces Amaryllida silvas.

[Tityrus, while you lie there in the shade of the spreading beech and practise a woodland melody on the slender pipe . . . at your ease in the shade you teach the forests to re-echo 'the beauteous Amaryllis'—Ed.] In his epigram, 'In Effigiem Oliveri Cromwell', Marvell recalls 'lentus in umbra':

> Haec est quae toties *Inimicos* Umbra fugavit,
> At sub qua *Cives* otia lenta terunt.

('Haec . . . umbra' means 'the effigy of the man who', and the next line plays on the double sense of 'umbra'.) For 'umbra' in Horace's *Odes*, see I 32 1f.; II 15 9–12.

7. Vergil, *Georgics*, IV 563f.

8. Cicero, *Pro Murena*, 30 (whence also the previously quoted sentence 'sit in civitate . . .'). Cicero is claiming that a man of military experience ought to be preferred, for public office, to a man of legal experience.

9. Lucan, *Pharsalia*, I 143ff. (with condemnatory expressions italicised):

> sed non in Caesare tantum
> nomen erat nec fama ducis, sed nescia uirtus
> stare loco, *solusque pudor non uincere bello,*
> acer et indomitus, *quo spes quoque ira uocasset,*
> ferre manum et *nunquam temerando parcere ferro,*
> successus urguere suos, instare fauori
> nominis, impellens quidquid sibi summa petenti
> obstaret *gaudensque uiam fecisse ruina,*
> qualiter expressum uentis per nubila fulmen
> aetheris inpulsi sonitu mundique fragore
> emicuit rupitque diem populosque pauentes
> terruit obliqua praestringens lumina flamma:
> in sua templa furit, nullaque exire uetante
> materia magnamque cadens magnamque reuertens
> dat stragem late sparsosque recolligit ignes.

[Caesar, on the other hand, had not only won the reputation of a successful general, but was burned with so restless a desire for conquest that he felt disgraced by inactivity. Headstrong, fierce, and never hesitating to flesh his sword, he stood prepared to lead his troops wherever hope to glory or personal resentment offered a battlefield. Confident in Fortune's continued favours, he would follow up each advantage gained, thrusting aside all obstacles that barred his march to supreme power, and rejoicing in the havoc he occasioned. Caesar may, indeed, be justly compared to lightning. Discharged by the winds from a pack of clouds, it darts out jaggedly with a crash that splits the daylight skies, dazzling every eye, striking terror into every heart, and blasting its own airy seats. Nothing may stand against it, either during that furious progress through the clouds, or when it bursts against the earth and at once recomposes its scattered fires—trans. Robert Graves, 1956.]

'Spes', coupled with 'ira' is 'bad hope', and may certainly be reckoned with the condemnatory phrases in this fine passage of Lucan. Marvell was probably influence, not only by the original passage, but also by Tom May's rendering of it in his version of the *Pharsalia*. This is quoted by Margoliouth (op. cit., 1 237). The neighbouring passage of this version of the *Pharsalia* (229–32) quoted by Margoliouth may have *inspired* Marvell in writing the Ode, but seems to me to have no bearing on the *meaning*.

    10. Ovid, *Metamorphoses*, II 848, and *Ibis*, 467.

    11. See S. K. Heninger, *A Handbook of Renaissance Metereorology*, pp. 174f. and 72ff., quoting Simon Harward, *A Discourse of the Several Kinds and Causes of Lightnings* (1605): 'First a viscous vapour joyned with

a hot exhalation is lifted up to the highest part of the middle region of the aire, by vertue of the Planets: then the waterie vapour by the coldness both of place and matter, is thickned into a clowd, and the exhalation (which was drawne up with it) is shut within the clowd, and driven into straights. This hotte exhalation flying the touching of the cold clowd, doth flie into the depth of the clowd that doeth compasse it about, and courseth up and downe in the clowd, seeking some passage out.' Then finally, '. . . it maketh a way by force, and, being kindled, by the violent motion it breaketh through the clowde'.

12. Marvell, as is clear from other poems, had studied, at least in part, Pliny, *Naturalis Historia*, xv f., and may have taken the immunity of the laurel to lightning direct from xv 135. Pliny has much to say of the association of the laurel with the ceremony of the imperial house (xv 127 ff.); but the standing right of the Emperor to wear the laurel wreath probably belonged to Marvell's general stock of information.

13. Horace, *Odes*, iii 1 1ff.:

> Odi profanum volgus et arceo;
> favete linguis: carmina non prius
>   audita Musarum sacerdos
>   virginibus puerisque canto.

[I hate the common herd and I warn them off; keep silence; I am the priest of the Muses and sing songs never heard before to maidens and young men—Ed.]

14. Sir Charles Firth, *Oliver Cromwell*, p. 469.

15. Horace, *Odes*, iii 3 1–12, esp. 9 ff.

16. 'Penetration' was used for 'a supposed or conceived occupation of the same space by two bodies at the same time' (*OED*, s.v.)

17. Reasons for disbelieving, in this case, in Cromwell's 'wiser Art': Firth, op. cit., p. 184 f.

18. G. M. Trevelyan, *England under the Stuarts*, p. 130.

19. *Odes*, i 37 21 ff.

20. Fairfax's lines abhorring the regicide (C. R. Markham, *A Life of . . . Lord Fairfax*, p. 352) may make us ask how he will have reacted to these stanzas; Fairfax's verses are no less significant because an adaptation of Statius, *Silvae*, v 2 88 ff.

21. Pliny, *Naturalis Historia*, xxviii 15; Plutarch, *Camillus*, 31 4; Dionysius of Halicarnassus, *Roman Antiquities*, iv 59–61; Varro, *De Lingua Latina*, v 41.

22. Professor J. M. Wallace, in *Destiny His Choice: The Loyalism of Andrew Marvell*, after citing contemporary evidence for a more

clement side to Cromwell's conduct in Ireland, concludes, 'the satisfaction of her people is plainly recalled to witness to Cromwell's fitness for another task' (p. 88). This is more to the point than reports from Ireland, which Marvell may or may not have studied. But the whole literary character of this part of the Ode is not, I think, sufficiently considered by Professor Wallace.

23. Erasmus's form of the adage (*Adagia*, Basle, 1520, Chil. 13 p. 21) is '*nemo bene imperat nisi qui ante paruerit imperio*'. The thought is traced from its first appearance by J. M. Wallace (op. cit., p. 88); but I cannot see here a proposal for a 'constitutional dictatorship' for Cromwell, as he argues in his political interpretation of the Ode (p. 69 ff.). Such suggestions in contemporary pamphlets are adduced in this interpretation; and, in Marvell, compressed allusion to contemporary pamphlet literature is conceivable. But, though conceivable, it is not necessary here; it would require the reader to come down hard on 'sway', like a political orator producing the punch-line in a nomination speech, and would give this couplet a sudden emphasis, alien to the series. Wallace's interpretation of the Ode generally starts from without, not within, the poem, and its many perversities may be left to the reviewers of his book.

24. Horace, *Odes*, III 5 1 ff.; 3 43 ff. & 53 ff.; I 12 & 53 ff. Cf. the similar utterances of other Augustan and later Roman poets discussed by H. D. Meyer, *Die Aussenpolitik des Augustus und die Augusteische Dichtung* (Kölner Histor. Abhand., no. 5).

25. Claudian, *On the Third Consulate of Honorius*, 54; the Royalist satirist Cleveland starts *The Rebel Scot* with 'You Picts in gentry and devotion'; Ray's *Collection of English Proverbs* (1670) includes 'false as a Scot'. 'Party-colour'd' is both 'versicolor' and, as we now say, 'party-dominated'.

26. In both which poems Horace uses the impetus of verse to convey warlike *impetus*, in a manner not attempted in the Ode.

27. 49 ff.; the parallel of '*perfidus* Hannibal' and the treacherous *Pict* may have occurred to Marvell.

28. Vergil, *Aeneid*, VI 261 f., with Servius's comments on 251 and 291. It is not altogether far-fetched to suppose Marvell may have recollected Servius; even boys used Servius, in his day, at Grammar School (see Foster Watson, *The English Grammar Schools*, p. 373). For Jugurtha's ghost in Horace, see *Odes*, II 1 25 ff. E. E. Duncan–Jones, 'The Erect Sword in Marvell's "Horatian Ode" (*Etudes anglaises*, 1962, pp. 172–4), in drawing attention to the Vergilian suggestion, might have omitted, as less probable and relevant, the idea of an allusion to *Odyssey*, XI and its νέχυια . Her suggestion is coupled with the sort of understanding of stanza 30 which I reject; but need not have been.

29. Sallust, *Catiline*, 2 4.

30. J. M. Wallace, *Destiny His Choice*, op. cit., p. 96.

31. Quoted in ibid, p. 97.

32. As the ancients, so Marvell's contemporaries were com-
pelled to see the hand of fickle Fortune at work everywhere, making or
breaking states or lives. But, in 'An Horatian Ode', 'Fortune's Son' is
surely an echo of the Latin and Greek expression. In Horace (*Sermones*, II
6 49) the use of 'Fortunae filius' is humorous, but the phrase as such
answers to παις της τύχης (as in Sophocles, *Oedipus Tyrannus*, 1080).

33. Abbott (ed.), *Letters and Speeches of Oliver Cromwell*, II p. 38.

34. Velleius Paterculus, II 89 4.

35. I disagree *toto coelo* with the approach of John S. Coolidge in
'Marvell and Horace' (*Modern Philology*, LXIII, III ff.) A dubious
reconstruction of the development of Horace is linked with a dubious
reconstruction of Marvell's development, and literary comparison goes
by the board; even with regard to the *vita umbratilis* and its bearing in
the early stanzas, Professor Coolidge seems to me to introduce confusing
refinements.

Frank Kermode   The Argument of 'The Garden' (1952)

I

'The Garden is an *étude d'exécution transcendante* which has been
interpreted by so many virtuosi in the past few years that a stiff-
fingered academic rendering is unlikely to be very entertaining.
However, since it appears that the brilliant executants have been
making rather too many mistakes, there may be some value in
going slowly over the whole piece.

It may be useful to point out in advance that these mistakes are
of three kinds. The first is historical, as when Mr Milton
Klonsky—writing in the *Sewanee Review*, LVIII (Winter 1950), 16–
35—seizes on a passage in Plotinus as the sole key to the poem. He
is wrong, not because there is no connection at all between

Plotinus and Marvell's lyric, but because he has misunderstood the relationship and consequently exaggerated its importance. He fails to observe that Marvell, like other poets of the period, uses philosophical concepts, including those of Neoplatonism in a special way, with reference not to the body of formal doctrine in which those concepts are originally announced, but to genres of poetry which habitually and conventionally make use of them. The process is familiar enough; for example, the nature of the relationship between pastoral poetry and philosophic material such as the debates on Action and Contemplation, Art and Nature, is tolerably well understood. It is not customary to find the only key to the works of Guarini or Fletcher in some Greek philosopher; but these poets have not, like Donne and Marvell, been distorted by the solemn enthusiasm of modern exegetes. In a sense all philosophical propositions in Marvell are what Professor Richards used to call 'pseudo-statements', and his is a 'physical' rather than a 'platonic' poetry. However, rather than risk myself in these deep waters, I shall support myself on a raft of Mr Wellek's construction: 'The work of art . . . appears as an object *sui generis* . . . a system of norms of ideal concepts which are intersubjective . . .' Above all, it is possible 'to proceed to a classification of works of art according to the norms they employ' and thus 'we may finally arrive at theories of genre'.[1] The point is that we must not treat these 'norms' as propositions, for if we do we shall fall into the toils of Mr Klonsky. Miss Ruth Wallerstein, who has worked so hard and so sanely to liberate seventeenth-century poetry from modern error, is none the less guilty of Mr Klonsky's fault, in her *Studies in Seventeenth Century Poetic* (Madison, 1950). Not only the indolent cry out against the suggestion that 'The Garden' needs to be explicated in terms of Hugo of St Victor and Bonaventura. Doubtless there is, for the historian of ideas, a real connection between the poem and the Victorine and Neo-Platonic systems of symbolic thought; for there is a connection between Plato and 'Trees'. However interesting this may be, it has nothing to do with what most of us call criticism. If we read 'The Garden' as historians of poetry, and not as historians of ideas, we shall resist all such temptation to treat the 'norms' as ideas, even if it proceeds from Diotima herself, to whom Professor Richards succumbed in a recent lecture on the poem.

The second kind of mistake is one which, particularly when it assumes its more subtle shape, we are all liable to yield to, though it appears to be seductive even in its usual grossness. Sufficient, however, to say that 'The Garden' must not be read as autobiography. 'What was Marvell's state of mind as he wandered in Fairfax's Yorkshire garden?' is a very bad question to ask, but it is obviously one which comes readily to the minds of learned and subtle interpreters; both Marvell and Donne have suffered greatly from this form of misapplied scholarship, and it is comforting to reflect that the date of 'The Garden' is quite unknown, so that it cannot be positively stated to be the direct record of some personal experience at Nun Appleton. It could conceivably have been written much later. The pseudo-biographical critic is wasteful and deceptive; he diverts attention from the genre just as certainly as Mr Klonsky does when he presents a picture of the poet torturing himself with Chinese boxes of Forms, or Mr Empson when he invites us to reflect upon the Buddhist enlightenment (*Some Versions of Pastoral*, pp. 119–20; in the United States, *English Pastoral Poetry*).

The third kind of critical failure is clearly, in this case, the most important, for the others would not have occurred had there not been this cardinal error. It is the failure to appreciate the genre (the system of 'norms' shared by other poems) to which 'The Garden' belongs. Despite the labours of Miss Bradbrook, Miss Lloyd Thomas,[2] and Miss Wallerstein, poets like Théophile, Saint-Amant, Randolph, Lovelace, Fane and Stanley have simply not been put to proper use in the criticism of Marvell. This is the central difficulty, and the one which this paper is intended to diminish. The first necessity is to distinguish between the genre and the history of the ideas to which the genre is related.

II

'We cannot erre in following Nature': thus Montaigne, 'very rawly and simply', with this addition: 'I have not (as *Socrates*) by the power and vertue of reason, corrected my natural complexions, nor by Art hindered mine inclination.'[3] This is a useful guide to that aspect of 'naturalism' in the thought of the late Renaissance which here concerns us. The like consideration governs all the speculations of the older Montaigne; Nature is to be distinguished from Custom; the natural inclinations are good, and sensual gratifications are not the dangerous suggestions that other and more orthodox psychologies hold them to be. Sense and instinct seek and find their own temperance without the interference of reason. It is good to satisfy a natural appetite, and it is also, of course, innocent. Thus men behaved, says Montaigne, in the Golden World, and thus they still behave in the Indies.

The question how far Montaigne believed in his own 'primitivism' seems to me a difficult one, but it scarcely concerns us at the moment. It is legitimate to use him as spokesman for naturalism; and before we leave him it will be prudent to glance at some of his references to Plato, in order to have at hand some record of the naturalist reaction to the Platonic theory of love. In short, as the foregoing quotation implies, Platonic love is rejected. No longer 'an appetite of generation by the mediation of beauty', love is in fact 'nothing else but an insatiate thirst of enjoying a greedily desired subject' (III 105). 'My Page makes love, and understands it feelingly; Read *Leon Hebraeus* or *Ficinus* unto him; you speake of him, of his thoughts and of his actions, yet understands he nothing what you meane . . .' (III 102). Much more sympathetic are 'the ample and lively descriptions in *Plato*, of the loves practised in his dayes' (III 82). If one is not over-careful—if, for instance, one fails to discriminate between the orations of Socrates and those who precede him, one may without much difficulty extract from the *Symposium* itself very different theories of love from those developed by Ficino or Milton. In Marvell's own youth antithetical versions of Platonism flourished contemporaneously at Cambridge and at Whitehall.

So far we have concerned ourselves, very briefly, with the informal naturalism of Montaigne, and hinted at a naturalistic version of Plato. What of the poetry which concerns itself with similar issues? One thinks at once of Tasso, and specifically of that chorus in his *Aminta*, *O bella età de l'oro* which was so often imitated and debated in the poetry of the age. In the happy Golden Age lovers concerned themselves with their own love and innocence, and not with honour, that tyrant bred of custom and opinion, that enemy of nature. In the garden of the unfallen just, whatever pleases is lawful. The paradise of these fortunate innocents is abundant in its appeal to the senses; law and appetite are the same, and no resolved soul interferes with the banquet of sense offered by created pleasure. Thus an ancient pastoral tradition accommodates new poetic motives, and poetry, though affirming nothing, strengthens its association with the freer thought of its time. The formal opposition to Tasso's statement is properly made in poetry which belongs to the same genre; and it may be found in the chorus in Act IV of Guarini's *Il Pastor Fido*. Parallel debates could go on in the great world, and in the little world of poetry: the debate about naturalism was a serious one, since it involved theological censures. The poetical debate is of a different quality. The proper answer to Tasso is Guarini's. A genre of poetry developed which assumed the right to describe the sensuality of a natural Eden, and a specialised kind concentrated on sexual gratifications as innocent, and the subject of unreasonable interference from Honour. The proper reply is, again, in terms of the 'norms' of the genre, and there is evidence that the very poets who stated the extreme naturalist case were quite capable of refuting it. One might call the 'norms' of the refutation an anti-genre. 'The Garden' is a poem of the anti-genre of the naturalist paradise.

Marvell therefore rejects the naturalist account of love, and with it that Platonism which was associated with the delights of the senses. The poets of the Renaissance were profitably aware of the possible antitheses in Platonic theories of love, just as they were aware of Plato's argument against their status as vessels of the truth.[4] Spenser makes comfortable bedfellows of two Platonisms in his 'Hymns'; the two Aphrodites easily change into each other in poem and emblem. Nothing is more characteristic of Renaissance poetry than the synthesis of spiritual and erotic in poetic genre and image. It was encouraged by centuries of comment on the *Canticum Canticorum* and the eclecticism of mystics as well as by the doctrinaire efforts of Bruno to spiritualise the erotic Petrarcan conceits. Much more evidence could be brought, if it were necessary, to establish the existence of genre and anti-genre in Platonic love-poetry. They not only co-exist, but suggest each other. Marvell could pass with ease from the libertine garden to the garden of the Platonic *solitaire*, soliciting the primary *furor* of spiritual ascent. (The ease of such transitions

was partly responsible for the development of another genre—
that of the palinode.)

'The Garden' stands in relation to the poetry of the gardens of
sense as the 'Hymn of Heavenly Beauty' stands in relation to the
'Hymn of Beauty'. It is poetry written in the language of, or using
the 'norms' of, a genre in a formal refutation of the genre. In fact,
this was a method Marvell habitually used, sometimes almost
with an affectation of pedantry, as I have elsewhere shown of
'The Mower against Gardens'.[5]

III

The garden is a rich emblem, and this is not the place to explore it
in any detail; indeed I shall say nothing of the symbolic gardens
of the Middle Ages which were still alive in the consciousness of
the seventeenth century. The gardens to which Marvell most
directly alludes in his poem are the Garden of Eden, the Earthly
Paradise, and that garden to which both Stoic and Epicurean, as
well as Platonist, retire for solace or meditation. The first two are
in many respects one and the same; the third is the garden of
Montaigne, of Lipsius, and of Cowley. I shall not refer to the
hortus conclusus, though at one point in my explication of Marvell's
poem I allude to a Catholic emblem-writer. Doubtless the notion
of Nature as God's book affects the poetic tradition; it certainly
occurs in poems about solitude at this period. But I think it is
misleading to dwell on the history of the idea.

Of the complexity of the Earthly Paradise, with all its
associated images and ideas, it is not necessary to say much: it is of
course a staple of pastoral poetry and drama, and the quality of
Marvell's allusions to it will emerge in my explication. But a
word is needed about the garden of the solitary thinker, which
Marvell uses in his argument against the libertine garden of
innocent sexuality.

It is to be remembered that we are not dealing with the
innocence of Tasso's Golden Age, where there is a perfect
concord between appetite and reason, or with the garden of
innocent love that Spenser sketches in *Faerie Queene*, IV x, where
'thousand payres of louers walkt, Praysing their god and yeelding

him great thankes', and, 'did sport Their spotlesse pleasures, and
sweet loues content'. The libertines use the argument of the
innocence of sense to exalt sensuality and to propose the abolition
of the tyrant Honour, meaning merely female chastity. This is the
situation of the *Jouissance* poetry which was fashionable in
France, and of which Saint-Amant's well-known example,
excellently translated by Stanley, is typical. It is equally the
situation of Randolph's 'Upon Love Fondly Refused' and his
'Pastoral Courtship', Carew's 'Rapture' and Lovelace's 'Love
Made in the first Age'. In Randolph's Paradise there is no
serpent—'Nothing that wears a sting, but I'[6]—and in Lovelace's

> No Serpent kiss poyson'd the Tast
> Each touch was naturally Chast,
> And their mere Sense a Miracle.[7]

And so it is throughout the libertine versions of sensual innocence. The garden, the place of unfallen innocence, is
identified with a naturalist glorification of sensuality. The garden
which is formally opposed to this one by Marvell is the garden
where sense is controlled by reason and the intellect can
contemplate not beauty but heavenly beauty.

It was Montaigne, this time in his Stoic role, who gave wide
currency to the pleasures of *solitary* seclusion. The relevant ideas
and attitudes were developed into a poetic genre. Many poets
certainly known to Marvell practised this genre, among them
Fane and Fairfax and the French poets, notably Saint-Amant,
whose *Solitude* demonstrates how easily he moved in this, the
antithesis of the *Jouissance* mode. This famous poem was
translated by Fairfax and by Katharine Phillips. This is the
poetry of the meditative garden, whether the meditation be
pseudo-Dionysian, or Ciceronian, or merely pleasantly
Epicurean, like Cowley's. There is, of course, a play of the senses
in which woman has no necessary part, though the equation of all
appetite with the sexual appetite in the libertines tends to ignore
it; this unamorous sensuality is firmly castigated by Lipsius in his
treatment of gardens. If the garden is treated merely as a resort of
pleasure, for the 'inward tickling and delight of the senses' it
becomes 'a verie sepulchre of slothfulnes'. The true end of the
garden is 'quietnes, withdrawing from the world, meditation',

the subjection of the distressed mind to right reason.[8] The true ecstasy is in being rapt by intellect, not by sex.

Retirement; the study of right reason; the denial of the sovereignty of sense; the proper use of created nature: these are the themes of Marvell's poem laboriously and misleadingly translated into prose. As poetry the work can only be studied in relation to its genre, though that genre may be related to ethical debates. To the naturalist *Jouissance* Marvell opposes the meditative *Solitude*. The fact that both these opposed conceptions are treated in the work of one poet, Saint-Amant, and a little less explicitly in Théophile and Randolph also, should warn against the mistaking of seriousness for directness of reference to ethical propositions. 'The Garden' uses and revalues the 'norms' of the genre: it is not a contribution to philosophy, and not the direct account of a contemplative act.

IV

Henry Hawkins, the author of the emblem-book *Partheneia Sacra*, adopts a plan which enables him, in treating the emblematic qualities of a garden, to direct the attention of the pious reader away from the delights of the sense offered by the Plants to a consideration of their higher significance. As in Marvell, sensual pleasure has to give way to meditation.[9] We now proceed to the explication of Marvell's poem, with a glance at Hawkins's wise disclaimer: 'I will not take upon me to tel al; for so of a Garden of flowers, should I make a Labyrinth of discourse, and should never be able to get forth' (p. 8).

The poem begins by establishing that of all the possible gardens it is dealing with that of retirement, with the garden of the contemplative man who shuns action. The retired life is preferred to the active life in a witty simplification: if the two ways of life are appraised in terms of the vegetable solace they provide it will be seen that the retired life is quantitatively superior. The joke is in the substitution of the emblem of victory for its substance. If you then appraise action in terms of plants you get single plants, whereas retirement offers you the solace of not one but *all* plants. This is a typical 'metaphysical' use of the figure called by Puttenham the Disabler. The first stanza, then, is

a witty dispraise of the active life, though it has nothing to
distinguish it sharply from other kinds of garden-poetry such as
libertine or Epicurean—except possibly the hint of a secondary
meaning 'celibate' in the word *single* and a parallel sexual pun on
close,[10] which go very well with the leading idea that woman has
no place in this garden.

The Innocence of the second stanza cannot itself divide the
poem from other garden-poems; for Innocence of a sort is a
feature of the libertine paradise, as well as of the Epicurean
garden of Cowley and indeed most gardens.

> Your sacred Plants, if here below,
> Only among the Plants will grow—

lines which are certainly a much more complicated statement
than that of *Hortus*—seem to have stimulated Mr Klonsky to
astonishing feats. But the idea is not as difficult as all that.
Compare 'Upon Appleton House'—

> For he did, with his utmost Skill,
> *Ambition* weed, but *Conscience* till.
> *Conscience*, that Heaven-nursed Plant,
> Which most our Earthly Gardens want.   (XLV)

Your sacred plants, he says, addressing Quiet and Innocence, are
unlike the palm, the oak and the bays in that if you find them
anywhere on earth it will be among the plants of the garden. The
others you can find 'in buise Companies'. The joke here is to give
Quiet and her sister plant-emblems like those of the active life,
and to clash the emblematic and the vegetable plants together.
The inference is that Innocence may be found only in the green
shade (*concolor Umbra* occurs at this point in the Latin version).
Society (with its ordinary connotations by 'polish' and 'company') is in fact all but rude (unpolished) by comparison with
Solitude, which at first appears to be lacking in the virtues
Society possesses, but which possesses them, if the truth were
known, in greater measure (the Ciceronian-Stoic 'never less
alone than when alone' became so trite that Cowley, in his essay
'Of Solitude', apologized for referring to it).

We are now ready for a clearer rejection of libertine innocence.

Female beauty is reduced to its emblematic colours, red and white (a commonplace, but incidentally one found in the libertine poets) and unfavourably compared with the green of the garden as a dispenser of sensual delight. This is to reject Saint-Amant's 'crime innocent, à quoi la Nature consent'.[11] A foolish failure to understand the superiority of green causes lovers to insult trees (themselves the worthier object of love) by carving on them the names of women. (This happens in Saint-Amant's *Jouissance*.) Since it is the green garden, and not women that the poet chooses to regard as amorous, it would be farcically logical for him to carve on the trees their own names. The garden is not to have women or their names or their love in it. It is natural (green) and amorous (green—a 'norm' of the poem) in quite a different way from the libertine garden.

Love enters this garden, but only when the pursuit of the white and red is done, and we are without appetite. (Love is here indiscriminately the pursued and the pursuer. Weary with the race and exertion (*heat*) it 'makes a retreat' in the garden; hard-pressed by pursuers it carries out a military retreat.) The place of retreat has therefore Love, but not women: they are metamorphosed into trees. The gods, who might be expected to know, have been misunderstood; they pursued women not as women but as potential trees, for the green and not for the red and white. Marvell, in this witty version of the metamorphoses, continues to 'disable' the idea of sexual love. Here one needs quite firmly to delimit the reference, because it is confusing to think of *laurel* and *reed* as having symbolic significations. It is interesting that this comic metamorphosis (which has affinities with the fashionable mock-heroic) was practised for their own ends by the libertine poets; for example, in Saint-Amant's 'La Metamorphose de Lyrian et de Sylvie', in Stanley's Marinesque 'Apollo and Daphne', in Carew's 'Rapture', where Lucrece and other types of chastity become sensualists in the libertine paradise, and very notably in Lovelace. Thus, in 'Against the Love of Great Ones':

> *Ixion* willingly doth feele
> The Gyre of his eternal wheele,
> Nor would he now exchange his paine
> For Cloudes and Goddesses againe.   (*Poems*, p. 75)

The sensuous appeal of this garden is, then, not sexual, as it is in the libertines. It has, nonetheless, all the enchantment of the Earthly Paradise, and all its innocence: this is the topic of the fifth stanza. The trees and plants press their fruit upon him, and their gifts are in strong contrast to those of the libertine garden,

> Love then unstinted, Love did sip,
> And Cherries pluck'd fresh from the Lip,
>   On Cheeks and Roses free he fed;
> Lasses like *Autumne* Plums did drop,
> And Lads, indifferently did crop
>   A Flower, and a Maiden-head.   (*Poems*, p. 146)

The fruits of green, not of red and white, are offered in primeval abundance, as they are in the Fortunate Islands or in any paradise. Everything is by nature lush and fertile; the difference between this and a paradise containing a woman is that here a Fall is of light consequence, and without tragic significance. ('Insnar'd with *flowers*, I fall on grass.') In the same way, Marvell had in 'Upon Appleton House' (LXXVII) bound himself with the entanglements not of wanton limbs, in the libertine manner of Carew, Randolph and Stanley, but of woodbine, briar and bramble. The same imagery is still in use for amorous purposes in the poetry of Leigh.

In this garden both man and nature are unfallen; it is therefore, for all its richness, not a trap for virtue but a paradise of perfect innocence. Even the fall is innocent; the sensuous allurements of the trees are harmless, and there is no need to 'fence The Batteries of alluring Sense'. It is evident that Empson and King were quite right to find here a direct allusion to the Fall.

Modern commentators all agree that the sixth stanza, central to the poem, is a witty Platonism, and of course this is so. The danger is that the Platonism can be made to appear doctrinal and even recherché, when in fact it is reasonably modest, and directly related to genre treatments of love in gardens. There is, however, a famous ambiguity in the first two lines: how are we to take 'from pleasure less'? It can mean simply (1) reduced by pleasure, or (2) that the mind retires because it experiences less pleasure than the senses, or (3) that it retires from the lesser pleasure to the greater.

The first of these might be related to the doctrine of the creation in *Paradise Lost*, VII 168 ff – 'I am who fill Infinitude, nor vacuous the space. Though I uncircumscrib'd myself retire, And put not forth my goodness . . .' This would be consistent with the analogy later drawn between the human and the divine minds. But the second is more likely to be the dominant meaning, with a proper distinction between mind and sense which is obviously relevant to the theme ('None can chain a mind Whom this sweet Chordage cannot bind'). The third meaning is easily associated with this interpretation. The mind withdraws from the sensual gratification offered in order to enjoy a happiness of the imagination. In terms of the genre, it rejects the *Jouissance* for the *Solitude*—indeed, Saint-Amant, in a poem which prefers the contemplative garden, writes of it thus:

> Tantost, faisant agir mes sens
> Sur des sujets *de moindre estofe*,
> De marche en autre je descens
> Dans les termes du philosophe;
> Nature n'a point de secret
> Que d'un soin libre, mais discret,
> Ma curiosité ne sonde;
> Et, dans ma recherche profonde,
> Je loge en moy tout l'univers.
> Là, songeant au flus et reflus,
> *Je m'abisme dans cette idée*;
> Son mouvement me rend perclus,
> Et mon âme en est obsedée. (1 32; my italics)

To put it another way, one prefers a different kind of ecstasy from that of the libertine, described by the same poet in his *Jouissance*, which Stanley translated. Saint-Amant represents his solitary as acquiring from nature knowledge of the forms, and the next two lines of Marvell's stanza seem to do likewise. The metaphor is not unfamiliar—'Some have affirm'd that what on earth we find The sea can parallel for shape and kind'—and the idea is that the forms exist in the mind of man as they do in the mind of God. By virtue of the imagination the mind can create worlds and seas too which have nothing to do with the world which is reported by the senses. This is the passage which seems to have caused such

trouble to commentators, who look to learned originals like
Plotinus and Ficino for the explanation: but in fact the Platonism
here is dilute and current.

It is a commonplace of Renaissance poetic that God is a poet,
and that the poet has the honour of this comparison only because
of the creative force of fancy or imagination. Nor is the power
exclusive to poets. The mind, which 'all effects into their causes
brings',[12] can through the imagination alone devise new and rare
things: as Puttenham says, 'the phantasticall part of man (if it be
not disordered) is a representer of the best, most comely and
bewtifull images or apparences of thinges to the soule and
according to their very truth' (p. 19). Puttenham shuns 'disordered phantasies . . . monstrous imaginations or conceits' as being alien to the truth of imagination, but it is conceivable that
Marvell, in his suggestion of the mind's ability to create, refers to
a more modern psychology and poetic, with its roots in the
Renaissance, but with a new emphasis. Thus Cowley in his
Pindaric 'The Muse' says that the coach of poetry can go
anywhere:

> And all's an *open Road* to *thee*.
>   Whatever *God* did say,
> Is all thy plain and smooth, uninterrupted *Way*.
> Nay, ev'n beyond his *Works* thy *Voyages* are known,
>   Thou hast a thousand *Worlds* too of thine *own*.
> Thou speak'st, great *Queen*, in the same *Stile* as *he*,
> And *a new World* leaps forth, when *thou* say'st, *Let it be*.

And in a note he obligingly explains this:

The meaning is, that *Poetry* treats not only of all Things that are, or can
be, but makes *Creatures* of her own, as *Centaurs, Satyrs, Fairies*, &c., makes
Persons and *Actions* of her own . . . makes *Beasts, Trees, Waters*, and other
irrational and insensible Things to act above the Possibility of their
Natures as to *understand* and *speak*; nay makes what *Gods* it pleases too
without *Idolatry*, and varies all these into innumerable *Systemes*, or
Worlds of Invention.

These other worlds are thoughts in the mind of man as the
world is a thought in the mind of God. Empson is probably right

in his guess that *streight* means 'packed together' as well as 'at once'. The whole idea is illuminated by a passage of extraordinary interest in Leigh (who was imbued with that passion for optics which later became common among poets) in which the reduced images of the eye are contrasted with the illimitable visions of the mind. The mind contains everything undiminished by the deficiencies of sense.[13] The mental activity which Marvell is describing is clear; it is the working of the imagination, which psychologically, follows sense and precedes intellection, and is therefore the means of rejecting the voluptuous suggestions of sense; and which 'performs its function when the sensible object is rejected or even removed'.[14] The mind's newly created worlds are, in the strict sense, phantasms, and without substance: and since they have the same mental status as the created world, it is fair to say that 'all that's made' is being annihilated, reduced to a thought.

But a green thought? This is a great bogey; but surely the thought is green because the solitude is green, which means that it is also the antithesis of voluptuousness? Here the normative signification of green in the poem is in accord with what is after all a common enough notion—green for innocence, Thus, in 'Aramantha' Lovelace asks:

> Can trees be green, and to the Ay'r
> Thus prostitute their flowing Hayr?   (*Poems*, p. 112)

But I cannot think the green has any more extensive symbolic intention. Green is still opposed to red and white; all this is possible only when women are absent and the senses innocently engaged.

The stanza thus alludes to the favourable conditions which enable the mind to apply itself to contemplation. The process is wittily described and the psychology requires no explanation in terms of any doctrinaire Platonism, whether pseudo-Dionysian, Plotinian, or Florentine.

The seventh stanza is also subject to much ingenious comment. The poet allows his mind to contemplate the ideas, and his soul begins a Platonic ascent. Here there are obvious parallels in the English mystics, in Plotinus, in medieval and Florentine Platonism; but we must see this stanza as we see the rest of the poem, in relation to the genre. Failing to do this we shall be involved in an endless strife between rival symbolisms, as we are if we try to find an external significance for *green*. As it is, there is no need to be over-curious about the fountain; its obvious symbolic quality may have an interesting history, but it is primarily an easily accessible emblem of purity. As for the use of the bird as an emblem of the soul, that is an image popularised by Castiglione,[15] and used by Spenser of the early stages of the ascent:

> Beginning then below, with th'easie vew
> Of this base world, subject to fleshly eye,
> From thence to mount aloft by order dew,
> To contemplation of th'immortall sky,
> Of that soare faulcon so I learne to fly,
> That flags awhile her fluttering wings beneath,
> Till she her selfe for stronger flight can breath.
>
> ('Hymne of Heavenly Beauty')

Spenser has just passed from the consideration of woman's love and beauty to the heavenly love and beauty. The bird which prepares its wings for flight is evidently a symbol with as settled a meaning as the dew, which Marvell also shared with many other poets.

The hungry soul, deceived with false beauties, may have 'after vain deceiptfull shadowes sought'—but at last it looks 'up to that soveraine light, From whose pure beams al perfect beauty springs' ('HHB'). Marvell's bird 'Waves in its Plumes the various Light'. Once more we might spring to Ebreo or Plotinus or even Haydocke, but we shall do better to note how this same image is used in literature more closely related to Marvell.

> Les oyseaux, d'un joyeux ramage,
> En chantant semblent adorer
> La lumière qui vient dorer
> Leur cabinet et leur plumage—

thus Théophile, in his Ode, 'Le Matin'.[16] In *Partheneia Sacra* Hawkins uses the dove as other poets use the dew or the rainbow:

Being of what coulour soever, her neck being opposed to the Sun will
diversify into a thousand coulours, more various then the Iris it-self, or
that Bird of *Juno* in al her pride; as scarlet, cerulean, flame-coulour, and
yealding a flash like the Carbuncle, with vermilion, ash-coulour, and
manie others besides. . . . (p. 202)

Marvell's use of the Platonic light-symbolism is therefore not
technical, as it might be in Chapman, but generalised, as in
Quarles or Vaughan, and affected by imagery associated with the
garden genres. We are thus reminded that the point about the
ascent towards the pure source of light is not that it can be
achieved, but that it can be a product of *Solitude* rather than of
Jouissance and that it is an alternative to libertine behaviour in
gardens. It is the ecstasy not of beauty but of heavenly beauty.

The eighth stanza at last makes this theme explicit. This is a
special solitude, which can only exist in the absence of women,
the agents of the most powerful voluptuous temptation. This has
been implied throughout, but it is now wittily stated in the first
clear reference to Eden. The notion that Adam would have been
happy without a mate is not, of course, novel; St Ambrose
believed it. Here it is another way of putting the case that woman
offers the wrong beauty, the wrong love, the red and white
instead of the green. Eve deprived Adam of solitude, and gave
him instead an inferior joy. Indeed she was his punishment for
being mortal (rather than pure Intelligence?). Her absence
would be equivalent to the gift of a paradise (since her presence
means the loss of the only one there is). This is easy enough, and a
good example of how naturally we read references to the more
familiar conceptions of theology and philosophy as part of the
play of wit within the limited range of a genre.

In the last stanza the temperate quiet of the garden is once
more asserted, by way of conclusion. (The Earthly Paradise is
always in the temperate zone.) The time, for us as for the bee (a
pun on 'thyme'), is sweet and rewarding; hours of innocence are
told by a dial of pure herbs and flowers. The sun is 'milder'
because in this zodiac of flowers fragrance is substituted for heat;
Miss Bradbrook and Miss Lloyd Thomas have some good
observations here. The time computed is likewise spent in
fragrant rather than hot pursuits. This is the *Solitude*, not the
Jouissance; the garden of the *solitaire* whose soul rises towards

divine beauty, not that of the voluptuary who voluntarily surrenders to the delights of the senses.

This ends the attempt to read 'The Garden' as a poem of a definite historical kind and to explore its delicate allusions to a genre of which the 'norms' are within limits ascertainable. Although it is very improbable that such an attempt can avoid errors of both sophistication and simplification, one may readily claim for it than in substituting poetry for metaphysics it does no violence to the richness and subtlety of its subject.

SOURCE: article in *Essays in Criticism*, II (1952).

NOTES

1. Wellek, 'The Mode of Existence of a Literary Work of Art', in R. W. Stellman (ed.), *Critiques and Essays in Criticism* (New York, 1949), pp. 210–23.

2. M. C. Bradbrook, 'Marvell and the Poetry of Rural Solitude', *Review of English Studies*, XVII (Jan. 1941), pp. 37–46; M. C. Bradbrook and M. G. Lloyd Thomas, *Andrew Marvell* (Cambridge, 1940).

3. Montaigne, *Essayes*, trans. John Florio (Everyman edition), III p. 316.

4. See F. A. Yates, *The French Academies of the Sixteenth Century* (London, 1947), pp. 128ff. From Plato (*Symposium*, 202A; *Republic*, 477 et seq.) through the Pléiade to Sidney there ran the argument that poets were not competent to make philosophical statements; they affirm nothing.

5. Frank Kermode, 'Two Notes on Marvell', *Notes and Queries*, CXCVII (March 1952), pp. 136–8.

6. Randolph, *Poems*, ed. G. Thorn-Drury (1929), p. 110.

7. Lovelace, *Poems*, ed. C. H. Wilkinson (1930), p. 147.

8. Lipsius, *De Constantia: Of Constancie*, trans. Sir J. Stradling, ed. R. Kirk and C. M. Hall (1929), pp. 132ff.

9. Hawkins, *Partheneia Sacra*, ed. Iain Fletcher (1950; reprint of 1633 edn).

10. Proposed by A. H. King, 'Some Notes on Marvell's Garden', *English Studies*, XX (1938), pp. 118–21.

11. Saint-Amant, *Oeuvres Complètes*, ed. Ch.-L. Livet (1855), I, p. 119.

12. Sir John Davies, *Nosce Teipsum* ('The Intellectual Powers of the Soul', stanza 5).

13. Leigh, *Poems*, ed. Hugh Macdonald (1947), p. 36ff.

14. Gianfrancesco Pico della Mirandola, *De Imaginatione*, ed. and trans. H. Caplan (1930), p. 29.

15. Castiglione, *The Book of the Courtier*, trans. Thomas Hoby (Everyman edition), p. 338.

16. Théophile, *Oeuvres Complètes*, ed. M. Alleaume (1856), I, pp. 174–5.

D. M. Friedman   On 'Upon Appleton House' (1970)

. . . The study of a poetic genre can often reveal more than the variations in the techniques and interests of the authors who have practised it. The development of the 'country house poem' from Jonson to Pope can tell us a great deal about such apparently unrelated matters as the changing opinion of the use of wealth in a capitalist state, the relationships between poets and patrons, the ways in which architectural styles reflect the *mores* of a social group, and even the kind of activities that civilisation feels to be most favourably representative of itself. Our view is limited, however, by the fact that all the major writers within the genre of the 'country house poem' are evidently sympathetic with the values represented by the landed gentry of England. The homes and the patrons that people these poems are not in all cases of the nobility, but they are all eminent examples of the English reliance on the land itself as the basic, stable, indispensable form of property that maintains a nation no matter what political, social, or religious convulsions may disrupt the constitutional order. The point of view shared by Jonson, Carew, Marvell, and Pope is in many ways related to the picture of the world I have characterised as 'pastoral'. Simplicity is the ultimate value in manners, artistic style, even in eating and drinking; and the reluctance to compete with the court and the city in pursuit of novelty and extravagance is equally essential in the world of old mansions and bountiful squires. Very often the apparent democracy of the manners of the 'great hall' is deceptive; it is really only a vivid demonstration of the meaning of *noblesse oblige*, and none of our poets would have understood the modern, pejorative meaning of 'condescension'. The rural gentry of England took very seriously their responsibilities toward their tenants; in this case the dictates of political economy coincided very happily with the Christian teachings of the parson's homilies. Indeed, the lordly owners of the great estates understood the mingled privileges and obligations of 'divine right' almost as clearly as Charles I. To shun ostentation became nearly as urgent a duty as to care for the welfare of the families under the lord's jurisdiction. In this sense the art of government was seen to mirror both the state of the soul and the condition of his early estate.

Nevertheless, certain significant changes can be observed in the century-long development of the 'country house poem' between Jonson and Pope. The great houses of the sixteenth century had been centred on the great hall, where most of the family lived and most of the estate's business was done. The life was communal and crude in its amenities; and its relation to the traditions of the Anglo-Saxon moot-halls was strong. Beginning with the late years of James I's reign and extending well into Caroline times, the country house became more and more a showplace, dependent upon the talents of architects imported from France and Italy, and dedicated to progressively more elaborate displays and celebrations of state occasions. Decoration grew more independent of utility, and the appointments, the entertainment, and the food and drink became sumptuous to the point of uncontrolled luxury. By 1731 Pope could write of his emblematic villa of Timon:

> To compass this, his building is a Town,
> His pond an Ocean, his parterre a Down.   (105–6)

> Is this a dinner? this a Genial room?
> No, 'tis a Temple, and a Hecatomb.
> A solemn Sacrifice, perform'd in state,
> You drink by measure, and to minutes eat.   (155–8)

One of the main points in Jonson's 'To Penshurst' and Carew's 'To Saxham' had been the measure and proportion that governed the tables of Sidney and Crofts—the 'good sense' that Pope celebrates in 'To Burlington'. But the earlier poets had also made a point of describing the entertainments at Penshurst and Saxham in terms of the rural feast, replete with capons, nuts, apples, and 'rurall cake'.[1] The tenant farmer was as welcome as an unexpected visit from the King, and 'no man tells my cups; nor, standing by,/A waiter, doth my gluttony envy'.[2] Thus moderation is enlivened by freedom and good-fellowship, and the excesses of exotic gluttony and social pretension do not mar the simple warmth of the great country houses of this Golden Age of English hospitality. It is not difficult to see many connections between Jonson's and Carew's visions of the ideal state of social man and the dominant concepts of the pastoral tradition. The facts of social hierarchy are softened by the inherent democracy of the rustic world, and the philosophy of moderation is constantly exemplified in the very material furnishings of the lord's hall and board. Where there is no cramping desire for superior place there can be no envy to warp and wizen the traditional structure of country society. And it is important to the overt assumptions of the 'country house poem' that the buildings themselves were often mere renovations of the original manor-houses of the distant ancestors of the family. Not until later in the century did the fad for new and architecturally elaborate country houses make itself fully felt. The older buildings, which in their solidity and square simplicity seemed to the conservative poets easily available symbols of the virtues of their owners, were replaced by structures that bore witness only to the ephemeral artifice of man, and had no visual relation to either the site or to the civilisation that had called them into being. This had not been true in the great days of Elizabethan and Jacobean domestic architecture, which had created a style that expressed both unmistakable Englishness and also the growing prosperity of a country in transition between its agricultural past and its future economic predominance in Western Europe. Foreign architects and craftsmen were brought in to introduce to the English the latest styles of cultures that had developed their artistic tastes at the top of a very steep pyramid of social position. And the advocates of the historical English virtues realised, or thought they realised, that the ornate French and Italian styles could never represent faithfully the spirit of a landed society that entertained, as a matter of course, farmers and villagers in the squire's hall. Much of this feeling may have been the kind of nostalgic chauvinism that does not hesitate to misrepresent historical fact, and to which England was especially subject in the late days of Elizabeth's reign and in the more troubled portions of James 1's. But Jonson, Carew, Drayton, Daniel and others were, in a way, creating a national mythology for England, a mythology in which the supreme virtues were those of modesty and generosity. We can see it at work in Jonson's climactic compliment to Penshurst.

> Now, *Penshurst*, they that will proportion thee
> With other edifices, when they see
> Those proud, ambitious heaps, and nothing else,
> May say, their lords have built, but thy lord dwells.
>
> $(99-102)$[3]

Marvell's poem takes account of at least two aspects of the idea Jonson puts forward. The first stanza of 'Upon Appleton House' begins a discussion of the moral significance of the proportions of a noble building. And in stanza IX, while referring to a poem written by Fairfax himself to stand at the entrance to Appleton House,[4] Marvell alludes to the religious view that sees man only as a temporary sojourner on earth.

> The House was built upon the Place
> Only as for *a Mark of Grace*;
> And for an *Inn* to entertain
> Its *Lord* a while, but not remain. $(69-72)$

The Protestant ethic had rejuvenated the belief that material wealth was given by God in 'stewardship' to its possessors on earth, and it was this idea that helped to support the tenets by which men like Fairfax guided their actions as landowners and great lords. Like the king himself, they had been granted by Divine Providence possessions and privileges that yet carried with them important responsibilities toward their dependents. Furthermore, the Protestant belief that each man rehearsed in some measure the life of Christ was also implicit in the image of the world as an inn; and Fairfax's poem makes it clear that in calling Appleton House an inn he was also referring to the world in which man lived so short a part of his eternal life.

But Marvell's poem is never overburdened by religious reference; the 'country house poem' was essentially a secular form, even though the social values it encompassed were usually related to a particular religious world-view. Again we observe how intimately the two sets of ideas were associated in Renaissance England. As Miss Røstvig points out,[5] the inspiration for the genre came originally from Roman poets, and particularly from Martial (*Epigrams*, III 58) and Horace (*Epodes*, II). Within the classical tradition, the praise of country life was based on the wholesome moderation of rural living, the possibility of contentment with a small, choice acquaintance, and on the continuation of familial and cultural traditions in a place and in a manner untouched by the shifting fads of the city. All this is incorporated into the seventeenth-century genre, but its scope is enlarged by the addition of Christian concepts of the virtue of contemplative retirement and the rejection of worldly temptations. The latter is no longer the pleasant duty of the man of intelligence and taste, but a duty enjoined upon him by God.

'Upon Appleton House', however, goes beyond these typical concerns into various digressions that are more pertinently related to the recurrent problems and ideas of all Marvell's poetry. It is for this that it has often been criticised for lack of coherent structure, and even for lacking the appearance of any internal principle of organisation.[6] Indeed, it would be hazardous to suggest one theme, one motif, or one dominant idea that can be described as central to 'Upon Appleton House'. The poem is divided, roughly, into six parts of varying length: the introduction on Appleton House itself; the story of Isabella Thwaites and William Fairfax; the description of Lord Fairfax's garden; the descent into the meadows; the poet's retreat into the woods; and the final address to Mary Fairfax, daughter of the Lord General and Marvell's pupil. There is no narrative or rhetorical device that holds these sections together in any very obvious way; but as the poet's mind and eye turn from one object of concentration to another, we shall see that the meanings he draws from what he sees and what he remembers *are* related, and that they constitute an inventory of most of his characteristic poetic subjects. In particular, the process and the concept of metamorphosis will assume great importance in this very long poem. . . .

Before Marvell can examine the natural scene that encloses the little world of the Fairfax home and family, he must give due attention to another requirement of the 'country house poem'— the genealogy of the hero. The convention has clear, if slight, connections with similar elements in the epic; but it is especially fitting in a poem dedicated to Fairfax. For one thing he himself was intensely interested in family history; and for another, the consciousness of personal tradition is an important part of the sense of legitimacy that supports the governance and ethos of the landed gentry. Marvell was obviously attracted by any idea or institution that promised a reasoned stability to any human system; one of the great problems he faced in writing 'An Horatian Ode' was the morality and wisdom of destroying 'the great Work of Time'. The recounting of the hero's ancestry in 'Upon Appleton House', especially since it was a history of such public and military distinction, was vital to the purpose of establishing Fairfax as a figure who might serve as a model to a warring and chaotic nation. . . .

. . . The order and serenity of the garden at Nun Appleton has summoned, irresistibly, the memory of the 'Garden-state' of Britain before the Civil War, and the comparisons between that age and the mythic state of Paradise are not veiled in the least by conceited diction. The image of England as a type of the Garden of Eden was sanctioned by traditional legends and sagas, as well as by the common Elizabethan practice. But Marvell's appeal is given added force by the verisimilitude of the analogy he draws while describing Fairfax's well-disciplined realm. The loss of Paradise is the tragic event that goes almost unmentioned, but it is interesting to notice that Marvell, as well as Milton,[7] thinks of Eden not only as Heaven's most perfect earthly creation, but also as a symbol of perfection constantly threatened by 'the World'. The conditions of external reality have for the moment impinged on the playful contentment of Fairfax's floral regiment, and we are reminded not only of the events of the Civil War itself but also of the failure of the convent to protect itself ultimately from the brute force (albeit legal and justified) of Fairfax's ancestor. To

see 'Upon Appleton House' as a fanciful retreat from political
reality into a world of rural mindlessness is to misread a poem
which at almost every moment is torn between the divergent
demands of the world and the self.

Nor would Marvell elevate the condition of the English polity
to an image of the fall of mankind if he were merely playing with
the analogy. England had indeed become a 'Wast',[8] and men
whose loyalties were attached to ancient institutions and the
stable procedures of monarchical successions found the knowledge of mortality in the events of 1642–1649. What Marvell
cannot say, and what the poem finally cannot tell us, is what was
the 'luckless Apple' that brought this all about—was it worldly
ambition, pride, or the nerveless taste for ease that banished
Englishmen from the paradise Providence gave to them
particularly?

When, in stanza XLII, the military metaphor is applied once
more to gardens and flowers, it is with the purpose of recalling
that imaginary Golden Age from which contemporary England
has declined. Then 'Gardens only had their Towrs,/And all the
Garrisons were Flowrs' (331–2); and the point is that this was
once the reality, not the mock-reality of Fairfax's flowery militia,
whose mimicking of the discipline of the Parliamentary army
becomes somehow sinister when seen against the background of a
true pastoral, where military discipline was a symbol only of
innate natural order. The change is a bitter one for Marvell, as is
evident in the tone of the transformations in stanza XLIII.

> The *Gardiner* had the *Souldiers* place,
> And his more gentle Forts did trace.
> The Nursery of all things green
> Was then the only *Magazeen*.
> The *Winter Quarters* were the Stoves,
> Where he the tender Plants removes.
> But War all this doth overgrow:
> We Ord'nance Plant and Powder sow.   (337–44)

. . . With the return to the natural setting we find a return to
the conceits and ambiguous diction of the lines on the flower-
garden.

> The sight does from these *Bastions* ply,
> Th' invisible *Artilery*;
> And at proud *Cawood Castle* seems
> To point the *Battery* of its Beams.   (361–4)

Now the armament of the flowery fortress is alleged to be the sense of sight itself, and the eye's beam is compared to the shot from a cannon. The idea allows Marvell a joke at the expense of the Archbishop of York, but it also redirects our attention to the world surrounding Nun Appleton, since the poet is about to descend into the meadows he has already mentioned, and thus begin the third major portion of the poem. He is moving (or 'escaping', as some critics will have it) from the world of ordered artifice to the realm of nature, the meadows; but he will find that the grass, as reflecting symbol of mortal life, is subject to the same vicissitudes that spoil the perfection of the garden and the greater world outside—and there will follow the further retreat to the solitude of the woods. But first he must undergo the transformations of the strange meadows.

> And now to the Abbyss I pass
> Of that unfathomable Grass,
> Where Men like Grashoppers appear,
> But Grashoppers are Gyants there.   (369–72)

Whether Marvell is remembering Lovelace's poem 'The Grasse–hopper'[9] or intending a biblical allusion,[10] the dominant ideas of the passage are the inversion of human and natural characteristics, and the suggestion of the strange visions that arise when the human consciousness immerses itself in the instinctive processes of growing things. Not only is the meadow an abyss, but it is easily and cogently compared to a sea, and the analogy obviously attracts Marvell. He imagines the mowers diving into the depths of the green sea, and the wit with which he compares sailors taking a sounding to the men who 'bring up Flow'rs so to be seen,/And prove they've at the Bottom been' (383–4), is a lighter version of the extraordinary but similar image in 'Mourning'.

It must be remembered that these are not the meadows with which the Mower Damon was so intimately identified; the poet sees them as a scene of successive wondrous changes, even comparing them to the elaborate stage machinery of the court masques. Marvell uses imagery of the theatre rarely, but always with clear intent;[11] and here his purpose is to strengthen the impression of kaleidoscopic variety in nature, which in turn contributes to our sense of patterns and discipline gone awry. The ordinarily sympathetic pastoral scene now presents itself as a shifting vision of man's history and human folly, so that it becomes more exemplary than comforting. Not only do the visions change as Marvell watches, but we must also be aware of the gradual but unswerving succession of the seasons that moves through the poem as the poet moves through the grounds of Nun Appleton. All of nature is in flux, constantly—and 'Upon Appleton House' is one major evidence that Marvell did not long conceive of the natural world as a static emblem of metaphysical truths. He shows himself unfailingly aware of the unceasing process of metamorphosis that dominates both nature and human society. . . .

. . . Marvell holds fast to his perception of metamorphosis in all natural changes. The river, for example, 'makes the Meadow truly be/(What it but seem'd before) a Sea' (467–8); and Marvell finds an instance of his favourite phenomenon, the inclusion of a thing within itself, as 'The River in it self is drown'd' (471). And with the overwhelming inundation,[12] Marvell brings down the curtain on the changing stage of the meadows at the moment of supreme chaos, when denizens of sea and land have exchanged their habitats and every semblance of natural order has disappeared from the meadows that not long before were marked by at least the mock-discipline of the pillaging hay-gatherers. The sea may, when calm, be a true and reflecting surface, but in moments of disorder it threatens human communities—and the world of the fields—with monstrous disruption. It is from this confused terror that the poet retreats in stanza LXI.

> But I, retiring from the Flood,
> Take Sanctuary in the Wood;
> And, while it lasts, my self imbark
> In this yet green, yet growing Ark.   (481–4)

There can be no doubt of the biblical allusions in these lines, and Marvell goes on to point out that Noah might well have chosen the wood for *his* Ark from this venerable forest. The mention of 'Sanctuary' shows that Marvell is aware of both the allusions to Noah's Ark and the Ark of the Covenant; and it is possible that the confidence with which he 'imbarks' himself (a pun on 'embark' and 'bark') is meant to be contrasted with the arrogance with which man, the 'Mote of Dust', 'imparked' himself in stanza III. But the word-play does not obscure the sense of safe and virtuous solitude that Marvell, once again, discovers amongst the trees.

The change in the poet's mood recalls the part in the poem that Fairfax and Nun Appleton are meant to play; the trees are made the subject of an extended conceit intended as a compliment to the families of Fairfax and Vere, which includes a reference to the military fame of both houses.

> Of whom though many fell in War,
> Yet more to Heaven shooting are:
> And, as they Natures Cradle deckt,
> Will in green Age her Hearse expect.   (493-6)[13]

Not only are the trees regarded as emblems of the bravery of their masters, but they are characterised as living pillars of continuity. To have 'deckt' 'Natures Cradle' is remarkable enough, but to live long enough to 'expect' 'her Hearse' is to accomplish a miracle of longevity that can be attributed only to the abstract essence of a political institution. Marvell adds to the wit of the concept by the paradoxical 'green Age', a quality that can be posited only of trees and other growing things.

The following stanzas display the accuracy of visual observation for which Marvell has often been praised.[14] But every detail of the description of the wood is made to serve the end of a metaphysical conceit. Seen from afar the trees seem to form a solid mass, so bulky and coherent that it suggests a *'Fifth Element'* (497-502); within the wood, the trees appear as columns supporting *'Corinthean Porticoes'*[15] and the wood itself a temple whose choristers are the singing birds. Once again the process of animating inanimate objects is reversed, and growing things are said to follow the designs of architecture. Marvell also distinguishes between the studious songs of the nightingale and the emblematic love-songs of the stock doves, which give him the opportunity for some plays on words in the style of his early hyperbolical, courtly verse. Stanzas LXVII and LXVIII are curiosities of ornithology; they tell us more about Marvell's interest in the humanseeming habits of certain birds than they do about the greater concerns of the poem. But he finds a sermon in the behaviour of the woodpecker (hewel), which reminds him both of the actual woodcutter and the allegorical effects of sin on the human soul.

> Who could have thought the *tallest Oak*
> Should fall by such a *feeble Strok'*!
>
> Nor would it, had the Tree not fed
> A *Traitor-worm*, within it bred.
> (As first our *Flesh* corrupt within
> Tempts impotent and bashful *Sin*.)   (551–6)

The hewel, like sin, is only the instrument that brings about the fall that our innate fleshly corruption has already made inevitable.

The thought, which in another context might be expected to elicit weighty pronouncements, propels the poet into an easy and supremely witty transformation of his own.

> Thus I, *easie Philosopher*,
> Among the *Birds* and *Trees* confer:
> And little now to make me, wants
> Or of the *Fowles*, or of the *Plants*.
> Give me but Wings as they, and I
> Streight floting on the Air shall fly:
> Or turn me but, and you shall see
> I was but an inverted Tree.   (561–8)

. . . Thus far in the poem Marvell has simply observed and interpreted nature, and has not extracted any of the 'mystical' truths that the created world was supposed to express about the structure of the entire intelligible universe. Nature, in 'Upon Appleton House', will not remain static and emblematic long enough for Marvell to launch the conventional disquisition on its divinely symbolic essence. The leaves and ivy behave like the fruits in 'The Garden', reaching out and enveloping the poet in an *'antick Cope'* of verdure so that he looks 'Like some great *Prelate of the Grove'* (592). But the disguise penetrates no deeper than the surface, since the poet's bishopric is populated only by trees. There is no place here for either the outward rituals or deeper religious meanings of the Church. Nor does the poet behave as a prelate when, 'languishing with ease' he rests on 'Pallets swoln of Velvet Moss' and enjoys the ministrations of the breezes which 'winnow from the Chaff [his] Head'. The unassertive and undemanding sympathy of nature clarifies his imagination and purges it of the disturbed images that had crowded in while he viewed the garden and the meadow. He discovers the final, impregnable retreat for the mind that can read *'Natures mystick Book'* but can discern only the mockery of true order and sanctity in the world that man has touched or despoiled.

> How safe, methinks, and strong, behind
> These Trees have I incamp'd my Mind;
> Where Beauty, aiming at the Heart,
> Bends in some Tree its useless Dart;
> And where the World no certain Shot
> Can make, or me it toucheth not.
> But I on it securely play,
> And gaul its Horsemen all the Day.   (601–8)

This is another version of the metaphorical fortress, but it does not betray its pretence, as does Fairfax's garden, by assuming the same shapes and proportions of the evils it is meant to exclude. The use of 'incamp'd' suggests that Marvell wanted to recall the military imagery of the opening stanzas, and also to refine the distinction he had made already between 'impark'd' and 'embark'd'. The two enemies against which the wood defends him are 'Beauty' and 'the World'; 'The Garden' shows how nature can purify the passion of sexual love, and the forest at Nun Appleton now shuts out the world of civil war, the world that was playfully but mistakenly symbolised by the mowers in the meadows. Secure in his retirement, and in amused defiance of the mortal dangers he has escaped, the poet gives himself for a moment to an image of vigorous activity: 'But I on it securely play,/And gaul its Horsemen all the Day' (607–8). The joke is that the poet has conquered the horrors of wartime savagery by triumphing over the cavalry that was the greatest weapon on both sides in the Civil War; he 'gauls' the riders as they have spurred their horses and as their image has driven the poet into his forest retreat.

But even this safety is precarious, and so he appeals to the plants to force their active sympathy still further and bind him permanently to the spot.[16] He is conscious, however, that the analogy between the human spirit and the natural forces that govern the plants is an abstraction whose source is in the imagination; and it is that mental faculty that divides the human and the natural ultimately and decrees that man will be both destroyer and gardener. In anticipation of his own inevitable defection, he pleads,

> But, lest your Fetters prove too weak,
> Ere I your Silken Bondage break,
> Do you, *O Brambles*, chain me too,
> And courteous *Briars* nail me through.   (613–16)

The last lines are shocking, not simply because Marvell seems to be alluding to the Crucifixion, but because any such reference is beside the point here. Only by stretching the limits of tolerance can we see that Marvell is asking to be martyred by the trees so that he can extend his triumph over the world eternally. The analogy is false in so far as his faith is supported by nature, and since the hostile world of war and society has been defeated in the very passage that leads to this climax. And the poet abandons it rather swiftly in order to return to the vision of the meadows, from which the flooded river has receded. . . .

. . . The appearance of Mary Fairfax in stanza LXXXII draws him back forcibly into the world of order and value that he left for the spiritual simplicity of the forest. In the final fifteen stanzas of 'Upon Appleton House' Mary will assume metaphorical proportions comparable to the Elizabeth Drury of Donne's 'Anniversaries'; she is now 'her *Ages Aw*' but more important she will become a figure of hopeful prophecy for the restoration of stable and ordered peace in England. In recognition of her imagined power, Marvell shamefacedly puts away his 'idle Utensils' lest Mary's 'judicious Eyes/Should with such Toyes a

Man surprize' (653–4). He defers to the necessity of returning to the ostensible concerns of the earlier part of the poem, and in doing so must assume a stance that belittles the delights and the surcease he had found in the wood. The pursuits are now called immature that a short while ago were the source of ecstasy; the hurried shift in viewpoint is almost a précis of the poem's method.

The decorum of compliment necessitates, in this case, the conceited diction that had begun the poem; but each conceit is used to advance the general argument of the compliment. Thus, since Mary must represent the civilised alternative to the wild and permissive disorder of Nature, Marvell first points out 'how loose Nature, in respect/To her, it self doth recollect' (657–8); and the pun on 'recollect' ('remember' and 'pull together again') intensifies the correspondence between the embarrassment of Nature and the poet's own shame at his idleness. The sun's behaviour in lines 661–4 both justifies the introduction of a night scene and does indirect homage to the innocence and chastity of the heroine.[17] . . .

. . . Mary shares the natural innocence of the trees, and thus justifies Marvell in calling her 'a *sprig of Misleto*' that 'On the *Fairfacian Oak* does grow'. The importance of lineal descent, the guarantee of legitimacy, is emphasised here as it had been in the long episode of William Fairfax and Isabella Thwaites earlier. And Marvell deals with the question of inheritance in lines that contrast illuminatingly with the final stanzas of 'The Picture of little T.C.':

> Whence, for some universal good,
> The *Priest* shall cut the sacred Bud;
> While her *glad Parents* most rejoice,
> And make their *Destiny* their *Choice*.   (741–4)

The implication, of course, is that this bud will be cut not for adornment but for grafting to another distinguished stock, as the Veres and the Fairfaxes combined to produce this unparalleled sprig. Marriage opens up the vistas of the future for Marvell, now that he has traced the history of the family and the estate from its source to its latest glory. He exhorts the 'Fields, Springs, Bushes, Flow'rs' to profit from Mary's presence while she remains unmarried (her chaste state is equated with 'studious Hours' as if

her pursuit of wisdom must cease with the end of her virginity),
and to 'preferr' themselves so that they will exceed the rest of
nature in the same degree that she surpasses all other women. To
substantiate the compliment Marvell adduces a number of
contemporary and legendary garden-seats of beauty—except
that Idalia and the Elysian Fields are scorned as unworthy of
being compared to the garden ruled by Mary Fairfax. But the
light arrogance of the exaggerated flattery dissolves in the
obviously sincere and hopeless sorrow of,

> 'Tis not, what once it was, the *World*;
> But a rude heap together hurl'd;
> All negligently overthrown,
> Gulfes, Deserts, Precipices, Stone.
> Your lesser *World* contains the same.
> But in more decent Order tame;
> *You Heaven's Center, Nature's Lap.*
> *And Paradice's only Map.*   (761–8)

Despite the demands made by the genre, this is not simply the
tone of courtly compliment. It is the pastoral lament for the lost
Golden Age; it could be a verse paraphrase of the tenor of Godfrey
Goodman's *The Fall of the World*, and it resonates to the same
notes of despair and disgust that inform Donne's 'An Anatomy of
the World'.[18] The bare, harsh stress on 'Stone' conveys exactly
the desolation of this view of the corrupt world of chaotic self-
seeking. And the integrity of Marvell's vision is assured in his
recognition that the 'lesser *World*' (which is both Mary Fairfax
and Nun Appleton) is made up of the same intractably decadent
materials as the great world, or macrocosm, that it has come to
symbolise through the various movements of the poem. 'More
decent Order tame' is the only bulwark, passive as it is, that can
shore up man's ruins against the assaults of the rude world; it
governs the military garden of Lord Fairfax, it directs the
seasonal transformations of the river and the meadow, and it
gives Mary Fairfax a pattern to impose upon unruly nature so
that it may best fulfil its potentialities. And because there is still
hope that Mary, or what she symbolises, will restore the garden-
state from which England has banished itself, she is called
'*Heaven's Center, Nature's Lap*'—the pole-star of spiritual value and

the nursery of all things green. The irony in the last line is neither
sharp nor critical; if anything, it is a pathetic admission that
beneath the high-flown flattery there is a disconcerting core of
truth. Although 'only' commonly meant 'foremost',[19] it has its
modern meaning as well in the last line—and Marvell's point is
that all there can be of Paradise for man is contained in the
'decent Order' of Nun Appleton, despite its stones and precipices.
The imposition of a meaningful pattern on nature is man's
peculiar ability; yet it can never eradicate the effects of man's evil
propensities or the mindless chaos of unformed nature.

The final stanza of the poem has attracted the same charges of
irrelevance and extraneousness that are usually laid to the end of
'The Garden'. It is true that after the profound and moving
statement of stanza LXXXXVI this conceited imitation of
Cleveland[20] is responsible for a disconcerting lapse of tone. But
the poem is framed in passages of precise observation, as if to
assure us that all the wide-ranging thoughts have started from a
firm centre of physical reality. That reality has undergone
uncounted transmutations within seven hundred-odd lines, and
even at the end of the long season's vigil Marvell's mind is still
alert to the analogical possibilities of the odd sight presented by
the fishermen carrying their coracles. With 'their *Heads* in their
Canoos' the fishermen provide yet another instance of the
principle of inversion that has motivated so many of the
metaphors and the incidents of 'Upon Appleton House'. And
'rational *Amphibii*' is indeed a pertinent phrase for the human
figure, which in this poem has been thrust below the seas, has
lived through harvest and massacre, and finally immersed itself
in nature and felt its soul released from the galling bonds of the
world. The poet's life, if not his consciousness, has shown itself to
be 'amphibious', and the deliberate confusion among the
elements and the senses has in some ways sustained the metaphorical modes of the entire work.

Thus there is no strain in the comparison with which 'Upon
Appleton House' ends; the night sky begins to look like the dark
shell that covers the men's heads, the hemisphere has become
dark, and the time has come for the poet to go back through the
woods and meadows he has known and described, and finally
through the emblematic door that opens the poem. We have
been given an exhaustive and varied picture of the dangerously

disordered state of England and the world; and we have learned
something of the 'green' virtues that may redeem them. The poet
has presented the opposed and complementary claims of the life
of public action and of private retirement; and to call his attitude
'complex' is to do a disservice to the way in which his reactions to
the two ways of life interact with and modify each other. The
safety and solitude of the woods attract Marvell almost irresistibly, yet his feelings for the profundity and worth of the roots of
human society will not permit him to dismiss responsibilities
outside the garden and the forests. The fluctuation of the poem
between poles of realism and symbolic extravagance reflects the
constant oscillation between these two poles of moral action. If
there is any resolution it is in the metaphors themselves that form
the substance of 'Upon Appleton House'.

SOURCE: extracts from *Marvell's Pastoral Art* (1970), pp.
210–14, 220, 227–9, 230–1, 234–7, 238–9, 241, 243–6.

NOTES

[The Notes here have been revised and
renumbered from those in the original
version—Ed.]

1. Jonson, 'To Penshurst', 51: *The Complete Poetry of Ben Jonson*,
ed. W. B. Hunter, Jnr (New York, 1963), pp. 77–81.

2. Ibid., 67–8.

3. Cf. Carew, 'To my friend G. N. from Wrest', 20–4: *Poems*,
pp. 86–9.

4. See Margoliouth (ed.), *Poems and Letters of Andrew Marvell*, I,
p. 231, for Fairfax's poem (from Bodleian MS Fairfax, 40).

5. *The Happy Man*, p. 90. Miss Røstvig actually cites Martial,
Epigrams, X 47, but this seems to me less useful as an illustrative source
than the description of Baiain villa. See also her article, 'Benlowes,
Marvell and the Divine Casimire', *Huntington Library Quarterly*, XVIII, I
(Nov. 1954), pp. 13–35.

6. Some recent critiques of the poem, while acknowledging its
apparent lack of coherence, attempt to provide a rationale for its
structure: see M. S. Røstvig, ' "Upon Appleton House" and the
Universal History of Man', *English Studies*, XLII (1961), pp. 337–51; D.
C. Allen, 'Upon Appleton House', in *Image and Meaning*, pp. 115–53;

Tayler, *Nature and Art in Renaissance Literature*, pp. 150–4; Toliver, *Marvell's Ironic Vision*, pp. 113–29; Kitty Scoular, *Natural Magic* (Oxford, 1965), pp. 120–90; M. J. K. O'Loughlin, 'This Sober Frame: A Reading of "Upon Appleton House" ', in G. DeF. Lord (ed.), *Andrew Marvell: A Collection of Critical Essays* (Englewood Cliffs, N.J., 1968), pp. 120–42.

7. See the long passage in *Paradise Lost*, IV, 268–85, where Eden is compared with numerous gardens where treasures were hidden and protected from external dangers.

8. Contrast this with the 'sweetly wast' park of Nun Appleton in line 78.

9. *Poems*, pp. 38–40; Lovelace's poem is a humorous address to the grasshopper on the dangers of life amidst nature.

10. Miss Joan Grundy, in 'Marvell's Grasshoppers', *Notes and Queries*, n.s. IV, 4 (April 1957), p. 142, cites Numbers *xiii* 32–3. Legouis later rejected more extensive suggestions of Old Testament parallels by Miss Grundy in 'Upon Appleton House'.

11. Cf. 'An Horatian Ode', 53–8; and 'A Poem upon the Death of O.C.', 7–12.

12. Cf. Horace, *Odes*, I 2; and Ovid, *Metamorphoses*, I.

13. Margoliouth (op. cit., I, p. 234) remarks that the lines probably refer to the felling of trees during wartime. The conceit applies equally well to the trees and to the scions of Fairfax and of Vere.

14. The lines on the hewel (woodpecker) and 'hatching thrastles shining eye' (537–44, 532) are most often quoted in this regard. Marvell's technique of passing from one observation quickly to another is illuminated by a remark of Miss Mourgues's (*Metaphysical Baroque and Précieuse Poetry*, pp. 93–4) on similar devices in the poetry of Théophile, Saint-Amant and Tristan. She says they 'consider nature as a succession of landscapes to be enjoyed for their own sake and depicted with some precision; and precision for them consists in putting the stress on concrete details in landscape. . . . The second noticeable aspect of their technique in landscape painting is to pass from one object to another without supplying the connection . . .'

15. The choice of the Corinthian order is exact, since its capitals are decorated heavily with leaves. Marvell even uses the technical architectural term 'order' in line 507.

16. As Margoliouth notes (op. cit., I, p. 235), 'gadding vines' seems to echo 'Lycidas', 40.

17. Cf. Milton's early, Italianate and notorious conceit in 'On the Morning of Christ's Nativity', 229–31: *Complete Poems*, p. 49.

18. There are verbal similarities in Henry More's 'Ad Paronem': 'A rude confused heap of ashes dead', *Philosophical Poems*, p.

136; and in a poem by John Joynes in *Lachrymae Musarum*, 'On the Incomparable Lord Hastings': 'and now this carcase, World,/Is into her first, rude, dark Chaos, hurl'd'. This image derives ultimately from Ovid, *Metamorphoses*, I, 7.

    19. Cf. *Hamlet*, III ii 132.

    20. Cf. Cleveland, 'Square-Cap', 19: *Poems*, pp. 43–5.

Joseph H. Summers   On 'The Picture of little T.C.' (1953)

. . . 'The Picture of little T.C. in a Prospect of Flowers' is not a graceful trifle which somehow goes wrong. It is a fine poem, and it elucidates Marvell's central vision of man and nature:

I

See with what simplicity
This Nimph begins her golden daies!
In the green Grass she loves to lie,
And there with her fair Aspect tames
The Wilder flow'rs, and gives them names:
But only with the Roses playes;
      And them does tell
What Colour best becomes them, and what Smell.

II

Who can foretel for what high cause
This Darling of the Gods was born!
Yet this is She whose chaster Laws
The wanton Love shall one day fear,
And, under her command severe,
See his Bow broke and Ensigns torn.
      Happy, who can
Appease this virtuous Enemy of Man!

III

O then let me in time compound,
And parly with those conquering Eyes:
Ere they have try'd their force to wound,
Ere, with their glancing wheels, they drive
In Triumph over Hearts that strive,
And them that yield but more despise.
                Let me be laid,
Where I may see thy Glories from some shade.

IV

Mean time, whilst every verdant thing
It self does at thy Beauty charm,
Reform the errours of the Spring;
Make that the Tulips may have share
Of sweetness, seeing they are fair;
And Roses of their thorns disarm:
                But most procure
That Violets may a longer Age endure.

V

But O young beauty of the Woods,
Whom Nature courts with fruits and flow'rs,
Gather the Flow'rs, but spare the Buds;
Lest *Flora* angry at thy crime,
To kill her Infants in their prime,
Do quickly make th' Example Yours;
                And, ere we see,
Nip in the blossome all our hopes and Thee.

The opening stanza of the poem tells us of the child's alienation
from and superiority to nature, as well as of her delight in it. Her
apparently successful imposition of her own order and value on
nature raises inevitably the question of the prospect of time, and
we see prophetically in the second stanza her future triumph over
'wanton Love'—and over man. Not a combatant, the speaker of
the poem resolves to observe the dazzling scene from the shade
which allows vision, for the god-like glories cannot be viewed

immediately by profane man. If he is to admire her triumph, it must be from a distance where there is no fear of its destructiveness. With the 'Mean time' of the fourth stanza we are back at the present prospect, and the observer from his advantageous point of view advises the present T. C. At the golden moment when 'every verdant thing' charms itself at her beauty, she is instructed to prepare for her future career by reforming the 'errours of the Spring'. At first it seems, or perhaps would seem to a child, an almost possible command. With the talismanic power of her 'fair Aspect' she already 'tames/The Wilder flow'rs, and gives them names', and she tells the roses 'What Colour best becomes them, and what Smell'. At least within the circle of her immediate view she may, perhaps, by a judicious bouquet arrangement cause the tulips to share in sweetness, and it is possible to disarm roses of their thorns with assiduous labor. But the thing which should be 'most' procured is impossible for the human orderer even within his small area. And all of it is, of course, impossible if all the 'errours of the Spring' are in question. For, in comparison either with the triumph of T. C. or the vision of Eden, Spring is full of errors; the decorative details suggest exactly how far nature fails to sustain human visions of propriety, delight, and immortality. T. C. and the idealising aspect of man wish delight and beauty and goodness to be single, but they cannot find such singleness within the promising verdancy of nature; if they desire it they must impose it on nature or must seek it in an 'unnatural' or supernatural world. The tulips show how improperly the delights of the senses are separated in this world; the roses with their thorns traditionally indicate the conjunction of pain and pleasure, the hidden hurts lying under the delights of the senses; and the transience of the violets is a perpetual reminder of the mortality of life and innocence and beauty. The description of the preceding triumph is placed in a doubtful light. If T. C.'s reformation of floral errors is so doomed, how much real hope or fear can there be of her reformation of the errors of that higher order, man? Is the former description a fantasy, ideal yet frightening, of what might happen if the superhuman power as well as the superhuman virtue were granted, a fantasy proceeding from the observer's sharing for one moment the simplicity of the nymph?

In the exclamatory warning of the final stanza the observer

and the reader see the picture of little T. C. in the full prospect of
time which the flowers have furnished. At the present moment
'Nature courts' her 'with fruits and flow'rs' as a superior being;
she represents the promise of an order higher than we have
known. But she is also the 'young beauty of the Woods', and she is
a 'Bud'. The child of nature as well as its potential orderer, she
shares the mortality as well as the beauty of the flowers; her own
being, in the light of the absolute, is as 'improper' as are the tulips
or the roses. The former vision of her triumph implied full
recognition of only one half of her relationship to the fruits and
flowers. The introduction of Flora reminds us more sharply than
anything else in the poem of the entire relationship. However
lacking in the ideal, Flora has her own laws which man violates at
the peril of self-destruction. Flora decrees that life shall continue:
the infants shall not be killed 'in their prime'—either in their
moment of ideal promise or in their first moment of conception.
The sexual concerns which have been suggested throughout the
poem are made explicit in the final stanza. The picture in the
central stanzas of the complete triumph of T. C., the absolute
rule of human notions of propriety, has inevitably meant that
'wanton Love's' bow will be broken, his ensigns torn: there will
be no more marriages. With a recognition of mortality and of the
power of Flora, we recognise also the doom of such a triumph, for
both the ideal and the reality will soon die, and there is no
prospect of renewal in future 'T. C.s' The conclusion, however,
is neither a Renaissance nor a modern 'naturalism'. Because
perfect fulfilment is impossible, man is not therefore to abandon
his attempts at perfection. T. C. is allowed and even commanded
to 'Gather the Flow'rs', to expend her present and her future
energies in ordering the natural nearer to the ideal pattern—so
long as she spares the buds. The qualification is all important.
Man must beware of attempting to anticipate heaven by
imposing the ideal absolutely on earth. The killing of the infants
in their prime is not only a crime against Flora but against all the
gods, for man is never free to commit either murder or suicide in
the pursuit of the abstract ideal. The human triumph must
function within and wait upon the fulness of time. It must
recognise the real and individual as well as the ideal and the
general or it becomes a horror. The ending of the poem revalues
everything which has gone before. 'Ere we see' may mean

something equivalent to 'in the twinkling of an eye'; it certainly means, 'Before we see what will become of you and the vision of a new and higher order.' What will be nipped 'in the blossom', in the first full flowering, unless the warning is heeded will be not only 'all our hopes' (our hopes of the idealised child and of a possible new order, our hopes of love and of a new generation), but also 'Thee', the living child.

'The Picture of little T. C. in a Prospect of Flowers' is characteristic of Marvell's poetry both in its complexity and in its subtle use of superficially 'romantic' or decorative detail. It may remind us of modern poetry, but ultimately Marvell is both more complex and more assured of his meanings than are most of the moderns. Marvell does not present a *persona* simply and finally torn between this world and the next, distracted by the sensuous while attempting to achieve a spiritual vision. For Marvell, as for most Renaissance poets, the perception of a dilemma was not considered a sufficient occasion for a poem. Marvell made precise the differences between the values of time and of eternity. He recognised that man exists and discovers his values largely within time; he also believed that those values could be ultimately fulfilled only outside time. The recognition and the belief did not constitute a paralysing dilemma. Each of his early poems implies the realisation that any action or decision costs something; yet each presents a precise stance, an unique position and a decision taken at one moment with a full consciousness of all the costs. The costs are counted, but not mourned; the position is taken, the poem is written, with gaiety. . . .

SOURCE: extract from 'Marvell's "Nature"' *Journal of English Literary History*, xx (June 1953), pp. 130–4.

SELECT BIBLIOGRAPHY

The following list does not include books or articles from which material is included in this Casebook.

TEXTS

E. S. Donno (ed.), *Andrew Marvell: The Complete Poems* (Harmondsworth, 1972).

W. A. McQueen and K. A. Rockwell (eds.), *The Latin Poetry of Andrew Marvell* (Chapel Hill, 1964).

H. M. Margoliouth (ed.), *The Poems and Letters of Andrew Marvell*, 2 vols (Oxford, 1927); 2nd edn (1952); 3rd edn revd by P. Legouis and E. E. Duncan-Jones (1971).

BIOGRAPHY

P. Legouis, *André Marvell, Poète, Puritain, Patriote, 1621–1678* (Paris and London, 1928); abridged, translated and revised as *Andrew Marvell: Poet, Puritan, Patriot* (Oxford, 1965; revised 1968).

CRITICISM

(a) *Books on Marvell*

A. E. Berthoff, *The Resolved Soul* (Princeton, N.J., 1970).

M. C. Bradbrook and M. G. Lloyd Thomas, *Andrew Marvell* (Cambridge, 1940; corrected, 1962).

R. L. Brett (ed.), *Andrew Marvell: Essays on the Tercentenary of his Death* (Oxford, for University of Hull, 1979).

J. Carey (ed.), *Andrew Marvell: A Critical Anthology* (Baltimore and

Harmondsworth, 1969). Wide selection, mainly of modern criticism with full and incisive introductions.

E. S. Donno (ed.), *Andrew Marvell: The Critical Heritage* (London and Boston, Mass., 1978). Quotations of critics from Marvell's own time to T. S. Eliot.

J. B. Leishman, *The Art of Marvell's Poetry* (London, 1966). His uncompleted work edited by the late John Butt: expands the article reproduced in this Casebook.

H. E. Toliver, *Marvell's Ironic Vision* (New Haven, Conn., 1965).

J. M. Wallace, *Destiny His Choice: The Loyalism of Andrew Marvell* (Cambridge, 1968). Includes consideration of 'An Horatian Ode' and 'Upon Appleton House'.

(b) *Books containing material on Marvell*

D. C. Allen, *Image and Meaning: Metaphoric Tradition in Renaissance Poetry* (Baltimore, 1960): 'The Nymph Complaining . . .' and 'Upon Appleton House'.

J. Bennett, *Five Metaphysical Poets* (Cambridge, 1964).

J. V. Cunningham, *Logic and Lyric—Marvell, Dunbar and Nashe: Tradition and Poetic Structure* (Denver, 1960).

J. E. Duncan, *The Revival of Metaphysical Poetry* (Minneapolis, 1959).

A. E. Dyson and J. Lovelock, *Masterful Images: English Poetry from Metaphysicals to Romantics* (London, 1976): 'The Picture of little T. C.'

R. Ellrodt, *Les Poètes Métaphysiques Anglais*, Vol. II, Part I (Paris, 1960).

W. Empson, *Seven Types of Ambiguity* (London, 1930; 2nd edition, revised 1947).

W. Empson, *Some Versions of Pastoral* (London, 1936; 2nd edition, 1950).

W. H. Halewood, *The Poetry of Grace: Reformation Themes and Structures in English Seventeenth-Century Poetry* (New Haven, Conn., 1970).

C. Hill, *Puritanism and Revolution: Studies in Interpretation of the English Revolution of the Seventeenth Century* (London, 1958). An attempt at Marxist interpretation of Marvell.

F. R. Leavis, *Revaluation: Tradition and Development in English Poetry* (London, 1936).

R. Nevo, *The Dial of Virtue: A Study of Poems on Affairs of State in the Seventeenth Century* (Princeton, N. J., 1963). 'An Horatian Ode' and the political poems.

M-S. Røstvig, *The Happy Man: Studies in the Metamorphosis of a Classical Ideal, 1600–1700*, 2 vols (Oslo and Oxford, 1958 and 1962): 'The Garden', 'Upon Appleton House' and 'Upon the Hill and

Grove at Billborow'.

K. Scoular, *Natural Magic: Studies in the Presentation of English Poetry from Spenser to Milton* (Oxford, 1965): 'Upon Appleton House'.

S. Stewart, *The Enclosed Garden: The Tradition and the Image in Seventeenth-Century Poetry* (Madison, 1966): 'The Garden'.

H. R. Swardson, *Poetry and the Fountain of Light: Observations on the Conflict between Christian and Classical Traditions in Seventeenth-Century Poetry* (New York, 1962).

R. Tuve, *Elizabethan and Metaphysical Imagery: Renaissance Poetic and Twentieth-Century Critics* (Chicago, 1947).

J. Wain (ed.), *Interpretations* (London, 1955): 'An Horatian Ode', essay by L. D. Lerner.

R. C. Wallerstein, *Studies in Seventeenth-Century Poetic* (Madison, 1950).

(c) *Articles*

Cleanth Brooks, 'Criticism and Literary History: Marvell's "Horatian Ode"', *Sewanee Review*, 55 (1947), pp. 199–222.

D. Bush, 'Marvell's "Horatian Ode"', *Sewanee Review*, 60 (1952), pp. 363–76. In part a reply to Brooks, who commented further in *Sewanee Review*, 61, pp. 129–35.

B. Everett, 'Marvell's "The Mower's Song"', *Critical Quarterly*, 4 (1962), pp. 219–24.

S. L. Goldberg, 'Andrew Marvell', *Melbourne Critical Review*, 3 (1960), pp. 41–56.

M. Klonsky, 'A Guide through the Garden', *Sewanee Review*, 58 (1950), pp. 16–35.

L. Spitzer, 'Marvell's "The Nymph Complaining for the Death of Her Fawn": Sources versus Meaning', *Modern Language Quarterly*, 19 (1958), pp. 231–43.

R. H. Syfret, 'Marvell's "Horatian Ode"', *Review of English Studies*, new series, 12 (1961), pp. 160–72.

NOTES ON CONTRIBUTORS

A. ALVAREZ: critic and poet. His literary criticism includes a study of Samuel Beckett, and *The Shaping Spirit* (1958), *The School of Donne* (1961), *Beyond All This Fiddle* (1968) and *The Savage God* (1971).

H. C. BEECHING (1859–1919): theologian (Dean of Norwich) and man of letters. He composed *The Yattendon Hymnal* (with Robert Bridges), edited Milton and published several volumes of religious writings.

A. C. BENSON (1862–1925): prolific writer of short fictional and biographical books, essays and *belles-lettres*, and an assiduous diarist. As Master of Magdalene College, Cambridge (whose fortunes he restored), he established the Honorary Fellowship there held successively by Thomas Hardy, Rudyard Kipling and T. S. Eliot.

E. K. CHAMBERS (1866–1954): civil servant and literary critic. He is best known for his studies of the Elizabethan drama in general and on Shakespeare.

HARTLEY COLERIDGE (1796–1849): son of the poet, he was himself a poet and essayist.

ROSALIE COLIE: Professor of English, University of Toronto. Her publications include *Paradoxia Epidemica: The Renaissance Tradition of Paradox* (1966) and '*My Ecchoing Song': Andrew Marvell's Poetry of Criticism* (1970).

J. V. CUNNINGHAM: Professor of English at Brandeis University. His publications include *Woe and Wonder: The Emotional Effects of Shakespearean Tragedy* (1951), *Tradition and Poetic Structure* (1960) and also several volumes of poetry.

JOHN DOVE (fl. 1830): a Whig and a Dissenter, who also wrote about the Wesley family.

T. S. ELIOT (1888–1965): poet, dramatist and critic. His most important works of criticism are *The Sacred Wood* (1920) and *The Use of Poetry and Use of Criticism* (1933).

D. M. FRIEDMAN: teaches at the University of California, Berkeley.

EDMUND GOSSE (1849–1928): civil servant and literary critic in the older tradition of the civilised amateur. He was an early devotee of Ibsen and wrote on, among others, Donne, Congreve, Gray, Patmore and Swinburne, as well as a novel, *Father and Son*, about his own childhood. Knighted 1925.

S. C. HALL (1800–89): indefatigable journalist of literature and art.

WILLIAM HAZLITT (1778–1830): essayist, literary critic and political writer. He is best known for his writings on Shakespeare.

LEIGH HUNT (1784–1859): poet, essayist, critic and political writer. He edited *The Liberal*, with Byron (1822), *The Examiner* (1808–13) and *The Tatler* (1830–32).

FRANK KERMODE, King Edward VII Professor of English Literature, University of Cambridge. His publications include *Romantic Image* (1957), *The Sense of an Ending* (1967), *Continuities* (1968), *Modern Essays* (1971), *Renaissance Essays* (1973) and *The Classic* (1975).

J. B. LEISHMAN (1902–63) was Fellow of St John's College and Senior Lecturer in English Literature, University of Oxford. His publications include *The Metaphysical Poets* (1934), *The Monarch of Wit* (1951), *Translating Horace* (1956) and *Themes and Variations in Shakespeare's Sonnets* (1961).

ALICE MEYNELL (1847–1922): poet, essayist and critic. Her essays were published in *The Rhythm of Life* (1893), *The Children* (1896) and *The Spirit of Peace* (1898).

MARY RUSSELL MITFORD (1787–1855): essayist, playwright and novelist. She is best-known for *Our Village*, a collection of sketches based on her life in a Berkshire village.

JOHN ORMSBY (1829–95): mainly known as an early Alpinist, he wrote extensively on travel for several Victorian reviews.

EDGAR ALLAN POE (1809–49): American poet, short-story writer and critic, he was educated at school in England and at the University of Virginia. His life and work have attracted increasing attention from modern literary critics.

MAREN-SOFIE RØSTVIG: Professor of English at the University of Oslo.

JOSEPH H. SUMMERS: Professor of English, University of Rochester, New York. His publications include *The Muse's Method: An Introduction to 'Paradise Lost'* (1962), *The Lyric and Dramatic Milton* (1964) and a study of George Herbert.

E. W. TAYLER: Professor of English at Columbia University. His published work is mainly on seventeenth-century topics.

ALFRED TENNYSON, 1st Lord Tennyson (1809–1892): Poet Laureate from 1850. In memoirs and recollections by his contemporaries, and in his letters, he often reveals great critical perception.

CAPTAIN EDWARD THOMPSON (? 1738–86): naval captain and minor writer, born in Hull. He published the first edition of Marvell's complete works, and was mainly interested in the poet as an advocate of liberty.

A. J. N. WILSON: Senior Lecturer in Classics, University of Manchester until his retirement in 1979. He has written on emigration in the Roman period.

INDEX

Poems are listed under 'Marvell'; bold-type references indicate the principal treatments of a given poem. Only selective reference appears here to matter included in Notes to reprinted items.